Laura Trowbridge

Excelsior Cook Book, and Housekeeper's Aid

Laura Trowbridge

Excelsior Cook Book, and Housekeeper's Aid

ISBN/EAN: 9783744785402

Printed in Europe, USA, Canada, Australia, Japan

Cover: Foto ©Lupo / pixelio.de

More available books at **www.hansebooks.com**

EXCELSIOR COOK BOOK

AND

Housekeeper's Aid;

CONTAINING RECEIPTS FOR

COOKING ALL KINDS OF MEATS, FOWL, FISH;

AND MAKING

GRAVIES, SOUPS, SAUCES, BREAD, CAKES, PASTRY, PUDDINGS, CUSTARDS, PRESERVES, ESSENCES;

CANNING FRUIT;

THE MAKING OF

BUTTER, CHEESE, SOAPS; THE ART OF DYEING; ANTIDOTES FOR POISON;

COOKERY FOR THE SICK;

FAMILY PHYSICIAN, GARDENING, HOUSE-PLANTS, THE TOILET; AND MANY MISCELLANEOUS RECEIPTS.

BY

Mrs. LAURA TROWBRIDGE

NEW YORK:
OAKLEY, MASON & CO.,
21 MURRAY STREET.
1870.

PREFACE.

In presenting this work to the public, the author ventures to hope that she is offering a book which will meet the demands of housekeepers in any sphere of life, and which will furnish rules and directions for the proper management of household matters and the skillful discharge of domestic duties. The receipts here given have all been thoroughly tested by experienced housekeepers, and have only to be strictly followed to prove their superior excellence. Economy, which at all times and under all circumstances should be practiced, has not been forgotten; therefore, one of the most common objections against cook books generally, namely, their extravagance, has been avoided. Beside rules for cooking, the book contains directions for the treatment of various diseases; also for making butter and cheese, soap-making, dyeing, and the toilet, which alone are worth four times the price of the book to every housekeeper. The result of twenty-five years' experience, and selections from the best and most approved authors, are humbly submitted to the public, and the writer feels confident that her work will be, what its name indicates, an "Excelsior Cook Book."

RULES FOR HOUSEKEEPERS.

Order is said to be "Heaven's first law;" at any rate, it should be the first of every household; and to maintain it, rules and regulations for the management of domestic affairs should be framed, and their observance strictly and punctually enforced upon each member of the family. It is just as easy to cultivate habits of neatness and order as those of an opposite character, and when once established, will contribute much to the happiness and comfort of their possessor. There should be regular hours for rising and retiring; persons in health do not usually require more than seven or eight hours' sleep, but in sickness or debility "kind nature's sweet restorer," is often the most efficient physician, and should be welcomed as long as he chooses to bless with his presence.

All important matters should be attended to in the early part of the day. If you have unpleasant duties to discharge, set about them resolutely and promptly, and not render their performance more difficult by procrastinating. Always have some convenient work at hand upon which to employ your leisure moments. By a judicious management of your affairs, you will have time for making and receiving calls, time for reading, time for evening and morning communion with your Maker—time for every thing. When the hands are occupied, the mind can be employed in recalling and meditating on something you have been reading. Have a place for every thing and put every thing in its place. Have a time to do each kind of work, and see that it is done at that time. Study to do every thing in the best possible manner.

Every house should have a dry, cool, store-room, convenient to the kitchen.

Have a box for every kind of spice, and have them labeled.

Put dried herbs in paper bags, and hang in a dry place.

Dried fruit should be tied in cloth bags, and hung up.

Vegetables should be put in sand in the cellar for winter use; those not wanted till spring, buried in the ground.

Flour should be kept in a barrel or bin, with a scoop to dip it with, kept covered, and always sifted before using, both for lightness of the food and cleanliness.

Indian meal should be sifted and put in a barrel where it will keep cool and dry, occasionally stirring it, particularly in warm weather, as it is liable to get musty or sour.

Rice should be kept in a dry tub, and when used, picked over and washed before using.

Hominy should be washed in several waters to get out the hulls.

Sugar should be bought by the barrel, as it is more economical than buying in small quantities. It can generally be purchased lower by the barrel, and is more convenient.

It is a good plan to purchase molasses when you can get part of a hogshead, then draw off the molasses and put in a firkin or demijohn for use. The sugar at the bottom can be used for some kind of preserves or pickling.

Coffee should be bought in quantities, as it improves by age.

Tea is cheaper to buy by the box, but should be well covered; if bought in small quantities, put it in a tin can.

Raisins and starch are cheapest bought by the box.

Zante currants should be washed and dried, then put in a jar for use.

Lemon and orange-peel should be dried and pounded, put in glass bottles, well corked, for use.

Nutmegs should be put in a box with the grater;

cinnamon, cloves, allspice, mace, and pepper should be bought whole, then ground fine and put in boxes for use. Mustard should be ground and kept tight.

Sweet herbs should be gathered on a dry day, spread until dry, then put in paper bags. It is well to grind some and put in bottles for use.

Hops should be kept in paper bags and hung up; they are not good after a year old.

Codfish should be purchased in small quantities, as it is unpleasant about the house. If put in a dry place it will get too dry, if too damp it will spoil; it must be changed from garret to cellar.

Cream of tartar, tartaric acid, essences, and sal volatile should be kept in glass bottles, particularly the sal volatile, which should have a ground stopper. Use cold water for dissolving it when used.

Keep cheese in a dry, cool place, and after it is cut, wrap a cloth around and put in a tin box. If it gets dry before using, grate it and pour on brandy, then pack tight in a jar, and it will be better than at first.

Butter should be kept in dry, cool cellars in the summer, and in the winter in an outhouse or out-doors.

Smoked beef should be kept in a bag and hung up. While using ham, put in a bag and hang up.

Keep bread and cake in a tin box, well covered; it will keep fresh longer than any other way.

Preserves and jellies should be put in glass, stone, or china, and kept in a cool place. Jellies should be put in moulds or tumblers. Strawberries, pine-apples, and all delicate preserves may be kept in a box, with sand or saw-dust filled around them, and they will keep longer.

All salted provisions should be watched, and see that they are kept under the brine, for if one piece of meat lies up it will spoil the whole barrel. If the brine looks bloody, it must be scalded, and more salt added; when cold pour back.

Tallow should be kept in a dry, cool place. All kinds of oil in the cellar. Salt should be kept in the dryest place that can be found.

No housekeeper should be without good vinegar;

the best is made from cider or wine. The washings from honey, (and after making jelly or wine,) should be poured into the vinegar. Cold tea should be saved for this purpose.

Jelly-bags should be made of flannel, pudding-bags of coarse, thick cotton cloth.

Pickles should be kept in a cool place, and often looked to; if the vinegar is too strong, they will get soft. A cloth should be put on top, and washed out as the scum rises. Put mustard, nasturtions, or horse-radish to keep them. Alum will harden them.

Wheat-starch is made by washing the wheat clean, then mash it fine, wash and strain, and the starch will settle at the bottom.

Potato-starch is made by grating the potatoes, then washing clean and straining. They should be pared first. Corn-starch is made in the same way.

Wheat washed and boiled as rice, and eaten with cream, sugar, and nutmeg, is nice, and a very good substitute for that article.

Poppy-leaves and rose-leaves should be gathered, and dried on paper, then put in paper-bags for poultices and washes.

Iron ware lined with enamel is superior to every other utensil, for preserving, and should always be used; but if brass or copper is used, it should be kept scrupulously clean.

To purify water, put common charcoal in a watering-pot, and fine sand over it. Let the water trickle through. An old sieve will answer.

Save all your suds for gardens. It is a great fertilizer for grape-vines.

German silver spoons should never be used; iron ones are preferable.

Marble fire-places nor oil-cloths should not be washed in suds. Wipe off the dust, then rub with a cloth dipped in oil. Buttermilk is good to wash oil-cloths.

To make flat-irons smooth, rub a little bees-wax over them, then rub with a cloth.

Count all your clothes-pins, spoons, knives and forks, towels, napkins, etc., once a week.

A little bees-wax or soap rubbed on the hinges of your doors to prevent their creaking, and on drawers, to make them run easy, is good.

Never put away your clothes or stockings without mending. A basket should be kept, and when the ironing is done for the week, any article that wants repairing should be put into it.

To keep hams: Wrap them in brown paper and pack loosely in barrels of dry ashes or oats set in a dry place, or rub them over with black pepper mixed with Cayenne, then put in bags and keep in a cool place. Another: smoke a barrel, set it in the attic, have nails driven around, and hang the hams in, then cover with a thick cloth, and a board on top. Another: put in bags and whitewash them; hang in a cool place. A very successful way of keeping them is to cut the ham in slices and pack them in a jar; melt lard and pour over; cover tight and keep in a cool place.

Soft soap should be kept in an out-house, and not used until six months old.

Onions should be tied in linen bags, and hung in a dry, cool place.

Eggs should be kept in lime-water or salt, with the small end down.

Use whiting or chalk to clean silver; if very black, wet with alcohol; rub with soft flannel or buckskin.

To bleach cotton cloth: Soak in cold water till wet through, then put in chloride of lime, say a pound to forty yards of cloth, with just sufficient water to cover it. Let it remain from three to five hours, then rinse well and dry.

Salt or brine is good to put on sidewalks or places where the grass is not wanted.

All herbs should be gathered on a dry day, and while in blossom.

Smart-weed is an excellent weed for many purposes, and should always be gathered.

Horse-radish leaves and burdock leaves should be dried for use.

Lettuce and motherwort are quieting to the nerves.

Boneset or thoroughwort is good for coughs, colds, liver complaint, and stomach derangement.

Spearmint is good to settle the stomach, and for bowel complaints.

Catmint and elderblows should always be gathered. Mayweed is good for many things.

Grapes should be packed in sawdust or dry sand to keep any time.

Apples keep better by wrapping them in papers, and keeping them in a cool place. This is some trouble, but large ones can be taken care of in this way. Dry sand and buckwheat chaff is good to pack them in, then put in a cool place.

Lima beans should be dried for winter's use, or they be packed in salt. Take them in the pods, just as they begin to turn yellow, and pack in a keg, with alternate layers of salt. Soak in cold water over night before using.

Tea and coffee should be made as soon as the water boils, or the gas escapes and the flavor is destroyed.

Molasses is improved by boiling, and should be boiled and set away for cake and other purposes.

Cranberries should have water kept on them, and changed every two weeks.

Scour zinc with sand and buttermilk.

Pour hot tallow on ink-spots, let it remain a few minutes before washing.

To give a gloss to shirt-bosoms and collars, add a piece of white wax and spermaceti, each about the size of a pea, to a pint of starch, while boiling. Iron until smooth, as friction puts on the gloss.

Another: pour boiling water on gum arabic, and when dissolved, put in a bottle, cork tight. When the starch is boiled add some, and it will give a fine gloss.

To choose nutmegs, prick them with a pin; if the oil comes out, they are good.

Keep lemons and oranges well wrapped in paper, and they will keep a long time.

To use cold starch, pour cold water on the quantity of starch required, stir well, then dip in the articles to be starched; roll them up in a dry cloth; iron in fifteen minutes.

To prepare rye for coffee: wash thoroughly, and soak over night. Brown the color of coffee in the morning.

Celery should be put in the cellar, in a box of dry sand, for winter use.

Fig. 1. Beef.

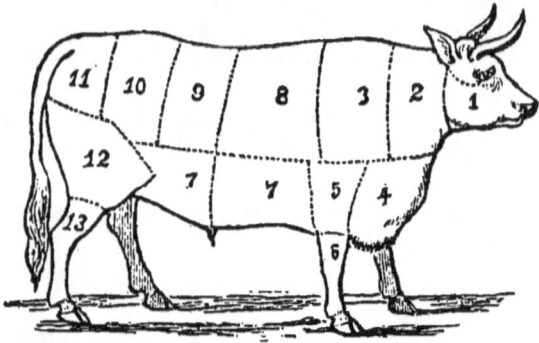

1, cheek; 2, neck; 3, chuck rib; 4, front of the shoulder; 5, back of shoulder; 6, fore-shin; 7, plate pieces; 8, standing ribs; 9, sirloin; 10, sirloin steak; 11, rump; 12, round; 13, hind-shank.

Fig. 2. Mutton.

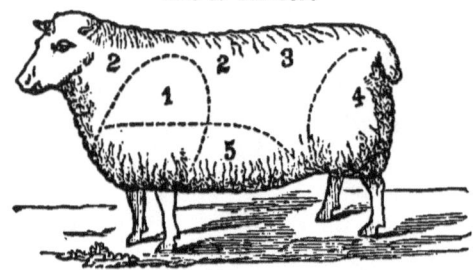

1, shoulder; 2, 2, neck or rack; 3, loin; 4, leg; 5, breast. A chine is two loins; a saddle of mutton is two legs and two loins.

A lamb is divided into two fore-quarters and two hind-quarters.

VENISON.—Two legs and two loins are a saddle. The fore-quarters are nice for a stew or for mince pies.

Fig. 3. Veal.

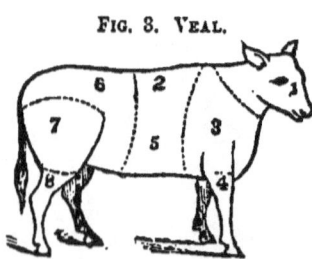

1, head and pluck; 2, rack and neck; 3, shoulder; 4, fore-shank or knuckle; 5, breast; 6, loin; 7, fillet or leg; 8, hind-shank or knuckle.

FIG. 4. PORK.

1, leg; 2, hind-loin; 3, fore-loin; 4, spare rib; 5, hand, 6, spring.

In selecting beef, the best pieces are cut from the shoulder to the rump, including the sirloin, the first, second, and third cuts of the fore-quarter. Steaks from the round are larger, but tougher and not as sweet as from the sirloin. The pieces near the fore-shoulder are always tough.

COOKING THE DIFFERENT PARTS OF BEEF.

The head and heart are used for mince pies; also the neck. The tongue for smoking, or corned and boiled. The sirloins roasted, or steaks. The round or buttock is used for steak, corning, and cooked *à la mode*, or dried beef. Edge-bone, boiled. Flanks, steaks or corned. Hock or shin is used for soups. Tallow tried for candles. Some of the suet should be taken care of for pies, puddings, etc. The neck may be used for soup.

VEAL.

The loin is used for roasting. The knuckles are used for broths and soups. The neck is used for soups, stews and pot-pies. The fillet is used for cutlets, or to stuff and roast.

MUTTON.

The loin is roasted. The leg is roasted, or corned and boiled, or cutlets made out of it. Neck or back, boil, roast, haricot, stewed, or soup. Shoulder, roast. Breast, grilled. Head, soup.

PORK.

Shoulder and ham are used for smoking. The spare-rib is used for roasting, ribs included. The lean pieces used for sausages, and the tenderloins for broiling. The head and feet for head-cheese, souse or scrapel; or the feet may be used for jelly. The rest may be corned.

EXCELSIOR COOK BOOK.

A SOUTHERN MODE OF CURING HAMS.

Take four quarts of salt, one and a half ounces of saltpetre, with sufficient molasses to make a paste; this quantity will salt a hundred and fifty pounds of meat. Rub well on the fleshy side; let it remain four weeks, then smoke. Two days before removing from the smoke-house, rub them over with black pepper and strong vinegar, to prevent the flies from touching them, then put in bags and hang up.

ANOTHER METHOD.

Take one and three quarters of a pound of good salt, half an ounce of saltpetre, one pint of molasses, one teaspoonful of saleratus, add one gallon of water. Bring the liquor to a boil, taking care to skim well. When cool, pour over the meat. Keep well covered with brine. After remaining six weeks, smoke them.

ANOTHER METHOD.

Take one pound of salt, one ounce of saltpetre, one pint of molasses, to twenty pounds of ham; water sufficient to cover well, then boil and skim as above.

CURING MUTTON HAM.

Cut a hind-quarter of mutton into the shape of a ham, then pound one ounce of saltpetre with one pound of salt and a quarter of a pound of brown sugar; rub the ham well with this mixture, particularly the hole of the shank; let it lie a fortnight, rubbing it every two or three days, then press it one day with a weight. Smoke it with sawdust ten days, or hang it to dry in the kitchen.

CURING HAMS. NO. 4.

To one hundred pounds of meat, take four pounds of fine salt, two ounces of saltpetre, and four ounces of brown sugar; mix well together, and rub the hams until they are covered; then lay them on a board and repeat the rubbing daily for several weeks, or till the meat is ready for smoking.

TO PICKLE BEEF.

Take four gallons of water, one pound of brown sugar, eight of salt, four ounces of saltpetre. Boil together, and carefully take off the scum as it rises. When clear, let it remain till cool, then pour over the meat. Increase the quantity according to the quantity of meat.

A PICKLE FOR BEEF TONGUES OR DRIED BEEF.

Take a pound and a half of brown sugar, six pounds of beef, ounce of saltpetre or saleratus, and four gallons of water, boil gently, skim well, and when clear, set away to cool. Put the meat in a tub, and pour on till covered; a weight should be put on to keep it under the brine.

TO PICKLE PORK.

It should not be salted until the meat is perfectly cold. It is best to let it remain one day before packing. Sprinkle salt on the bottom of a clean, sweet barrel; rock-salt is the best for this purpose. Put in a layer of pork with the rind down, pack closely, then a layer of salt alternately till all is in. Make a strong brine, boil, skim, and when cold, pour. Keep a stone on top to keep the meat under. If there is not sufficient salt, it will not keep during the warm weather; in that case, it must be scalded over, adding more salt. It should be looked to from time to time, to see that it is well covered with brine, for, if not, the top pieces become tainted, and will extend to the whole barrel. In salting down new pork the old brine may be used, by scalding and skimming.

DIRECTIONS FOR CUTTING UP A HOG.

Take off the head, split the hog through the spine; take out the leaf-fat, then take off a piece of the shoulder for sausage-meat; the lean meat called spare-rib should not be taken off. Cut a narrow strip from the belly for sausage-meat. Take off the ham and shoulder for smoking, the remainder for salting; the cheek may be used for sausages.

TRYING LARD.

Cut up the leaf-fat, take off the skin, put over a gentle fire, stirring occasionally to prevent its sticking at the bottom. No water should be added, as it will make it sputter, and will not keep so well. When a nice brown, strain through a strainer, using a pair of squeezers. Care should be taken not to let it burn.

The fat taken off the intestines should be soaked in salt and water two days, changing each day. This fat should be used first, as it will not keep as long as the leaf-fat.

TO PREPARE CASES FOR SAUSAGES.

Empty the cases, the smaller intestines of the hog; wash well; cut in lengths of two yards; scrape, and turn with a stick each day for five days, soaking in salt and water, changing each time.

TRYING TALLOW.

Cut in small pieces, put over a slow fire without any water, frequently stirring. When brown, squeeze through a strainer.

ON CARVING.

Your knife must not be too heavy, nor too large, but of middling size, and of a fine edge. Less strength is required than practice. The dish should be sufficiently near to enable the carver to reach it without rising, and to give an appearance of ease and ability. Cut your pieces, asking him or her what part they prefer, and showing no partiality to your guests. Fish requires but very little carving. It should be carefully helped with a fish-knife, which is not sharp, and being broad, it prevents the flakes from being broken, and, in salmon and cod, adds much to their beauty. A portion of the roe should be given to each person, as well as liver.

In salmon, the choice parts are next the head, and the thin part towards the tail is less savory. This is seldom sent to the table whole. A piece cut from the middle parts is the best flavored. Make an incision along the back; then cut the thickest part for the lean, and the thin for the fat. A cod's head and shoulders, when in season, is a very genteel dish. All the parts are eaten, except the green jelly of the eye; that is never served. The tongue and palate are considered great delicacies, for which you must insert a spoon into the mouth to obtain. Insert the knife from the back of the head, through the back; and help each person to a piece of the sounds, which line the under side of the backbone, together with a piece of the fish. Mackerel should have the head cut off, as being unsavory; then divide down the back, and give a side to each, if small; and, if less is required, give the thickest end. Give some of the roe, if liked. In the male it is hard; in the female, soft.

Turbot: The under part is most esteemed, and should be placed uppermost on the table. The middle is the choicest part, and an incision should be made directly through. It is difficult to divide the backbone; and it must be raised with the fork, until you separate a portion of it with the fish-knife. It is preferred by some, though less delicate than the under side.

To carve a calf's head: Cut along the cheek-bone, and let the knife penetrate to the bone. The sweet-bread lies at the thick part of the neck, which should be cut in slices. If the eye is asked for, take it out with the point of a knife. The palate is esteemed a delicacy, and some nice lean pieces may be cut from under the jaw-bone. A tongue should be cut through the thickest part, and slices cut from that, as it is more juicy. The fat is at the root of the tongue.

To carve a pig: This is generally divided by the cook before sending to the table. First, separate the shoulders from the body; then the leg; then divide the ribs into two or three parts. Put a piece of stuffing on each plate. Some prefer a bit of the ear.

Spare-rib: Cut from the thick meat near the backbone, slicing off. If a rib is preferred, they are easily cut through, after the meat is taken off.

A ham should be cut through the thick part, where the best pieces are; or you may commence at the knuckle, and proceed towards the end.

Poultry: Put your fork into the middle of the fowl, or breast; take off the wing and leg on both sides; then cut slices from each side of the breast. Ask which part each person prefers, and give a piece of dressing to every one.

MEATS.

In every branch of cookery experience is necessary, particularly in meats. Almost all kinds of meats are tenderer and better flavored by being a day or two old, in summer; and in cold weather they require a longer time. Beef and mutton do not ripen so soon as veal or lamb. When frozen, it should be laid in a warm place to thaw, before using, or it will be dry, and will not cook well. It is not so sweet if put into cold water to take out the frost. It can be kept frozen, by packing in snow; but as soon as the snow melts, it should be cooked. I have sometimes kept meat in the ice-house, but as soon as taken out it must be used; it would not keep long. Warm, damp weather is bad for keeping meats. South winds and lightning are very unfavorable. After a storm meat should always be examined. I have sometimes kept it successfully by putting in flour, in a dry place, as it keeps the flies from it, and also the air. Meat will keep longer by hanging than by laying down, if kept from the flies. If it does not smell perfectly sweet, add a little saleratus while boiling, and, if not bad, it will remove every unpleasant taste or smell. Fowls should never be cooked if there is the least taint about them.

BOILING MEATS.

While boiling meat, care should be taken to keep it constantly boiling, and well skimmed. The scum should be taken off just before boiling; and if not all taken off, throw in a little cold water, and skim again. Fresh meat should be put into hot water, salt into cold water. Never crowd the meat, but leave room for plenty of water. A quarter of an hour is allowed for a pound of meat. A chicken will cook in half an hour, or, if six months old, it will require an hour. An old fowl requires from four to five. Meats should be boiled gently, as fast boiling hardens meat. The part that is to be uppermost on the table should be laid down in the pot, as the scum is apt to give it a dark look, if not all taken off. When half boiled, throw in salt—say a large spoonful to three quarts of water. The water can be used for soup; if too greasy, skim off part of the fat. Meat or poultry lose their flavor by standing in water after they are done. The cover should never be taken off, except to take off the scum or examine the meat, and should be immediately put on again. When meat is put into cold water, it should be heated gradually; for, if boiled too soon, it will shrink and harden, and will not throw up the scum so readily.

ROAST OR BAKED MEATS.

Meats are better roasted than baked; but it is more convenient to bake, since fire-places have become obsolete. It must be frequently basted, and baked slowly. Before putting in the oven, rub salt and pepper all over the meat, and put water in the dripping-pan, always adding more when required, occasionally turning the meat over, and basting often. When tender, take up, and stir in a little flour and water, having previously mixed it, so as to get out all the lumps. Lean meats require butter put into the gravy. Game and pork require sweet herbs.

FRIED MEATS.

Fried meat is the most convenient method of cooking, but not as digestible as other modes, and should be avoided as much as possible. In frying fresh pork, plenty of pepper and salt, also sweet herbs, should be sprinkled on, and it will fry itself. Lean meats require butter or lard put into the spider, previous to putting in the meat. Pork is always preferable to lard, which can be fried first, then taken out, when the meat can be put in. It should fry quick, otherwise it will be hard and greasy. Take up the meat and stir in a spoonful of flour; mix well, so it will not be lumpy; turn in a little hot water, stir up, and turn on the meat. It must be seasoned while cooking.

BROILED MEATS.

Broiling is considered by epicures to be decidedly the best mode of cooking meats, particularly beef and chickens. Meats should not be cooked on the same gridiron as fish, unless great care is used in cleaning—which should always be done in either case. It is well to have the bars of the gridiron concave and terminate in a trough; otherwise the juice will drop into the fire, and smoke the meat. If the meat is not fat, it is well to grease the bars before using, or the meat will show the impression and injure the looks. The quicker meats are boiled without burning, the sweeter they will be. Have your platter warm; lay on your meat when done; sprinkle salt, pepper, and melted butter; turn over two or three times; then send to the table hot.

BROILING BEEF.

Steaks from the round are generally used, but are not as good as the sirloin. Be careful to have it cut the right way of the grain. It should be laid on a board and pounded, before broiling. Have nice hot coals, and the gridiron warm, before putting on; broil quickly, without burning. When the juice begins to rise, take a knife and fork, having your platter at hand; take it carefully up and lay on the platter; when the juice has drained out, put back on the gridiron, the other side down; let it remain a moment, when it must be turned again. This saves the juice, which otherwise goes into the fire. It should look red when done, and then it will be sweet and tender; if done too much, it becomes hard and tough, without that sweet taste for which beef is noted. Season with melted butter, pepper and salt. If liked, add a spoonful of hot water. It should be eaten the moment it is cooked. It requires from ten to fifteen minutes in cooking.

FRIED BEEF.

The same pieces that are used for broiling are good fried. It should be fried in butter or beef-drippings; put in when hot, sprinkle a little salt and pepper over; turn immediately or it will cook too much. When done, take up and stir in flour, then pour in hot water to make a gravy; send to the table at once.

ROAST OR BAKED BEEF.

In selecting beef care should be taken to get that, that is tender, and of a bright red color, the fat white. The sirloin of the cuts from the fore-quarter are the best pieces for roasting or baking. Rub salt and pepper on the meat; lay in the dripping-pan; put in water, and baste frequently with a large spoon. Roast slowly at first, then increase the heat, turning the meat occasionally over, and adding more water if needed. Do not let the water get out. If thick, allow twenty minutes to a pound; if thin, less time will be required. When done, make a gravy according to the directions given.

FRICASSEED BEEF.

Take any piece of beef—such as will not answer for any other purpose, will do; put in water sufficient to cook it tender; when half done, throw in salt and some pepper; fry down to a nice brown; then make a gravy of flour and water. Serve with apple-sauce, vegetables, and salad.

MOCK DUCK.

Take as large a slice of beef as you can get; pound thin; then make a stuffing prepared as for a turkey; fill it, and sew up; fry one hour in the drippings of beef or butter; turn it and keep covered until done; after taking up, pour in hot water, and the stuffing that falls will thicken it. You must season it with salt and pepper when first put over.

BEEF COOKED IN ONIONS.

Fry a few slices of pork quite brown, then take tender beef and slice thin; put a layer of beef and pork with onions sliced; season with salt and pepper. Put on sufficient water to cover it, and, when done, take up; then stir flour and water to make the gravy. They that are fond of onions will find this a savory dish.

ALAMODE BEEF.

Take five or six pounds of the round of beef; then soak one pound of bread in cold water; drain off the water, (or only put enough on to soak the bread;) mix a large spoonful of flour, the same of melted butter, a teaspoonful of salt, two eggs, pepper, cloves and allspice to the taste, or, if preferred, sweet herbs. Cut gashes in the meat, and fill with part of the meat; stew gently two hours, in just sufficient water to cover it; then take up and put in a dripping-pan with the liquor; lay the reserved dressing on top, and bake two hours, or until tender, basting occasionally. When taken up, make a gravy, as directed, and, if liked, add a wineglass of wine, and a little butter.

BOUILLI.

Boil about seven or eight pounds of beef in more water than enough to cover it. Take off the scum as it rises; then put in two carrots, two onions, two heads of celery, turnips, two cloves, a little parsley, and sweet herbs. Let it boil gently four or five hours. Put a turnip, an onion, and a head of celery to cook whole, and when done, take out and cut in squares. Take out the meat carefully, and skim off the fat, and lay the sliced vegetable in the soup, and add a spoonful of catsup, then serve as other soup.

ROLLED BEEF.

Take the inside of a sirloin; soak in a glass of port wine and a glass of vinegar mixed for forty-eight hours; make a stuffing, and fill it; then bind up tight, and roast before the fire, if convenient; if to be cooked in the stove, put in a pan with a pint of water, and cook gently; baste with a glass of wine and vinegar together, also, a tea-spoonful of pounded allspice. Larding improves the look and flavor. Make a gravy, and serve with currant-jelly or cranberries.

BEEF CAKES.

Pound some beef that is under-done with a little fat ham; season with pepper and salt, also onions, (if you like;) mix well and make into cakes, and fry a nice brown. Serve them in a good gravy.

A FRICANDEAU OF BEEF.

Take a piece of lean beef, lard it with bacon seasoned with pepper and salt, cloves, mace, and allspice. Put in a kettle with a pint of broth, a glass of white wine, all sorts of sweet herbs, a garlic or onion, four cloves, pepper and salt. When the meat is tender, cover it close and skim the liquor; then strain it, and let it boil till it is reduced to a glaze. Glaze the larded side with it.

TO MAKE HUNTER'S BEEF.

Take a round of beef that weighs twenty-five pounds, let it hang two days in summer, and longer in winter, then take one ounce of saltpetre, three ounces of brown sugar, an ounce of clove, and the same of nutmeg, half an ounce of allspice, three handfuls of common salt, and rub well into the meat; turn and rub every day for two or three weeks. The bone should be taken out first. When to be cooked, dip into cold water, to take off the loose spice; then bind with cord or tape, and put in a pan with a tea-cupful of water; cover the top of the meat with shred suet, and cover the pan with brown crust and paper; bake six hours; when cold, take off the paste and tape. The gravy is nice; it will keep a long time.

ANOTHER MODE OF DRESSING BEEF.

Take the bones out of three ribs; sprinkle with salt; roll tight, and roast it. It looks nice. It can be done as hunter's beef.

ITALIAN BEEFSTEAK.

Cut a steak as for broiling; pound well, and season with salt, pepper, and onion; put in a stew-pan, cover tight, and set where it will cook slowly, and without burning. Cook two or three hours, and then make a gravy.

BEEF OLIVES.

Take beef half cooked, cut in slices half an inch thick, and four inches square; lay then on a force-meat of bread-crumbs, a little suet, pepper and salt; roll them, and fasten with skewers; put in a stew-pan, with some gravy, and a spoonful of water, and stew until tender.

TO DRESS THE SAME—SANDERS.

Chop beef or mutton, with onion, pepper and salt; add a little gravy; put into saucers, making them two thirds full; fill up with mashed potatoes; put a piece of butter on the top, and brown in an oven.

CECILS.

Mince-meat of any kind, crumbs of bread, onion, anchovies, lemon-peel, salt, nutmeg, chopped parsley, pepper, a piece of butter; stir well together over a fire for a few minutes. When cool, make up into balls the size of a turkey's egg; roll in eggs beaten light, then sprinkle with bread-crumbs; then fry a nice brown, and serve with gravy.

HASH BEEF.

Chop up pieces of beef that has been cooked, with boiled potatoes, half and half, put in a spider; season with pepper and salt, also a piece of butter. Salt pork is nice for this purpose.

BEEF CAKES. NO. 2.

Chop pieces of roast beef very fine, mix bread-crumbs, chopped onions, and parsley; season with pepper and salt; moisten with drippings or catsup; cold ham or tongue may be added; make in broad flat cakes, and spread a coat of mashed potatoes on the top; put a piece of butter on every cake, and set it in the oven to brown. Other cold meats may be prepared in the same way.

BEEF LIVER. NO. 1.

Cut in thin slices and lay on a gridiron, with good live coals under; when cooked on one side, turn over; sprinkle a little salt and pepper over it, and in ten minutes it will be done; lay on melted butter, or make a gravy of flour and water. It is very nice fried. But the best way to use beef liver is to corn it, and then smoke it, as you would smoked beef; then cut in thin slices, and fry in a little butter; it will not need much cooking. This is very nice for tea.

TO BOIL A TONGUE.

Put a tongue into a pot over night, with water on; let it remain until next day, about three hours before dinner.

FRIZZLED BEEF.

Cut dried beef in thin slices, and warm, with a little water in the pan; stir in a little flour and water mixed, a piece of butter, and take up, as much cooking hardens it; add eggs, if liked.

TRIPE.

Very few persons understand dressing tripe. It should be cut in squares, nearly a quarter of a yard long; then scraped every day for nine days in succession; and put in fresh water with salt thrown in. It should then be boiled in milk until tender; if it can be kept frozen it is better; if not, it must be kept in salt and water, and changed every day while it lasts. It can be pickled in spiced vinegar, or broiled like steak, or fried in butter, or a nice stuffing made and filled; then sew up and fry.

TO STEW BEEF.

Take a good piece of fresh beef, not too fat, boil until an hour before taking up, then season with pepper and salt; pare potatoes and parsnips; cut one in two; cook until tender; then make a gravy. If you have sweet potatoes, they are better.

FROZEN BEEF.

If beef is frozen, shave off what you require with a sharp knife; put in a spider with butter, a few onions or not, just as you like, cover close; when nearly done, season with salt and pepper; make a gravy as directed.

VEAL CUTLETS.

Cut your veal, as for steaks; that cut from the round is the best; put some butter in the pan, and let it be hot; beat up an egg, dip one piece of veal in at a time; have some flour on another plate; dip into the flour next, both sides, lay carefully into the pan, sprinkle salt and pepper over them. Another way is to fry the veal first, and then dip in the egg and flour, and fry gently five minutes.

VEAL STEW.

Cut veal into strips or small pieces, a few slices of salt pork, potatoes pared and sliced thin; put on water to cover the whole; when nearly done, season with pepper and salt. About five minutes before taking up lay on the top slices of bread, and cover again closely until the bread has steamed through; then take up.

A FILLET OF VEAL.

Take out the bone and fill with a nice stuffing; close the meat up tight, season with salt and pepper, put in a dripping-pan with water, and bake two hours; thicken the gravy, adding butter, and if liked, a glass of wine. Veal is very nice cut in gashes, and slices of pork laid in and cooked. The loin is the best part for roasting. The neck is good for soup. The bones, after cutting off the meat, are nice for pot-pies.

FORCE-MEAT BALLS.

Chop pieces of veal up fine, with a very little pork; add a couple of eggs, and season to the taste; do up into balls the size of an egg, and fry brown.

CALF LIVER.

It is good fried or broiled, stuffed and baked; but the best way is to take the liver, heart, and under-jaw, boil together until tender, then take out of the liquor and chop fine; season with butter, pepper, and salt; you may add sweet herbs if you like.

COLLOPS.

Cut veal into thin slices, dip into flour and fry brown; then turn in water to cover the veal, and when it boils put in two or three sliced onions, pepper and salt; when tender take up, thicken the gravy and squeeze in the juice of a lemon and turn on the collops; garnish the dish with lemon cut in slices.

FRESH MEAT GRIDDLES.

Chop all the bits of cold fresh beef or veal, season with salt and pepper, make a nice batter, grease your griddle and put on a spoonful of batter, then one of meat, then another of batter, when fried on one side turn over; these are nice for a breakfast dish.

A BEEF OR VEAL PIE.

Take the cold pieces after baking and make a light crust, quite short; lay it in your basin, put in your pieces of meat with butter, pepper, and salt, adding a little water; put on a cover, and bake an hour.

A BEEF'S HEART.

Cut it open on both sides, (this is usually done by the butcher,) wash clean, make a nice stuffing, and fill up, then tie with a bit of twine, and roast or bake until tender; it is better if boiled about twenty minutes before stuffing; garnish with cloves and eat with jelly. It is nice boiled and fried in butter, or smoked, and then fried, in which case it must be corned first.

CALVES' HEAD.

Clean well and soak in water to make it look white, leave the skin on, take out the tongue to pickle, and the brains; boil the head tender, put in some parsley and a little butter, brown nice and take up. The brains must be boiled by themselves, then put in butter, sage, pepper, and salt. Another way: Boil the head almost tender, take off nearly all the meat off the bone and put in a dish; beat up the yolks of two eggs and turn over, then cover with bread-crumbs, a little summer savory or sage nicely sifted, pepper, salt, and one nutmeg if you like; mix well together before putting on; put the dish in the oven and brown it, then slice the rest of the head and skin the tongue, then slice it; put some gravy in a pan with parsley, sage, savory, pepper, and salt, stir in some flour while boiling hot, having previously wet it with cold water to prevent it being lumpy, turn over the rest, then beat up the brains, and add two spoonfuls of catsup; simmer the whole together.

CALVES' FEET.

Boil them tender, roll in flour, and fry brown, make a gravy and season with salt, pepper, and mace, add wine if you like. They can be boiled with the head if liked, and then split open to garnish it by laying around the head.

SWEETBREADS.

Boil them tender; then add cream, butter, pepper, salt, and nutmeg, if you like, stir in a little flour to thicken the gravy; or they may be parboiled, then dip in flour, with sweet herbs, pepper, and salt. They are also nice fried with liver.

MUTTON.

The saddle is the best to corn, and then boil, and eat cold. It is also the best to roast or fry. It is also nice broiled. The neck is best made into soup. For roasting the saddle, you can cut gashes, and fill with a stuffing made of bread soaked soft, a spoonful of butter, two eggs, with sweet herbs. Rub the outside with salt, pepper, clove, and allspice. Put water in the dripping-pan, and baste often. Turn the bony side down first, then turn after cooking awhile. Allow a quarter of an hour to each pound; if done too much, it will be tough. After taking up, thicken the gravy with flour, and season with spices and catsup. Wine or currant-jelly is nice in the gravy. Celery is nice to garnish the dish. Onions are nice served with mutton.

HOTCH POTCH.

Take a little corned beef, or a ham-bone, peas, lettuce, and onions in a little water. While stewing, fry some mutton or lamb-steaks, seasoned to a good brown. Put the steaks in a spider, and turn the vegetables over them, and let them stew three quarters of an hour.

MUTTON ROASTED.

Take the fat out of a loin, and joint it at every bone, dip it into the yolks of three well-beaten eggs, and dip into a mixture of bread-crumbs, salt, pepper, nutmeg, and sweet herbs; place them together as they were before, tie them, and roast quick. Make a gravy, and serve hot.

GRILLED LAMB.

Cut it in squares, about an inch long, (not cut in pieces, only hashed,) rub with butter, the yolk of an egg, pepper, salt, and bread-crumbs, any kind of sweet herbs you like; put in the dripping-pan, with a pint of water, and baste often. It will not require much roasting. Season the gravy with the juice and grated rind of a lemon, and a spoonful of tomato catsup. It is also good roasted, without the egg.

VENISON.

Venison should not be overdone, as it tends to dry the meat. It is nice fried, broiled, or roasted. In the latter case, it should be eaten with currant-jelly.

CHICKENS.

Chickens six months old are the best, as they are more tender; but if a year old, they are still nice. After having the head chopped off, they should be hung by the feet, so as to bleed freely. When boiled, they should always be put into cold water, as they are less liable to break. When roasted, they should be stuffed, sewed up, and laid on a dripping-pan, with water, and baste often. Lay slices of salt pork on top while cooking.

FRICASSEE.

Cut them up, or rather joint them; wash well; then put in a kettle—a quart of water to a chicken; let them boil until half done; then put in a lump of butter, salt, and pepper; let it cook down, to about a tea-cupful of gravy; then stir in flour, wet with water. Toast bread, and butter it; turn on boiling water enough to soak; then turn on the chicken. Pork may be put in, instead of butter, but it will require less salt, and should be put in when the chicken is put over, say two small slices to one chicken.

BROILED CHICKENS.

Take out the breast-bone, and beat well; then lay on the gridiron, and turn a tin on top; let it half broil; turn over, and finish cooking. It must broil slow, or it will burn; season with butter, pepper, and salt. It may be fried in butter, after dipping in bread-crumbs or flour, or dipped in egg first.

CHICKEN PIE.

It must be jointed, and boiled until tender; have a pudding-dish, lined with pie-crust; put in the chicken, with salt, butter, and pepper; sprinkle flour over the top; then turn on the liquor which the chicken was boiled in; put a crust on; cut in the middle; and ornament the top with pastry. Bake in a slow oven an hour. Any pieces of cold meat, beef, veal, venison, or mutton, may be made the same.

CHICKEN PUDDING.

Stew a pair, as above; then take out of the liquor to cool; then beat five eggs; turn in a quart of milk; stir in a quart of wheat-flour, a tea-spoonful of salt; cover the bottom of the pudding-dish; then a layer of chicken, (having previously seasoned it while cooking,) and so on, until the dish is filled; lastly, a layer of pudding. Bake three quarters of an hour, or until brown. Stir an egg into the liquor, which can be served hot with the pudding.

CHICKEN POT-PIE.

Joint the chickens, and boil until tender; season with butter, salt, and pepper. Take an egg and beat it light; put it into a pint of sour milk, half cream is better; if not, melt some butter, and turn in; stir in flour, a tea-spoonful of salt, add half a tea-spoonful of saleratus; stir well, and drop with a spoon into the kettle, while boiling. Let it boil half an hour, and take up. If it remains too long, the crust will be heavy. Two potatoes should be added before the crust is put in. Another method, and still better, but more trouble: Take light bread-dough, and mould in half a tea-cupful of butter, and let it rise; then cut in squares, and put a layer of crust, then a layer of chicken, until filled; cover the whole with a crust. It may be made of cream of tartar, like biscuits. Veal or mutton can be made the same.

CHICKEN SALAD.

Boil chickens tender, and cut up in small bits, or chop in a chopping-bowl. Take heads of celery and chop, then wash clean in cold water. Take double the quantity of celery that you have chicken. Put in a dish and make a dressing of two thirds of a tea-cupful of vinegar, two eggs beat to a froth, two spoonfuls of melted butter, a tea-spoonful of mixed mustard, the same of salt, and a little black pepper. This quantity is for two chickens. Stir the whole over a slow fire until thick. When cold, mix with the chicken and celery.

ROAST TURKEY.

Having washed the turkey clean, prepare the following dressing: Take light bread and soak in cold water; mix a spoonful of butter, salt and pepper, a spoonful of powdered sage, the same of savory. An egg makes the dressing cut smoother. If you like, cook the liver, heart, and gizzard tender, and chop with a few cold potatoes. Fill crop first and sew up, then the body. Tie up the legs and wings. Rub on butter and salt. Put a tea-cupful of water in the dripping-pan, and roast from two to three hours, according to their size; baste often. Make a gravy when done of the drippings. If the inwards are not put in for stuffing, they can be cooked tender and added to the gravy.

BOILED TURKEY OR CHICKEN.

Prepare them the same as for roasting. Tie in a cloth to have it look white. A bit of pork boiled with them improves the flavor. Use drawn butter for sauce. The liquor can be made into soup. They should be put into cold water, not hot.

A very nice way to cook turkey or chicken: Take a sharp knife, and scrape downwards. Begin at the wings, but do not break the skin, nor tear the flesh. Loosen the flesh from breast, back and thighs. Draw the skeleton by the neck from the flesh, then stuff with a nice dressing, and sew up. Bake three hours and serve cold. This mode requires some experience, but when done is very nice.

TO ROAST GEESE AND DUCKS.

They should be put into boiling water and stir around two or three minutes, when the feathers and down will come off as easy as off a chicken if right done. The feathers will not wet through, but they will steam. Then singe by lighting a bit of paper and holding over until all the fine hairs are off. Then dress nicely and wash clean. Boil an hour or more, according to their age. When some tender take them out and have a stuffing made as for a turkey; fill the body and sew up. Roast a nice brown, turning on the water they were boiled in. Make a gravy of the drippings. Eat with onions or apple-sauce.

TO ROAST SNIPES OR WOODCOCKS.

The flavor is best preserved without stuffing; but flour and baste until done. Toast a couple of slices of bread and dip in the dripping to lay on the dish. Put them on and make a gravy of butter and flour. To take away the fishy taste which some wild fowls have, take an onion, salt and hot water, and baste a few times, then with butter.

TO BOIL A DUCK OR RABBIT.

Use a good deal of water, and skim often. When done put in a little cream, butter, pepper, salt, parsley, chopped; stew a few minutes, then add flour and take up. A rabbit is nice made into a pot-pie or fricasseed like chickens. They may be stuffed and roasted, and will only require an hour; baste often with butter.

PIGEONS.

Make a dressing as for a turkey, and fill and sew up. Put them in a pot, breast side down, season with salt and pepper. If old, they will require a great deal of cooking. When nearly done, put in butter and stew down. Thicken the gravy with flour. They are nice stewed or made into a pot-pie, or made with a crust and baked like a chicken pie.

TO STEW BIRDS.

Make stuffing of bread, butter or salt pork, pepper and salt; fill and sew up. Lay in slices of bacon or pork and a quart of water. Add onions and sweet herbs if you like. Make a gravy.

BEEF OR VEAL STEWED.

Put a piece of butter in a stew-pan, cut the meat in small slices, and lay in with apples sliced thin, add pepper and salt. If liked, add onions. Cover tight and stew until done.

A SAUSAGE STEW.

Put a layer of peeled potatoes sliced in a kettle, then a layer of sausage, then another layer of potatoes, and so on until all are in. Season with pepper and salt; then pour on water, and if the sausages are very lean, add bits of ham or butter. Cook until the potatoes are well cooked.

TO BOIL CORNED BEEF.

Put in cold water enough to cover it nicely. Cover closely and boil slowly. Some think it much improved by letting it remain in the liquor all night. The liquor is good to boil cabbage and turnips, also potatoes. Corned beef is the best for hash.

VEAL OR MUTTON HARICOT.

Put some slices of veal or mutton in a stew-pan, season with pepper and salt. Drippings or butter should be put in first. Then add celery, onions, carrots; having previously cooked them tender, add tomato catsup and spice if you like. Let them stew ten minutes, then lay the meat in a dish and turn the vegetables over. Peas and cucumbers may be used instead.

VEAL BALLS.

Chop cold veal, as much salt pork, mix with as much bread-crumbs. Moisten with white wine and two eggs, season with salt, pepper, nutmeg, sweet herbs. Make into balls and fry in butter. They should be dipped in flour first.

TO POT VEAL.

Take veal that has been boiled and sliced, smoked tongue boiled and the skin taken off, also sliced. Pound each separately very fine, and moisten with butter as you proceed. Put in a stone jar and mix well. Press down and turn on melted butter. When cut it must look variegated. Keep it covered in a dry place. When used cut in slices. Ham is nice used instead of tongue.

CURRIED DISHES.

Chickens and veal are best for curries. But they can be made, and are nice, of mutton chops, pigeons, and other meats. Chicken should be jointed and boiled tender. Take them up and put some butter in a stew-pan, fry them brown; then pour on part of the liquor in which the meat was boiled, nearly enough to cover it. To two chickens or to four pounds of pork, put in a tea-cupful of boiled rice, a table-spoonful of curry-powder, one of butter, one of flour, a little salt, and a tea-cup of the liquor, mix all together, and pour over the meat. Let it cook twenty minutes slowly. Eat boiled rice with it.

PHEASANTS AND PARTRIDGES.

Stuff and roast like turkey, and serve with onions. They are nice stewed. When cold, they may be made into patties.

TO POT BIRDS.

Clean them well, then season with allspice, mace, pepper and salt. Rub every part well, and lay them in a pan, the breast downwards, and pack close. Put plenty of butter on them and make a coarse flour-paste, with a paper over, and bake. When cold cut into pieces and pack close in a jar. Cover with butter. The butter will answer for basting or for meat-pies.

GUINEA AND PEA FOWL

are dressed like a turkey, and eat very much like pheasants.

BAKED OR ROASTED PIG.

Take a young pig, which should be fat, five or six weeks old, cut off the first joints, and wash thoroughly outside and inside. Prepare a stuffing as for a turkey. If you have any fresh meat cooked, put some in the dressing, with a quarter of a pound of salt pork. Fill up and fasten tight. Put it into a dripping-pan, tie the legs, and put a grate or something in the dripping to keep it up. Turn in a pint of water. Swab every fifteen minutes with salt and water. Rub a little butter over it to keep it from blistering. It must bake from two to three hours. When done, expose to the air a few minutes to make it crispy. Make a gravy of flour and the brains, cooked, if you like.

BOILED HAM.

Take a ham weighing twenty pounds, and boil five hours; then take out and skin the whole. Put it in a slow oven half an hour; then cover it with bread-crumbs and put in again; let it remain half an hour longer. Garnish with cloves. Baking ham an hour after boiling is a great improvement to the flavor.

FOR COOKING COLD HAM.

Take all the bits and pieces, put in a frying-pan; if lean, put in some butter; cover close until warmed through; then break in some eggs, and stir constantly until they are cooked.

BROILED HAM.

Cut in slices, take off the rind and lay on the gridiron over hot coals two minutes; turn over and let it remain as long; take up and season with pepper, butter, and turn on a table-spoonful of hot water.

TO ROAST A SPARE RIB.

This should be cut thick; rub flour, salt, sage, and pepper on; lay on a dripping-pan, with a little water in, the bony side down; baste often, and cook an hour and a half. It must cook slowly.

TO COOK BOILED HAM.

Make a batter of eggs, milk, and flour, add a little salt, pour some on a dripping-pan, and fry three minutes, having put a little butter in; then cover the batter with thin slices of ham, and pour on more batter. Let it fry until a nice brown, then cut in squares, and turn over and let it fry on the other side.

TO KEEP HAM.

Cut in slices to broil or fry, and pack in jars; heat lard and turn on top, cover close, and keep in a cool place.

TO FRY HAM.

Cut in slices and fry quickly, but not too much; when done, take up, and fry eggs in the gravy.

SOUSE.

Clean pigs' feet, and ears if you like, (although there is not much meat on them,) soak them in salt and water three days, changing the water every day; boil six hours, then turn on hot, spiced vinegar. Fry in lard or eat out of the vinegar; a nicer way is to dry them after taking out of the vinegar, and dipping in a beaten egg, then in flour or bread-crumbs, then fry.

HEAD-CHEESE.

Clean the head, feet, and bony pieces, after cutting off sausage-meat, and boil all together until tender; then put in a chopping-bowl and take out all the bones, chop fine; add pepper, salt, sweet herbs, put in a bag, put on a weight, and let it remain till cold. It can be eaten cold, sliced up, or warmed up with vinegar.

SCRAPEL.

Save the liquor after boiling the head and feet, strain to get out all the bones, take off some of the fat, pour the liquor back into the kettle. If you have six quarts of liquor, add two quarts of chopped meat, season with pepper and salt to the taste; when boiling hot, stir in Indian meal, or buckwheat flour, or half and half, just as you like. When as thick as hasty pudding, take up, and when wanted for use cut off slices and fry; there should be fat enough to fry itself. This makes a nice breakfast dish.

ROAST PORK.

Take a sharp knife and cut in squares, or all one way, through the rind; rub on salt, pepper, and sage; put in a dripping-pan, with a cupful of water; set in the oven and bake from two to three hours. If a leg is to be baked, take out the bone, and fill with a stuffing of bread, pepper, salt, and sage; fasten it up; roast a fine brown, and serve with apple-sauce; make a gravy of flour. This is called mock goose, and is very nice.

HAM ROASTED.

Make a stuffing as for a turkey, take out the bone and fill up with the dressing, put into a dripping-pan with water, and cook until tender; make a gravy of flour. It is better to boil two hours in a cloth before baking, then take off the skin and rub bread-crumbs on top.

TO FRY SALT PORK.

Soak in cold water until freshened sufficient, then dip in flour and fry brown, or make a batter and dip in. You can cut it in slices and put in a spider, pour cold water on and just let it boil, take out and turn out the water, then put the meat back and fry to a nice brown. Take up, and stir up a large spoonful of flour with a pint of rich milk, (water will answer,) and pour in; when thick, take up.

PORK STEAKS.

Cut in slices and broil the same as beef, only slower and longer. When done, season with butter, pepper, and salt; add catsup if liked. They are nice fried, seasoned with sage, pepper, and salt, or dip in egg and flour, like veal cutlets.

A PORK STEW.

Take a few slices of fresh pork, a dozen potatoes pared, put into a kettle with water to cover them; let them cook an hour and a half; keep well covered while cooking; add salt and pepper, and put on top slices of bread; this is a nice way to use up the dry pieces which may have been left; let it simmer five minutes, and take up. Salt pork may be used, but in that case no salt will be required. A pie may be made of pork the same as a veal or a chicken pie, only slice a few potatoes in.

TO MAKE A CHOWDER.

Cut a few slices of pork and fry brown, then take them out and lay in fish cut lengthwise, then a layer of crackers, very thin sliced potatoes, sliced onions, with some of the pork, and then a layer of fish again, and so on; add a little salt and pepper over each layer, also a sliced lemon; pour over the whole a bowlful of flour and water well stirred up; it must cover the whole; cover tight, that the steam can not escape; it must not be opened until done.

PORK SAUSAGES.

Take one third fat to two thirds of lean pork; take out all the bones; cut in strips, and run through a sausage-cutter; to every pound of meat, add a large spoonful of sweet herbs, a heaping tea-spoonful of salt, and the same of pepper; mix well, and fill your casings, or pack in jars, turning melted lard to keep the air from it. When used, make into little cakes, by flouring your hand to keep them from sticking; also, to make them fry better. Fry slowly, and when done, make a gravy of flour.

ANOTHER RECEIPT.

To twelve pounds of meat, add twelve large spoonfuls of sage, eight of salt, six of black pepper; you may add half a tea-cupful of brown sugar, if you like, and a very little saltpetre; they will keep better. It is always well to take out some of the meat after mixing, and fry, and if not seasoned sufficient, add more.

BOLOGNA SAUSAGES.

Take equal quantities of pork, ham, beef or veal, run through a meat-cutter; then season highly with salt, cloves, pepper and allspice; do not put in sweet herbs, as they will not keep as well. Try a little before filling the casings; put them in brine, and let them remain nine or ten days; then smoke them, or boil until tender; then dry them. Another method is, to boil beef, chop fine, and season with Cayenne and black pepper, and cloves; put in bags, and cut off for tea.

SAUSAGES IN SUMMER.

Chop salt pork one third, to two thirds of beef; season with salt, pepper, cloves, and allspice; do up the meat into small cakes, and fry them brown.

HAM SANDWICHES.

Spread thin slices of bread with butter; lay thin slices of boiled ham between; add mustard, if you like. Cold tongue, sliced, will answer. Lay on plates. It is nice for tea or for luncheon.

A VEAL HASH.

Cut veal into strips, (either baked or roasted;) flour and fry to a light brown, in butter; take them up, and pour in a little water; season with salt, catsup, pepper, and lemon-juice; then put in the meat, and heat hot.

COLD MEAT TURNOVERS.

Roll bread-dough very thin; have meat chopped fine, seasoned with pepper, salt, sweet herbs and catsup; roll in little balls; then fry in lard until the dough is well cooked. The catsup may be left out, if not liked.

POTATO PIE.

Take mashed potatoes, seasoned, and line a baking-dish; put in slices of cold meats, with butter, catsup, pepper and salt; then potatoes, and so on; lastly, a cover of potatoes; bake until all warmed through.

A MEAT HASH.

Take six large tomatoes; pour on boiling water to take the skins off; then slice them with or without an onion; put in a stew-pan, with a spoonful of sugar, a piece of butter, pepper, and salt, and half a pint of cold water; shave up the meat as thin as possible; put in a little flour, and cook slowly one hour. It is delicious.

RICE CHICKEN PIE.

Line a pudding-dish with slices of boiled ham; joint a boiled chicken, and put in; pour in melted butter, a little curry-powder, or onions; fill up with boiled rice, and cover the top; pour in a little water; bake three quarters of an hour.

VEAL HASH, WITH TOAST.

Chop the veal fine, adding half as much stale bread as meat; put in a basin, and turn on the following sauce: mix a tea-spoonful of flour with cold water; turn on a tea-cupful of hot water; let it boil until thick; two spoonfuls of butter, salt, and pepper: pour on to the meat, and let it stand where it will keep warm; toast some bread, and lay on a dish; turn the hash over; cut slices of lemon to lay on the top, and garnish the dish.

BOILED PORK.

Take salt pork, and wash well in cold water, and boil until the rind is tender, when the pork will be done; skim the fat off, and boil such vegetables as are in the season, and serve with it.

LOIN OF PORK.

Cut the rind in squares, and boil until almost tender; then take up and skin; rub the yolk of an egg over it, and sprinkle on bread-crumbs.

TO DRESS A RUMP OF BEEF A LA BOUILLIE.

Take the high bone out of the rump of beef, and pour on a gill of vinegar, after having washed it well; dredge it with flour, and put in a pot, with three pints of water, and put over the fire until it boils; prepare and slice potatoes, carrots, cabbage, turnips, nearly a pint-bowl of each; two onions sliced, and a sprig of sweet marjoram; put into the pot, with a table-spoonful of pepper, and two of salt; when boiled, set where it will just stew, five hours, frequently turning it, as there will not be liquor enough to cover it. Pickled capers and cucumbers are a great improvement to the sauce.

RISSOLES.

Mince fine a quarter of a pound of any kind of cold meat; add a table-spoonful of suet or butter, and as much of bread-crumbs, pepper, salt, lemon-peel, parsley and spice, if you like; mix all together with two whites of an egg with a little gravy; make into balls, and fry a light brown; or omit the bread-crumbs, and put between a puff-paste, cut round; do them over with eggs and bread-crumbs; then fry a light brown. Serve on a napkin.

A RICH CHICKEN PUDDING.

Cut up a pair of chickens, and put into a pot, with just water enough to cover them; put in two table-spoonfuls of butter, pepper, salt, mace and nutmeg; stew gently until half tender, or a little more; then take them out, and set away to cool; reserve the gravy to be served up separately; make a batter of six eggs, well beaten; a pound of sifted flour stirred into a quart of milk; add a little salt; put a layer of chicken in a pudding-dish; turn on some of the batter, then a layer of chicken, and so on, until full, having a layer of pudding on top; bake until brown; break an egg into the gravy, and boil up; then serve with the pudding

OYSTER SAUSAGES.

Beard three dozen of oysters, and chop up, but not too fine; add half a pound of fine bread-crumbs; the same of suet, chopped fine; a tea-spoonful of mace, a salt-spoonful of salt, pepper, and the same quantity of Cayenne; moisten the whole with the yolks of three unbeaten eggs and the whites of one; work well together, and let it remain three or four hours before using; make up in little cakes, and flour well; then fry in butter to a light brown.

BEEF COBBETS.

Take fresh beef, and cut into pieces the size of an egg; put into a kettle of water, and when it boils take off the scum; then put in cloves, mace, allspice, and whole pepper, tied in a bit of muslin; six heads of celery cut an inch long; a carrot cut in slices; two turnips, cut small; a bundle of sweet herbs, pepper and salt, and a crust of bread; stew till the meat is tender; then take out the spice and herbs; have some French rolls crisped before the fire; put them in a dish, and put the meat over them.

MOCK GOOSE, OR LEG OF PORK.

Parboil it; take off the skin, and put it down to roast; baste it with butter, and make a savory powder of finely minced or dried and powdered sage, ground black pepper, salt, bread-crumbs rubbed together through a colander; add a little finely-minced onion; sprinkle it with this when nearly done; put half a pint of made gravy into the dish, and a goose-stuffing, under the knuckle-skin, or garnish the dish with balls of some of it, fried.

HAM WITH MADEIRA.

Soak in water a ham two hours, then boil it two hours; take off the skin, and put it into a stew-pan, with thin slices of veal at the bottom; add carrots and parsley, and season with spices; pour over it a pint of rich stock, and a pint of Madeira, and boil two hours; then strain and take the fat off the sauce, and serve hot.

LOAF HAM.

Soak a ham in cold water a day; then put it into a kettle, with no more water than will cover it, and add a pint of wine; skim it carefully till done; when done, take out the bones, remove the skin, pare off some of the fat; make a force of the fat, with veal or game, and sweet herbs pounded, and all minced fine; line a pan with quite thick paste; then cut your ham in thin slices, and place alternate layers of it and of the force in the pan, till nearly full; put a crust over the top, and bake nearly two hours.

CHICKENS FRIED. NO. 2.

Cut up a chicken in quarters; take off the skin, and dip in beaten egg; cover with grated bread; season with salt, pepper, grated lemon-peel, chopped parsley; fry in butter; thicken a little brown gravy with flour, and add lemon, pickle and mushroom catsup, if you like.

CHICKENS AND OYSTERS.

Fill young chickens with oysters, cut small, parsley, spices and truffles; then roast them; blanch two dozen oysters, and toss them up with melted butter and chopped herbs; when they have been on half an hour, add a glass of white wine and half a glass of good stock; thicken it over the fire, and when the chickens are done, pour the sauce over them, and garnish the dish with the oysters and lemon. A turkey may be dressed in the same way.

FRIED CHICKEN. NO. 1.

Cut in pieces, and fry in butter until cooked through; season with pepper and salt; then beat an egg light, dip the chicken in, then in flour, and fry brown.

FROGS.

The hind-quarters only are used; they should be seasoned with pepper and salt, and fried in butter, after rolling in flour. Another way is to fricassee them, and make a gravy of flour and butter.

A UNION DISH.

Chop up cold beef or veal; season with pepper and salt, adding a piece of butter, and gravy, if you have it, if not, pour in a little water; then put on a covering of mashed potatoes, and bake three quarters of an hour.

MEAT CAKES.

Take whatever meat you may have, game or poultry, —it is better for being under-done—mince it fine, adding a little salt pork, or ham, or anchovy; season with pepper and salt; mix together, and make into small cakes, about three inches in length, and an inch and a half in width, and half an inch thick; fry them of a light brown, and serve with a good gravy; or they may be baked.

TO MINCE VEAL.

Chop cold roast veal, add a little nutmeg, lemon-peel, (shred,) salt, and four or five spoonfuls of broth, milk, or water; simmer gently, but do not let it boil; add a bit of butter, rolled in flour; put pieces of thin toasted bread, cut into a three-cornered shape, round the dish. Fried crumbs of bread, strewed lightly over, is an improvement to the look and flavor.

MATELOTE MEAT.

Take equal quantities of beef, veal, pork, and mutton, a slice each, and a small leg of lamb, cut them in small pieces, which put into a saucepan with equal quantities of stock and champagne, salt and pepper; cover close, and set them on hot ashes six hours, then serve.

MINUTE DISH.

Cut thin slices of veal, and about four inches long; season with pepper and salt; lay them in a deep dish, pour over them half a pint of wine, let it stand three hours; cover the bottom of the stewpan with butter, and dredge each piece of the veal with flour; add a little more white wine and as much good stock as will cover it, and the juice of a lemon; cover the pan closely and let it simmer five minutes, and remove instantly, or it will become hard.

CHICKEN SALAD. NO. 2.

Chop the white meat of three boiled chickens, the same quantity of salad not too fine, mash the yolks of ten hard-boiled eggs, and chop the whites of the eggs very fine; mix half a tea-cup of mustard, and stir in gradually, with melted butter, into the yolks, then add the whites; just before serving, add salt, and pour over the chicken and celery; add vinegar. Lobster salad is made in the same way. Salads may be made of almost any kind of meat or vegetables. Extract of celery may be used if the vegetable can not be procured.

PICKLED BEEF.

Take beef, and season with salt, pepper, and stick it full of cloves; cover the meat with good vinegar, let it remain a fortnight, turning it every day and keeping it well covered with vinegar; then put it in a stewpan with vinegar and water, cover tight, and if a large piece, stew six hours. Eat with cooked onions. Good cold.

AN EXTRA METHOD OF COOKING SIRLOIN.

Take about two or three pounds, boil in one pint of water, with pepper and salt, till done; then roll in a mixture of butter, sweet herbs, parsley, shallots and crumbs of bread, all minced fine, and put in buttered paper; twist the ends, and broil over hot coals, with another sheet of paper laid on the gridiron.

TONGUE.

Tongue may be corned and smoked, or boiled and sliced cold for tea or sandwiches. It may be stewed or stuffed, or it may be boiled, then sliced and mixed with bread-crumbs, sweet herbs, pepper and salt, and baked.

FRICASSEE TRIPE.

Having it nicely dressed and cut in squares, then put in a stewpan with a little water; and add cream and butter with flour made smooth just before taking up. It does not require cooking long. It is nice rolled in bread-crumbs and fried in butter or drippings, or dipped in egg and then in flour or crumbs, and fried.

BEEF RISSOLES. NO. 2.

Chop a pound of lean tender beef, and a quarter of a pound of suet; pound well together, and mix a quarter of a pound of bread-crumbs, a little onion, a head of garlic bruised; season with salt and pepper, then beat three eggs light, and mix in; make in small cakes and fry of a light brown, then stew them in gravy fifteen or twenty minutes.

FRENCH VEAL CUTLETS

Cut from the loin and cover with a mixture of bread-crumbs, onions, parsley, salt, pepper, and an egg well beaten; butter foolscap paper, and inclose each cutlet, twisting the paper at each end; broil slowly on the gridiron, then turn over to cook on the other side. Veal-steak may be cooked in the same way.

VEAL A LA MODE.

Take a round of veal, and lard closely with fat pork cut thin; season, salt, pepper, and spices; put in a large stewpan with water and a little butter; stew gently three or four hours. It may be put in a deep dish and baked, in which case it should have a cover of paste, made of flour and water.

FRICANDEAU OF VEAL.

Take a fillet of veal, or a round slice from the leg two inches thick, lard it with thin slices of pork previously seasoned with salt, pepper, sweet herbs, and spices; blanch the whole in boiling water, then put it in a stewpan with boiling water, well seasoning the meat, and cook slowly till done. Put it in a dish, strain the gravy, take off the grease, and boil down; put in the veal on the larded side, and glaze well; when of a good brown, take up and cover with what gravy you have left. Good cold.

TO COLLAR VEAL.

Take the bone out of a breast of veal, and beat it flat; cover the inside with a nice stuffing, moistened with eggs; roll tightly and bind it, bake in an oven, with some weak stock in the dish; when done make a gravy with flour and pour over the veal. Serve with force-meat balls or without, and garnish with cut lemon.

VEAL, COLD DRESSED.

Mince cold roast veal, and season with pepper, salt, nutmeg and lemon-peel, moisten it with white stock and a beaten egg; butter a pudding-dish, put in the meat, press it firmly, cover tightly, and set it in a pan of boiling water, let it stand an hour or two; serve it with a white gravy thickened, or rub it over the top with the beaten yolk of an egg; sift bread-crumbs thickly over it and brown in an oven; baste with melted butter; garnish with fried parsley or cut lemon.

VEAL LEG IN SURPRISE.

Lard the veal with slips of fat pork, and a little lemon-peel cut very thin; make a stuffing as for a fillet of veal, only add half a pint of oysters chopped small; stuff your veal and stew gently (with just sufficient to cover it) till tender, then take up, and skim off the fat, and add lemon-juice, mushroom catsup, crumbs of bread grated fine, half a pint of oysters, the same of cream, and a piece of butter rolled in flour; thicken this over the fire and serve with the veal; garnish the dish with oysters, dipped in butter and fried, and thin slices of broiled ham.

MINCED COLLOPS.

Take raw beef and chop very fine, pepper and salt it, then pan in small jars and pour clarified butter over it. When used put the butter into a stewpan, and slice some onions into the pan and fry them; add a little water to it, and put in the meat. Stew it well, and in a few minutes it will be fit to serve. This is a Scotch dish, and will keep well and always be ready for use.

MUTTON CUTLETS.

Cut the thickest part of a leg of mutton into cutlets; beat well. Mix grated bread-crumbs, pepper, salt, (and if liked) finely chopped parsley and sweet marjoram. Dip the cutlets into melted butter and cover with the bread; then fry in butter or drippings ten or fifteen minutes.

MUTTON LEG STUFFED.

Make a stuffing with beef suet chopped, pepper, salt, sweet herbs, a little lemon grated, nutmeg, if you like, and a few bread-crumbs, mix all together with the yolk of an egg, put this under the skin in the thickest part of a leg of mutton under the flap, then roast it and serve it with gravy in the dish.

MUTTON LEG STUFFED WITH OYSTERS.

Make a force-meat of beef suet chopped, the yolks of hard-boiled eggs, thyme, savory, a little onion with three anchovies, (or not, just as you like,) a dozen oysters cut fine, pepper, salt, grated nutmeg, crumbs of bread, mixed up with raw eggs. Put this force-meat under the skin in the thickest part of the leg of mutton, under the flap and at the knuckle. For sauce, some oyster-liquor, a little red wine, an anchovy, some more oysters stewed and served under the mutton.

MUTTON STEAKS BROILED.

Cut from the thickest part of the mutton half an inch thick, beat well, and as soon as the gridiron is hot rub it with a little suet, lay on the steaks and turn frequently until done; then put them in a hot dish, adding pepper, salt, and butter; add a little catsup or tomatoes cooked if desired, and send hot to the table.

TO COOK MUTTON HAM.

If it has been smoked, soak several hours in cold water, then put into cold water and boil gently two hours. It is nice eaten cold for breakfast, luncheon or tea.

MUTTON CHOPS.

Cut the chops off a loin or the best end of a neck of mutton, pare off the fat, then dip them into the yolk of eggs beaten, and strew over them grated bread seasoned with pepper, salt, and parsley; fry them in butter and lay them upon the back of a sieve before the fire to drain. Thicken the gravy, add a table-spoonful of catsup and one of port wine; put the gravy into the dish and lay in the chops; garnish with fried parsley or cut lemon.

HUNG MUTTON.

Take a leg of mutton, rub well with pepper, salt, sweet herbs and vinegar; let it hang three or four days in a dry, cool place, then roast, basting with vinegar, water, and sweet herbs. Strain the gravy and stir in flour, butter, and currant-jelly. Serve in a boat.

SHOULDER OF MUTTON A LA TURQUE.

Boil a shoulder of mutton in sufficient water to cover. Season with cloves, sweet herbs, shallots, garlic, carrots, celery, parsley, pepper and salt. When done take out the meat and place over a kettle of hot water to keep it warm. Strain the broth and add one tea-cupful of rice, and boil till thick. Place the meat in a dish, cover over with cooked rice and brown in the oven. Mix two tea-spoonfuls of curry-powder in the broth after straining.

HARICOT OF MUTTON.

Take a shoulder of mutton, cut in strips or pieces two or three inches long; have a stewpan ready with a piece of butter and a table-spoonful of flour; brown it, and then put in the meat; stir around, and add a pint of water; season with pepper, salt, and sweet herbs. Boil slowly. If too fat, skim and then add turnips pared and cut in quarters. Stew till done. Serve in a deep platter, placing the turnips round the meat; pour the gravy over.

MUTTON LEG STUFFED. NO. 2.

Take a leg of mutton, cut off the fat, take out the bone, preserve the skin whole, mince the meat fine; add about a pound of fat pork and some parsley, season with pepper and salt, then put the meat into the skin and sew up on the under side; put it into a stewpan with some gravy made from the bones, two or three slices of veal, some sliced carrots and onions, a bunch of parsley, and a few slices of pork. Stew three or four hours and drain the liquor through a sieve; when reduced to a glaze, glaze the mutton with it and serve in stewed French beans.

MUTTON SAUSAGES.

Take pieces of cold mutton, some suet, two anchovies, one pint of oysters, mince the whole very fine. Season with pepper, salt, mace or nutmeg, and add two well-beaten eggs, and four ounces of bread-crumbs. Put in a jar and press down. Keep in a dry, cool place, and when used roll in cakes and fry brown.

ROAST LAMB.

Take the leg of a lamb, rub on pepper, salt, and flour; lay in a dripping-pan with water, and roast from one to two hours; then make a gravy. It is nice larded with pork. Mutton is very nice roasted down in a ketttle; boil tender first and season.

MUTTON WITH CREAM.

Stew some steaks in milk and water till tender, then season with pepper, salt, and mace if you like. Make smooth a spoonful of flour, and add some cream. Scald up and send to the table.

MUTTON FILLET STEWED.

Put a fillet of mutton or beef, weighing seven pounds, into a stewpan with a carrot, a turnip, and an onion with three or four cloves stuck in it, and a quart of water; season with pepper and salt. Cover close and stew from three to four hours, then take out the meat and strain the gravy; thicken with flour and garnish with sliced gherkins. It is nice stewed without the vegetables.

MINCED MUTTON.

Take the meat of the neck, mince fine, and add two onions, a few green peas, a piece of butter, a gill of water, pepper and salt. Simmer slowly two hours, keeping it well covered. Have ready some rice boiled dry. Put in a deep dish and dress on top with the rice.

A SHOULDER OF LAMB.

Boil till tender, then take out the bones and broil; season with butter, pepper, and salt. Send to the table hot.

ROLLED MUTTON.

Take out the bone of a shoulder carefully, so as not to injure the skin, mince the meat very fine; season highly with pepper, salt, sweet herbs, or any thing you like, roll very tightly in the skin, tie it round, and bake from two to three hours in a dripping-pan with a little water in; serve with a gravy.

BEEF BAKED WITH POTATOES.

Boil peeled potatoes and mash them with two small onions, moisten them with an egg beaten, and a little milk, add salt and pepper. Season slices of beef or mutton chops with salt and pepper, rub the bottom of a pudding-dish with butter, and put a laying of mashed potatoes, then a laying of meat, and so alternately till the dish is filled, ending with potatoes. Bake one hour in an oven.

CORNED BEEF. NO. 2.

Cover with water after washing it, and boil slowly from three to four hours, according to the size; vegetables or dumplings may be served with it.

BEEFSTEAK PUDDING.

Take nice steaks, season with pepper, salt, and butter, roll in a good soda biscuit crust, and boil two hours.

BEEF LIVER. NO. 2.

Scald the liver in two or three waters for an hour, then cut in slices, wipe dry; dredge with flour, pepper, and salt, and fry in pork drippings. Serve hot and garnish with fried potatoes.

BŒUF A LA MODE.

Take six or eight pounds of good tender beef, lard it with thin strips of fat pork, which has been seasoned with sweet herbs, cloves, pepper, and salt. Put in a stewpan one glass of wine, water or tomato juice, six small peeled onions, and six carrots, put the meat on top of all this, cover tight, and stew five or six hours slowly; serve all together in a deep dish.

PRESSED BEEF. NO. 1.

Take a flank or piece of brisket, rub with a mixture of salt, a little saltpetre, spices and sugar; let it remain a few days, then boil slowly till tender; press under a weight till cold. Slice off and cut as headcheese or sandwiches.

PRESSED BEEF. NO. 2.

Take a piece of beef near the neck, wash clean and boil till tender, take out the bones, mince the meat, season with salt and pepper, spices if liked, add some of the liquor to make quite soft, then press as head-cheese. Serve cold, sliced, or in sandwiches.

BEEF A LA MUSKMELON.

Take cold beef or any other cold meat, mince it with cold potatoes, sweet herbs, pepper, salt, and onions if desired, add two well-beaten eggs and flour enough to mould as a melon, put it in a dripping-pan with butter or drippings, and baste occasionally; bake one hour.

BEEF BALLS.

Mince good tender beef, lean and fat, add grated bread-crumbs, season with salt and pepper, moisten with beaten eggs, roll it into balls, flour, and fry them in hot drippings. Serve with fried bread-crumbs or with a thickened gravy. Spices and lemon-peel may be added if liked.

TO WARM COLD STEAKS.

Lay pieces of cold steak in a stewpan, slice up an onion, add six berries of allspice, the same of black pepper, pour on a little water, cover tight, and stew one hour gently; thicken the liquor with butter and flour rubbed together; take all up together on the same dish.

JELLIED BEEF A LA MODE.

Take six or eight pounds of beef, a knuckle of veal, lard it with fat pork, previously seasoning the pork with spices and sweet herbs. Put the meat in a large stewpan with water, pepper, and salt, cover closely and simmer three hours, then add two carrots, and two onions cut in slices, and boil two or three hours more; when done, take up the meat, and clarify the gravy with the white of an egg, boil a few minutes and pour it over the meat. To be eaten cold. Wine can be added if liked. It is an elegant dish.

VEAL A LA FRANCAISE.

Take a breast of veal, put in a deep dish with a pint of water, a table-spoonful of vinegar, salt, pepper, shallots, parsley, a bay-leaf, a clove of garlic, three cloves and two carrots; cover tight with paste around to keep close, bake three hours in a moderate oven.

COLD VEAL.

Cut veal in small pieces, with onions, pork and a little veal-gravy or water, pepper, and salt; have ready some mashed potatoes, in which put cream, pepper, salt, and one egg; put the meat in a deep dish, and put the potatoes on top, raising it from the sides in the shape of a pyramid; smooth nicely and bake brown. Another way is to mince cold veal with ham, season and roll in good paste, in the form of a ball, then fry in hot drippings.

MARBLED PRESSED VEAL.

Take equal quantities of cold veal, and boiled tongue, pound separately in a mortar, adding melted butter as you proceed; have a mould ready, and put in alternate layers of veal and tongue, till used up; let veal be the last layer; cover with melted butter. When pressed it is ready for use. Cut in slices, makes good sandwiches.

VEAL CONES.

Mince a pound and a half of veal, one slice of ham, two ounces of butter, pound them in a mortar, and mix five table-spoonfuls of cream, two tea-spoonfuls of pepper, one of salt, and some grated lemon-peel, make it up into cones about three inches high, rub them with an egg beaten up, sift grated bread-crumbs over them, and fry them of a light brown; put fried bread-crumbs in a dish and place the cones upon them, or serve with a brown gravy instead of the crumbs. Cold fowl or rabbit makes nice cones.

VEAL PATTIES.

Mince some under-done veal with a little parsley, onions, and sage leaves; season with lemon-peel, nutmeg, pepper, and salt; moisten with a little gravy, heat it up and put into the patties.

A JERSEY DISH.

Take fresh pork and put in a bake-oven, or stewpan, season with salt and pepper, cover over with apples which have been peeled, quartered, and cored, (pippins are best,) cover tightly, then stew gently three hours.

ROLLED PORK.

Take the neck, or backbone; take out the bones; make a dressing, as for a goose, and roll in the meat; tie firmly; roast or bake; baste with melted butter, flour, and water.

TO ROAST A HAUNCH OF VENISON.

Rub well with warm water, then with port wine or claret; put buttered paper around, to prevent its scorching; secure the paper with pack-thread, soaked in water; roast as you would a sirloin of beef, or bake; baste with wine and water, or currant-jelly; season with pepper and salt; cook about three hours. Before serving, baste with butter and flour to froth it; trim the venison with paper. Eat with cranberry sauce or currant-jelly.

VENISON HASH.

Take some of the gravy which it has previously been cooked in, if not, use water; add butter and a little flour made smooth, currant-jelly; let it boil up; then put in the minced venison, and when warm, take up. If it boils it will be tough.

SQUIRRELS STEWED.

Parboil, and wipe dry; then put in another water, and stew till most dry; then season with butter, pepper, and salt; thicken the gravy with flour, made smooth. Rabbit stewed the same way. They may be stuffed with a force-meat, highly seasoned, and roasted.

CHICKENS FRIED. NO. 3.

Take a young chicken; beat with a pounder; then fry in pork drippings; fry gently and turn over; when done, dip each piece into a fritter-batter, and fry brown. Fried oysters served with it are nice.

BOILED CHICKEN.

Stuff a well-dressed fowl with oysters, bread-crumbs, parsley, butter, pepper, and salt; roll in a floured cloth; put in a pot of cold water, with a head of celery, and a half tea-cup of water; boil slowly one hour and a half. Eat with oyster sauce or plain drawn butter. Garnish with hard-boiled eggs and curled parsley.

PICKLED GOOSE.

Make a pickle of vinegar and water, equal parts, salt, pepper, sweet herbs, garlic, and onions; put in your goose, and let it remain four days, turning three or four times every day; when ready to cook, drain and wipe dry; lard with salt pork; bake or stew slowly; baste with currant wine or jelly, and water. Seasoned goose is excellent cooked as Bœuf à la Mode.

A BONED TURKEY.

Have the turkey nicely dressed; then take a sharp knife, and commence at the wings, carefully separating the flesh from the bones, scraping it down as you go; do not break the skin. Next loosen the flesh from the breast, back, and thighs lastly. When all the flesh is loosened, take the turkey by the neck, and pull the skeleton out; take a needle and sew up the skin, if broken; then commence stuffing, first the wings, next the body, and then the thighs. It must be stuffed hard, and if properly done, will assume its natural shape. Sew up the breast, and skewer it into its proper form. Bake three hours. Any large fowl may be boned and stuffed in the same way.

TO FRY RABBITS.

Have well cleaned and washed; scald from ten to fifteen minutes; cut up in pieces; then dip in beaten eggs, and roll in bread-crumbs, pepper, and salt; fry in butter or drippings till done; make a gravy with flour, and pour over.

HAM TOAST.

Pound cold cooked ham, (or chop it, just as you like;) mix with beaten egg and cream; pour over toasted bread; serve hot. Any other kind of meat may be prepared in the same way.

GRAVIES AND SAUCES.

DRAWN BUTTER.

Take a table-spoonful of flour, with just water enough to mix well, then pour in a little more, (after the lumps are out,) and stir up; then stir in one tea-cupful of boiling water; let it boil up; then remove to where it will keep warm, but not boil; put in a quarter of a pound of butter, and let it stand until melted, when it will be ready for use. It must be free from lumps. If used for fish, put in boiled eggs, sliced up, or capers. If required for curry sauce, sprinkle in curry-powder.

BURNT BUTTER.

Heat three ounces of butter, until it is a nice brown; add half a tea-cupful of good vinegar, half a tea-spoonful of salt, and a third of a tea-spoonful of pepper. This is a nice sauce for fish or eggs.

DRAWN MEAT GRAVY, OR BROWN GRAVIES.

Put into a saucepan, a pound of fresh chopped meat, two table-spoonfuls of melted butter, salt, and pepper; let it brown nicely, taking care that it does not stick; pour on a pint of boiling water, and let it simmer three hours; skim well; then strain it, and cover up tight till wanted. When used, thicken with brown flour, a teaspoonful to half a pint.

OYSTER SAUCE.

Take a quart of oyster sauce, a stick of mace, pepper, and salt. If you have not juice sufficient, put one third water; then take two table-spoonfuls of flour, wet smooth with a tea-cupful of milk. When it has boiled up, put a quart of oysters in, and a piece of butter the size of a hen's egg; take up after boiling a few minutes, as boiling makes oysters shrivel up. Serve with poultry.

CELERY VINEGAR.

Pound in a mortar two gills of celery seed, and add good vinegar; shake every day for a week or two. It must be kept corked and sealed.

CELERY SAUCE FOR BOILED FOWLS.

Take the green tops off of four heads of celery, and cut into small pieces, and boil in half a pint of water, until tender. Mix two table-spoonfuls of flour with half a cup of milk; stir in with salt, and butter. When it boils, take up.

LIVER SAUCE FOR FISH.

Boil the liver of the fish, until tender enough to mash fine; stir it into drawn butter; add a spoonful of catsup, salt, and pepper. A little lemon or vinegar is an improvement.

CRANBERRY SAUCE.

Stew them in water, until tender; then add sugar, and let it scald well. Strain if you like, but I prefer without.

APPLE SAUCE.

Pare and core tart apples; stew until tender, then sweeten, and add a little butter; a little lemon or nutmeg is an improvement. Another way is to take sweet apples, pare and quarter nicely; then dry one day; then take new cider, which has been boiled down rich, one quart to one and a half of water, and stew slowly from two to three hours, in brass or tin. This will keep six months if made rich; a few quinces add very much to the flavor.

LOBSTER SAUCE.

Take the yolks of two hard-boiled eggs, two spoonfuls of melted butter, or salad oil, a mustard-spoonful of mustard, some of the lobster spawn, six spoonfuls of vinegar, salt, and pepper.

BROWN SAUCE FOR POULTRY.

Peel two or three onions, slice them, fry them brown in butter, sprinkle salt, pepper, flour, and sweet-marjoram or thyme; add half a pint of the liquor in which the poultry was boiled or roasted, some of the drippings, and a large spoonful of catsup.

RICE SAUCE.

Boil half a tea-cupful of rice; put in a blade of mace; slice up an onion, and when tender, and the water all absorbed, stir in a gill of milk, a tea-spoonful of salt, and strain it. This is nice for game.

HERB SPIRIT.

Take sweet herbs, such as sage, summer savory, thyme, sweet basil, sweet marjoram; dry them; then pound, and steep in brandy two or three weeks. This is convenient to use.

SAUCE FOR TURTLE, AND CALVES' HEAD.

Take half a pint of drawn butter; put in sweet marjoram, pepper, and salt, the juice and rind of half a lemon. When taken from the fire, add a wine-glass of white wine.

WINE SAUCE FOR VENISON OR MUTTON.

Warm half a pint of the drippings; wet a little flour to thicken; and season with salt, pepper, and cloves, just removing from the fire a glass of wine, or currant-jelly.

BROWNING FOR MADE DISHES.

Put a pound of good brown sugar in a saucepan, stir it constantly over a slow fire; boil till quite thick and brown, but do not burn it; take it off the fire, and stir in slowly a quart of boiling water; set it on the fire, and boil up, then turn out, and when cold, bottle it. This will keep a year, and a very little serves for soups, gravies or sauces.

TOMATO SAUCE.

Take one peck of green tomatoes, slice them, one dozen small onions, sliced; sprinkle over them a little salt, then let them remain twenty-four hours; drain them and add one quarter of a pound mustard-seed, whole, one box ground mustard, one ounce of pepper, one of allspice, the same of ginger; cover them with vinegar and boil slowly three hours, or until transparent.

SALAD DRESSING.

Take one cup of good vinegar, a tea-spoonful of oil, or melted butter, one of made mustard, the yolk of a hard-boiled egg rubbed fine, a salt-spoonful of salt; pour over the salad and send to the table.

PEPPER SAUCE.

Take a dozen ripe pepper-pods, cut them in two, lay them in a kettle with three pints of vinegar, and boil to one quart; strain through a sieve. This gives a flavor greatly superior to black pepper: it is also nice when added to catsup for fish-sauce.

DRAWN BUTTER. No. 2.

Take a few spoonfuls of flour, wet with cold water until all the lumps are out, then turn in a little more water; stir up, and then turn on boiling water enough to make a thick paste; put in one third as much butter as you have of gravy; let it remain where it is warm until melted, when it is fit for use. If used for fish, put in boiled eggs sliced up, or capers. Curry-sauce is the same, by sprinkling in a little curry-powder.

BURNT BUTTER. No. 2.

Put a quarter of a pound of butter in frying-pan, and brown nicely without being burnt, then add a cupful of vinegar; season with salt and pepper. This is nice for fish, salads, or eggs.

CURRANT SAUCE FOR VENISON.

Boil an ounce of dried currants in half a pint of water, add a tea-cupful of bread-crumbs, a glass of port wine, six cloves, and a piece of butter; stir until smooth.

SAUCE FOR COLD MEAT, FISH, OR SALAD.

Boil a couple of eggs three minutes, take off the shells, and then mix them with half a tea-cupful of vinegar, half a cup of butter or salad oil, a tea-spoonful of made mustard, a little salt and pepper; if you like, add catsup.

PUDDING SAUCE.

Stir half a tea-cup of butter to one of sugar to a cream; the more it is stirred the nicer it is; flavor with nutmeg, lemon, or wine, according to the taste. Another way of making sauce is to stir butter and a spoonful of flour together until free from lumps; turn on hot water sufficient to thicken to the proper consistency; add sugar, and any kind of flavoring you like. Brandy is nice for this kind.

CURRY-POWDER.

Mix an ounce of black pepper, mustard, ginger, each, three of coriander seed, the same of tumeric, one quarter of an ounce Cayenne pepper, half an ounce cardamus, the same of cummin-seed and cinnamon; pound the whole fine, sift, and keep in a bottle corked tight.

TOMATO SOY.

Put ripe tomatoes in a dish, (having previously pricked them with a fork,) to each layer sprinkle a little salt; let them remain three or four days, then put them in vinegar for one night; the next day drain off the vinegar; put the tomatoes in a jar with sliced onions in alternate layers, sprinkle spices between each layer, allowing half a pint of English mustard-seed, half an ounce of ground cloves and pepper to each peck of tomatoes. They are good in ten or twelve days.

TO MIX MUSTARD.

Take a cup of ground mustard, mix with cold vinegar, enough to make a paste, add a tea-spoonful of salt, a heaping tea-spoonful of sugar; then thin with scalding hot vinegar, otherwise it will have a raw taste.

FRENCH SAUCE FOR PUDDING.

Take half a pound of butter, the same of brown sugar, and stir to a cream; beat the yolk of an egg, and put in with a gill of wine; let it simmer on the stove a few minutes, stirring all the time; when taken up, grate in a little nutmeg.

Sweet cream, seasoned with nutmeg or lemon, wine or brandy if you like, is a nice sauce for puddings. Sweet cream and jelly alone is nice.

SAUCE FOR GOOSE, DUCK, OR LAMB.

Chop green mint and add vinegar, with a little sugar.

DRESSING FOR A GOOSE OR DUCK.

Bread-crumbs, onion, sage, pepper, salt, cold potatoes, parsley and egg, to make it cut nice. The same for a turkey except the onions.

CLARIFIED BUTTER.

Put the butter in a kettle over the fire, when melted skim off the buttermilk; let it stand two or three minutes, and then strain into a jar for use. Butter prepared in this way is as sweet as marrow.

OYSTER DRESSING FOR BOILED FOWLS.

Take one pint of oysters, bread-crumbs, butter, pepper and salt; mince the oysters, and add an egg.

FOR BAKED FISH.

Fat pork or ham, crumbs of bread, parsley, pepper, and salt; bind with an egg. Onions may be added, if liked.

DRESSING FOR A ROAST PIG.

Mince pork liver, sweet herbs, cold potatoes, butter, pepper, salt, and the yolk of an egg.

HORSE-RADISH TO EAT WITH HOT OR COLD MEAT.

A table-spoonful of mustard, one of vinegar, three of cream, a little salt and as much horse-radish as it will take. Horse-radish mixed with vinegar alone is excellent.

LEMON SAUCE.

Slice lemons thin, then cut very small and put into melted butter.

SCORCHED FLOUR.

Brown some flour in a spider, then bottle. Excellent to brown gravies of roast meats, soups or stews.

MUSHROOM SAUCE.

Pick and peel half a pint of mushrooms, the smaller the better; wash clean, put them in a saucepan with half a pint of veal gravy or milk, pepper and salt, an ounce of butter rubbed with a table-spoonful of flour;

mix together and set them over a gentle fire till tender, then skim and strain it.

ONION SAUCE.

Take half a dozen large white onions, peel and cut in half; put them in a pan of water half an hour, then boil a quarter of an hour; pour off the water and boil till tender; strain and mash in a bowl; add butter, salt and cream; heat before serving.

STOCK FOR GRAVY OR SOUP.

Cut a knuckle of veal into slices; slice a pound of lean beef, a pound of lean ham; put all into a saucepan with three carrots, two onions, two turnips, two heads of celery and two quarts of water; cook till all are tender, but not brown.

A SAUCE FOR ROAST BEEF.

Take a table-spoonful of finely grated horse-radish, a desert-spoonful of made mustard, the same of brown sugar, then add vinegar until thick as made mustard.

AN EXCELLENT SAUCE FOR VENISON.

Take half a pint of good white vinegar, a quarter of a pound of loaf-sugar, put in a tin basin and warm slowly, or simmer gently; skim it carefully, and send to the table in a sauce-tureen.

WHITE SAUCE FOR FOWLS.

Thicken half a pint of cream with flour and butter, four shallots minced, a little mace and lemon-peel; let it boil, and a little before serving add a spoonful of white wine, the yolk of an egg beaten, and a tea-spoonful of anchovy liquor, with a squeeze of a lemon.

ANOTHER.

Melt in a tea-cupful of milk a large spoonful of butter kneaded in flour; beat up the yolk of an egg with a tea-spoonful of cream; heat it over the fire, stirring it constantly, add a little chopped parsley.

SOUPS.

If uncooked meat is used, allow a pound to one quart of water. Put the meat into cold water and heat gradually. If cooked too fast the albumen coagulates and hardens the meat; prevents the water from penetrating, consequently the flavor is lost and the meat tough. Be careful to skim as soon as any thing rises on the top, and then throw in a little salt to bring up the scum. Keep it well covered up to prevent the flavor from escaping. If more water is needed, add boiling water, as cold spoils the soup. When tender, take it out and skim well, and then season with pepper and salt, adding any vegetables you like, or sweet herbs; thicken with rice, barley, vermicelli, or little flour-balls. As potato-water is not considered healthy, it is not best to put in much, or else boil by themselves and add afterward. Cold roast beef or beefsteak may be made into soup.

BEEF SOUP.

Boil the shank of beef in sufficient water to cover it until tender; take up and take off the fat. Put in a cup of rice or macaroni broken into small bits, or little flour-balls. Season with pepper, salt, and catsup; if you have not catsup, add a few powdered cloves. Slice up two onions, one potato, and one carrot. Boil until tender.

PORTABLE SOUP.

Take the liquor in which beef or veal has been boiled, and skim off the fat; then boil down the liquor to thick consistency. Season highly with pepper, salt, cloves, and allspice; add wine or brandy, and turn on platters, not over three quarters of an inch in thickness. When cold cut in squares and set in the sun to dry, turning often. When perfectly dry, put in an earthen vessel, with a piece of white paper between each layer. Whenever you wish to make a soup, take one of them to a quart of water, heating it scalding hot; add vegetables if you like. These will keep a long time.

VEGETABLE SOUP.

Take the liquor in which any kind of fresh meat has been boiled; but mutton or lamb is the best; skim off the fat, and to four quarts of liquor put in two carrots sliced, and let them boil twenty minutes; then add two onions, two potatoes, two turnips, two tomatoes, sliced thin; season with salt and pepper to the taste. When tender take up.

PEA SOUP.

Take dry peas and soak over night in cold water, the next morning boil in the same water an hour; just before taking up, add a tea-spoonful of saleratus; then turn into a colander to drain, and then put back again with a piece of pork, pouring on fresh water; boil until soft. Green peas need not boil more than an hour. Dry beans may be cooked the same way.

TOMATO SOUP.

Boil beef or veal until tender, then skin well and cut up half a dozen ripe tomatoes or green, just as you prefer; pare them first. Season with sugar, pepper, and salt; cloves, if you like.

CHICKEN OR TURKEY SOUP

After boiling tender, skin off the fat and put in a cupful of rice and a head of celery, pepper, and salt. Pour on crackers or toasted bread.

VERMICELLI SOUP.

Make a rich soup of any kind of meat; old fowls are nice. Add a few slices of ham, two onions, one head of celery, pepper, and salt, sweet herbs, if you like. Strain it and add a quarter of a pound of vermicelli which has been scalded in boiling water. Put in Cayenne pepper, and let it boil five minutes. The meat must be boiled until it falls from the bones. Turn on toasted bread.

FORCE-MEAT BALLS.

Take two thirds lean veal, one third raw, salt pork, chop fine; season with curry-powder, pepper, salt, or leave out the curry and add cloves. Make up into balls the size of an hen's egg; boil half in the soup fifteen minutes, and fry the remainder and serve in a separate dish. For beef soup, add beef and eggs, it will make them hold together better.

OYSTER SOUP.

Put two quarts of water in a stewpan, and when boiling, add three pints of oysters. Season with salt, pepper, and stir smooth two large spoonfuls of flour; add with it a quarter of a pound of butter. Let them boil five minutes and no longer; as much boiling makes them hard and tough. You may add a pint of milk if preferred, or half milk and half water. Salt should not be put in until ready to take up, as they shrink from the effects of it.

MOCK-TURTLE SOUP.

Take a calf's head and divide the upper from the lower part, also a knuckle of veal to make force-meat balls to be added; put in a gallon of water and boil until tender. Skim carefully, and season with pepper, salt, mace, sweet herbs, curry-powder or cloves. Three sliced potatoes may be added, and the juice of two lemons, also the yolks of six eggs boiled hard. Just before taking up add half a pint of white wine; add half your force-meat balls, and fry the remainder. The brains can be put in the balls after cooking them tender.

ANOTHER METHOD.

Boil a knuckle of veal in a gallon of water, down to two quarts; strain the juice of the oysters to get out the pieces of shell. Put in the oysters, season with pepper, salt, adding two spoonfuls of flour, or eight rolled crackers, and half pint of rich milk. Butter the size of an egg. Be careful not to cook the oysters until they shrink.

CLAM SOUP.

Wash a peck of clams and put them in a stewpan with a pint of water, and when they open strain the juice, and add a pint of milk, the same of water; when they boil, stir in two spoonfuls of flour and a lump of butter the size of an egg; add pepper and mace if you like.

MACARONI SOUP.

Make a nice veal soup and season with salt, pepper, parsley, and onions. Break in pieces a quarter of a pound of macaroni, and simmer in milk until tender. Strain and add to the soup. Stir in two large spoonfuls of flour and a pint of cream.

MACARONI SOUP. NO. 2.

Boil six pounds of beef with two onions, one carrot, half a turnip, and a head of celery. Boil until tender. Turn into a pan and let it cool. Skim off the fat and pour off into the kettle half an hour before used, leaving out the sediment. Add half a pint of macaroni, broken into small pieces. Season to the taste, and add a table-spoonful of tomato catsup.

GIBLET SOUP.

Take the giblets of two fowls, the feet, neck, and pinions, add a pound of veal and a piece of ham. Cut the giblets and meat into half-inch pieces. Pour on cold water and boil until tender. Strain the liquor, and when cold take off the fat. Add a table-spoonful of flour and one of butter, with sweet herbs tied in a bag; season with salt and pepper. Boil a few minutes and then serve.

PEPPER POT.

Take an ox-heel or any other part of the beef, and boil till tender, not forgetting to skim well; when nearly done, add carrot, turnip, two onions, and two potatoes sliced. Put in Cayenne pepper, black pepper, and salt. Make a crust as for pastry, and roll thin, then cut in strips half a finger long, and half an inch in width. Put in half an hour before taking up.

LOBSTER SOUP.

Take three young hen lobsters, spit the tails, take out the fish and crack the claws, cut the meat into mouthfuls; take out the coral and the soft part of the body, bruise part of the coral in a mortar, pick out the fish from the chines, beat part of it with the coral, and with this make force-meat balls. Have three quarts of veal broth, bruise the legs and the chine; put them into it to boil twenty minutes, then strain it, and to thicken it, take the live spawn and bruise it in a mortar with a little butter and flour; rub it through a sieve, and add to it the soup with the meat of the lobster and the remaining coral, let it simmer very gently ten minutes. Do not let it boil or the color will fade; turn into a tureen and add the juice of a lemon.

WHITE SOUP.

Take a turkey or chicken, have it nicely dressed and cut up; boil slowly until tender, then add celery, carrots, onions, salt, rice, and pepper. When done, add a tea-cupful of sweet cream. This is a nice method of cooking old fowls.

OCHRA SOUP.

Fry a chicken, cut up, to a light brown, also a slice of ham. Pour on hot water, and add two onions with sweet herbs tied up in a rag. Simmer until tender, then add two dozen ochras cut in slices, and half a tea-cup of rice. Boil half an hour, and then put in a dozen oysters and a wine-glass of wine. This is nice.

GUMBO SOUP.

Make as ochra soup; and when the meat is boiled in shreds, strain, and thicken with pulverized sassafras leaves, about two tea-spoonfuls; after the oysters are put in, take off the fire, and add the powder, and stir in till it ropes, without being too thick; eat with rice. The sassafras leaves should be gathered when tender, and dried in the shade; then pulverize and bottle.

EEL, OR FISH SOUP.

Take four pounds of small eels, (having previously cleaned them;) boil in four quarts of water; add two carrots, one onion, parsley, celery, allspice, cloves, Cayenne pepper, and salt; when the vegetables are done, thicken with a little flour; add a cup of sweet cream, or, if preferred, add one glass of wine, or catsup. Any kind of hard fish may be made in this manner, but will require a little butter. Good fast-day soup.

BROWN SOUP.

This is generally made of beef. Boil till tender, then some onions, either roasted, brown, or fried, carrots, parsley, celery, sweet herbs, cloves, allspice, pepper, salt, and some rice; when the meat is boiled to shreds, strain on toasted bread; add to this, if desired, port wine, or currant-jelly.

BEAN SOUP.

Clean and wash the beans over night, then pour boiling water on them, and let them remain till morning; then take out of the water, and put over the fire, with plenty of water; wash clean a small piece of corned beef, about half as much pork, and throw in; cover tight, not forgetting to skim carefully; then put in one carrot, sliced, parsley, celery, and pepper; boil slowly, till done; strain on toasted bread. Pea soup or dry corn may be made in the same way.

EGGS.

TO CHOOSE EGGS.

A very good method of choosing eggs is to drop them in cold water, and if they sink readily, they are good; if not, throw them away. Another way is to hold them to the light; if clear, they are fresh, if not, they are not good.

FOR PRESERVING EGGS.

They may be greased, so as to stop up the pores, and packed in a box of bran, or oats, small end down. The easiest and best way that I have kept them, is to take them, when fresh, and put them in a tub, with a layer of salt at the bottom, small end downward; then a layer of salt, and a layer of eggs, until your jar, or tub, is filled. A cracked one will spoil the whole, or a bad one. They must be kept in a cool place. This is the most acceptable way of keeping them that I have ever tried. Another method is good to keep them, if rightly done. Pour a gallon of boiling water on two quarts of quicklime, and half a pound of salt; when cold, stir into it an ounce of cream of tartar, part of the lime will remain at the bottom. Put in the eggs, small end downward, and they will keep for a long time.

BOILING EGGS.

Put into boiling water, and boil three minutes, or put into cold water, and let them remain five minutes; then turn off the water, and pour on more, and let them remain five minutes longer, without boiling. For salad, or to garnish a dish, boil eight minutes. A nice way to cook them is to drop them into boiling water, and let them remain a moment, to prevent their sticking, then set on the stove until the white is set; then take up with a spoon, and lay on buttered toast.

SCRAMBLED EGGS.

Warm a little butter in a pan; then beat up eggs light, and pour it in; stir until thick, and turn on a hot dish, without allowing any to stick.

TO FRY EGGS.

Eggs are usually fried after frying ham. If there is not gravy enough, add a little lard. Break one in a saucer, at a time, and drop in; then take a spoon and turn the hot fat over, until the white is nicely set, without turning over, as they look much nicer. Lay on the ham, if you like, but a nicer way is to put them on a plate by themselves.

OMELETTE.

Take half a dozen eggs, and beat to a froth, strain through a sieve, if you like; then resume the beating until light; put in the frying-pan a piece of butter, pour in the eggs, and, as soon as firm, put a plate over, and turn the pan bottom side up; fold the omelette together, and serve hot. From five to ten minutes will cook it.

BREAD OMELETTE.

Put a handful of bread-crumbs in a sauce-pan, a little cream, salt, and pepper, nutmeg if you like; when the bread has absorbed all the bread, pour in eight eggs well beaten, and fry like an omelette. Another method is to use chopped ham or beef, instead of bread-crumbs, and fry as above.

OMELETTE.

Mix a large spoonful of flour smooth, and add a cup of milk, add a large spoonful of butter, a tea-spoonful of salt, and six eggs, the white and yolks beaten separately; heat a little butter in a pan, and turn in until cooked, then take it up as directed. It should be fried in a small spider, so that the omelette should be an inch thick.

A SWEET OMELETTE.

Beat up four eggs, add a little salt and sugar, and fry in butter; make a half a pound of preserve liquid, by shaking it over the fire; spread half of it on the omelette; double up like a turnover, and pour the rest on the top.

CUPPED EGGS.

Put a spoonful of highly seasoned gravy, or butter, in tea-cups, set the cups in boiling water, and when the gravy heats, drop a fresh egg into each one, and take off the stove, and cover the pan tight, until nicely cooked; dredge with nutmeg, and salt. Serve in a hot-water plate, covered with a napkin.

TO POACH EGGS IN A CUP.

Put a little butter, or drippings, in a spider; break the eggs gently into cups of different sizes; with a slight turn of the hand, turn the cup with the egg into the pan, until all are turned over; have a very slow fire; raise the cups a little to ascertain when done. Serve with toasted bread, or spinage.

POACHED EGGS.

Break fresh eggs into boiling water, and let them stand on the stove till the white is set, then take up carefully; trim the edges nicely, and send to the table hot.

EGGS DONE WITH CHEESE.

Put some butter in a spider, cover it with bread-crumbs; on that, lay slices of cheese; then beat eggs light; season with pepper and salt; cover tight till the eggs are done, then take up.

EGG OMELETTE.

Take one spoonful of flour, wet it with one of milk, a small piece of butter, to one egg; fry till done.

BAKED EGGS.

Melt some butter in a patty-pan; break in your eggs; add a little salt and pepper; bake till the whites are done, then serve with toast.

ŒUFS BROUILLES.

Put a little butter in a saucepan; sprinkle over it some salt; add a little gravy, which makes the eggs softer; stir them over the fire until thick. Serve with toasted bread. Ham, mushroom, etc., are nice minced and added. The difference between this and an omelette is, that an omelette is more compact, and turns out smooth.

SOUFFLE FRANCAIS.

Put into a stewpan an ounce of butter; stir in two spoonfuls of flour, and cook well, but not colored; add by degrees a wine-glass of boiling cream and four of milk; stir smooth, and take off the fire; add the yolks of four eggs, a little sugar, and a table-spoonful of orange-water; whip up lightly the white of eight eggs, and mix with the batter; put the whole in a souffle-dish, and bake an hour.

FISH.

Fish should be well cleaned, and cooked while fresh. If the least tainted, they should be thrown away. Fresh fish are better soaked in salt and water a few hours before cooking. In boiling, they should be rolled in a cloth, and put in cold water, with salt thrown in the water. A very little boiling will answer; if over-boiled, they will be watery and unpalatable. Salt fish should be soaked over night, or longer, if not fresh enough. Buttermilk is the best to soak them in, but they require longer soaking; then wash clean before cooking. Fish should always be eaten as soon as cooked. For a garnish, use parsley, hard-boiled eggs, or lemons cut in slices. Always fry pork first, and then fry the fish in the gravy, if you can. Most all cook-books recommend lard instead of butter, but I prefer butter, if you are careful not to burn it, as it will make the fish look bad. After frying fish a gravy may be made by stirring in a little flour and water, with butter, if you like, wine or catsup; turn on the fish. For boiled fish, always make a sauce, as directed for fish. For baked fish, use a dressing of bread, soaked soft; then mix butter, salt, pepper and spices, if you can. An egg or two will make the dressing cut smooth. Wash the fish perfectly clean; fill with the dressing, and sew up; put in a dripping-pan, with a little water, a slice or two of pork. Bake from half an hour to an hour.

HALIBUT

is nice cut in slices and dipped in Indian meal; peppered and salted; then fried, or it may be broiled. The dried is nice for tea, or soaked in cold water a little while, and broiled.

CODFISH.

Fresh cod is good cooked almost in any way, except broiled. Salt codfish may be cut in small pieces, and soaked in cold water, putting it where it will warm, about half an hour; take out and put in milk and a piece of butter—or cream is the best; stir in a little flour, made smooth, but do not let it boil—only simmer—boiling will harden it. It will cook in fifteen minutes. A few eggs will improve it. Pour on buttered toast. It may be laid on a few coals till brown; then soak in cold water a few minutes to soften.

BUTTERED CODFISH.

Shred it fine, and soak in cold water until fresh enough; then drain and put in a piece of butter the size of an egg, with a spoonful of flour; stir a few minutes; then lay on the platter, and sprinkle pepper over it. Eat hot.

BAKED SHAD.

Make a stuffing of the head and cold boiled ham; season with salt, pepper, cloves and sweet herbs; moisten with an egg; stuff the fish and rub some on the outside; put it in a deep pan, with its tail toward its mouth; pour on water and a piece of butter; bake two hours; make a gravy and pour around it, and garnish with lemons sliced.

TO BOIL CODFISH.

Soak two or three hours in cold water; or a better way is to soak it over night, if wanted for dinner; then put in a pot, with cold water on it, and let it cook slowly, but not boil, for two hours. Serve with potatoes, and make a gravy of drawn butter, or egg sauce. If you prefer, it may be chopped up together, the fish and potatoes. Vinegar added to the sauce is nice. Another method is to mash the potatoes and fish together, adding cream, or milk and butter, with pepper, and make in round flat cake, an inch thick, and fry in butter, having previously dipped them in flour, or egg and flour. These are nice fried for tea.

BROILED CODFISH.

Sprinkle salt and pepper on the outside and inside; let it remain six or seven hours, before broiling or frying; split, and dry in a cloth; grease the gridiron, and put the fish on outside uppermost, and broil a quarter of an hour; be careful not to burn it; butter well, and send to the table hot. Fried shad must be rolled in Indian meal or flour, or rubbed over with egg and bread-crumbs, before frying.

TO BOIL FRESH SALMON.

Salmon requires more cooking than most any other kind of fish; scald and clean nice; put in a kettle of cold water, with a handful of salt; let it boil slowly, allowing a quarter of an hour to a pound of fish. As soon as done, take carefully up in a napkin, and wrap it close, to absorb the moisture; lay on a hot dish, and garnish with horse-radish and curled parsley, or boiled eggs, cut in rings, laid round the dish. Oyster sauce is best with fresh boiled fish. For broiling, cut in thin slices.

SMOKED SALMON.

Scale and cut the fish up the back; take out the roe and the bone; rub inside and out with equal parts of sugar and salt; add a little saltpetre; press flat with a board and weights on it two days; drain from the salt, and wipe dry; stretch it open, and fasten with a stick; hang up and smoke four or five days; when used, soak in warm water, and broil.

SOUNDS AND TONGUES.

Soak in lukewarm water three or four hours; then scrape off the skin, cut in two, and stew in milk; stir in a little butter and flour just before taking up. Another way is, to dip in egg, and then in flour, and fry in buttter. Use drawn-butter gravy.

TO BOIL FRESH CODFISH.

Put into water boiling hot, and boil twenty minutes, or according to the size of the fish. Use oyster sauce for gravy.

TO COOK EELS.

Skin, and wash clean; cut in small pieces two inches long; put in cold water, or milk and water, with a handful of salt, and boil until a fork will go in easy; then take up, and dip in flour, and fry in butter or lard a nice brown. Catfish are cooked in the same way, and are not good unless parboiled first.

STEWED EELS

must be parboiled and cooked with a very little gravy, and butter, if you have not the gravy. Put in a couple of spoonfuls of water, pepper, and salt. Just before taking up, stir in a little flour made smooth.

BLACK FISH.

They must be boiled or fried, as directed for other fish.

MACKEREL.

If salt, soak over night in cold water; then boil the next day. They will not require much cooking. If for frying or broiling, they must be soaked twenty-four hours at least, and in warm weather should be kept in buttermilk, and when required for broiling, should be rinsed and drained an hour or two before broiled. Salt shad may be soaked in the same way, only require longer soaking, as they are much thicker.

TO COOK FRESH FISH.

Have the fat hot, and, with a pastry-brush, rub egg over the fish, and sprinkle bread-crumbs on, or else dip them in flour or Indian meal. Allow them to cook well on one side before turning.

STURGEON STEAKS.

Take off the skin, and cut slices half an inch thick; rub with salt and the beaten yolk of an egg; sprinkle on bread-crumbs; wrap up in butter papers and broil; take the papers off before sending to the table; or broil without the egg, just salt rubbed on, and season with butter and Cayenne pepper.

STURGEONS BAKED OR FRIED.

They are good baked or broiled, but better fried. It should be boiled fifteen minutes previous to baking, to extract the oily taste which they are liable to have. The part next the tail is best. Bake as other fish. To fry, cut in slices nearly an inch thick, and fry where pork has been fried; when brown, take up, and stir in a little flour, with pepper, salt, catsup, butter, and wine, if liked; put back in the pot, and stew a few minutes. While cooking, make force-meat balls out of some fish reserved; fry, and use them as a garnish for the fish.

FISH FORCE-MEAT BALLS.

Chop some of the uncooked fish with salt pork; mix two raw eggs, some bread-crumbs, and season with pepper and spice, if you like; do up in balls, and fry brown.

TROUT.

These are very fine fried, dipped in flour or egg and bread-crumbs. They should be cooked with the head on, merely cut open and washed clean. They are good stewed with a very little water and salt pork; or they may be broiled, or put in a cloth and boiled, using a fish sauce.

FISH CAKES.

Take salt pork and chop with fresh fish that has been previously cooked; mix with eggs and breadcrumbs; season with pepper and salt; then make up into small cakes, and fry brown. Flour the hands while making them. The fat must be hot.

SCOLLOPS.

Boil them, and take out of the shells; take out the heart, and throw the rest away, as that is the only part fit to eat; dip in flour, and fry brown. They may also be stewed with a little water, seasoned with pepper and salt.

TO CRIMP FRESH FISH.

Cut in slices and put in water, vinegar, and salt, three hours; then fry or broil them.

LOBSTERS AND CRABS.

Put them in boiling water with a handful of salt. Boil half an hour or more, in proportion to its size. It must not be boiled too long or it will be hard. When done, take out and wipe dry; then take off the shell and take out the blue veins and the lady-fingers, as they are unwholesome. Send to the table cold with the body and tail split open and the claws taken off. Lay the claws next the body, the small ones outside; garnish with parsley. They must never be cooked after they are dead, but put alive into boiling water.

TO DRESS LOBSTERS COLD.

Take the fish out of the shell, divide it in small pieces, mash up the scarlet meat, then mix mustard, Cayenne pepper, salt, vinegar, sweet oil, and mix the lobster with this mixture and serve in a dish.

CLAMS.

Wash them clean and put in a pot with water enough to prevent their burning, and boil until the shells open, then take out and remove the shells. Cook in the same water, adding pepper and butter. Stir in rolled crackers, or toast slices of bread and lay in a tureen, and pour the clams over. Long clams are nice taken out of the shells and broiled.

CLAM PANCAKES.

Make a batter of milk, flour and eggs, and if small, stew the clams and put in whole; if large, chop them without stewing; season with pepper and salt, and fry on a griddle. Oysters may be made in the same way, only not cooked nor chopped. Part of the oyster-juice may be added to the milk. They are nice kept frozen in the winter-time and used when wanted;. freezing makes them more tender.

FRIED OYSTERS.

Take those that are large, wipe with a napkin, and then dip in beaten eggs, then in bread-crumbs or flour, and fry in lard or butter. They are nice dipped in a batter and fried. They can be kept several months by frying while fresh, seasoned with salt and pepper, then corked tight in a bottle. When eaten, warm in a little water. They are nice to garnish fish.

OYSTER PATTIES.

Stew oysters with cloves, nutmeg, yolks of hard-boiled eggs, a little butter, liquor enough to cover them; when stewed a few moments take out to cool. Have shells of puff-paste baked in patty-pans, and three or four oysters in each.

STEWED OYSTERS. NO. 1.

Rinse off the oysters and strain the liquor to get off the bits of shell that adhere to the oyster. Heat the liquor and add water, if not enough; then turn in the oysters; stir in a little flour made smooth or rolled crackers. Let them boil up two minutes and pour out. No salt should be added until taken out, or they will shrink and be hard. Eat with crackers or buttered toast.

OYSTER PIE.

Line a deep plate with pastry, fill it with pieces of bread, cover with nice pastry, and bake of a light brown. Have the oysters stewed and seasoned just as the pastry is baked. Take off the upper crust, remove the bread, and put in the oysters; cover with the crust and serve while hot. Another way is to line the dish with pastry and put in the oysters, and cover with pastry, and bake from half an hour to three quarters.

SCOLLOPED OYSTERS.

Pound crackers or rusk fine. Then butter small tin pans and put in alternate layers of oysters and crumbs, having a layer of crumbs on top; season with butter, salt, and pepper; add oyster-juice to moisten the whole. Bake until brown.

TO PICKLE OYSTERS.

Take them out of their liquor and pour boiling water on them; then take them out and put in a kettle with just water enough to cover them, with a large spoonful of salt to a hundred oysters; let boil up and take out, then spread on a board and cover with a cloth. With every pint of the liquor add a quart of good vinegar, a tea-spoonful of mace, a table-spoonful of whole cloves, the same of black pepper. Heat the whole together, and when it boils stir in the oysters five minutes. Let them cool and then put in jars and seal up.

Another way, is to scald the oysters in their own liquor. Take vinegar and heat scalding hot, with whole cloves and pepper-corns, also mace. When the oysters and vinegar are lukewarm, mix them. Then bottle them and cover tight.

SOUSED MACKEREL.

Clean, and boil in salt and water; take equal quantities of vinegar and water that they were boiled in. Heat scalding hot with cloves and pepper-corns, then turn on the fish. They will be eatable in two or three days.

STEWED OYSTERS.

Strain all the liquor from the oysters; thicken a very little with bread-crumbs or crackers; season with pepper and butter. Have ready a tureen with either toasted bread or crackers laid in the bottom; place the oyster on top, and when the liquor boils up, pour it over the oysters, then cover the tureen and let it remain five or six minutes before sending to the table. Cooking oysters in this way will prevent their shrinking. The butter, when put in, may be rolled in flour if liked.

PICKLED LOBSTERS.

Boil them in the usual manner, and after taking out of the shells, cut into pieces three inches long. Take vinegar, salt, cloves, allspice and pepper-corns, and boil ten minutes; then put in the lobster and scald up. Put in a jar and keep in a cool place.

TO PICKLE SHAD OR PIKE.

Have them well cleaned, then make a pickle by mixing half a pound of brown sugar, four quarts of rock salt, one of common salt, and two ounces of saltpetre. This quantity will pickle a dozen shad or fifteen pike. Put a layer of the mixture at the bottom of a keg, then a layer of fish with the skin-side down. Continue this until full, having the salt mixture on top. Have a heavy weight on to keep them under the brine.

PICKLED SALMON.

Salmon should be cut into a number of pieces and boiled in salt and water until sufficiently cooked to eat. Take three quarts of vinegar, an ounce of pepper-corns, allspice whole, scald together, and when strongly spiced take from the fire, and when cold, pour on the salmon.

PICKLED TROUT.

If large cut in pieces, boil with salt and water. Put in cold vinegar with whole cloves, allspice and pepper-corns, between each layer of fish. Keep in a stone jar in a cool place. They should be wrapped in a cloth or they will boil to pieces. These are excellent.

SPICED OYSTERS.

Take one hundred large fresh oysters, put them with the liquor into a large earthen vessel; add two table-spoonfuls of good vinegar, a dozen cloves, one nutmeg grated, a few blades of mace whole, one tea-spoonful of salt, one of whole allspice, and a little Cayenne pepper; stir well together and set them over a slow fire, keeping them well covered. Take them off occasionally and stir well from the bottom, to prevent their burning. As soon as they boil they are done. Pour them out into a pan to cool. When cool, they will be fit for eating. If to be kept any time, should have less spice, as they will taste too much of it.

TO KEEP OYSTERS IN THE SHELL.

Lay them in a heap in the cellar with the concave side upward to hold in the liquor. Sprinkle them every day with salt and water, and then with Indian meal. Cover with an old carpet.

STEWED OYSTERS. NO. 2.

Strain the liquor, and add a glass of white wine, some crumbs of stale bread and pepper. Put in the oysters and let them stew a few minutes. Have ready some toasted bread well buttered, then dip the toast in the liquor and lay around the sides and bottom of a dish. Pour the oysters on and send to the table hot.

BROILED FISH.

Rub a little salt on the bars of the gridiron to prevent its sticking; have a clear fire; score your fish and cook slowly; when done on one side, turn over and cook on the other. Season with salt, pepper, and melted butter.

HADDOCK.

Clean well and rub dry; then rub salt over it and let it hang two days; skin and rub beaten egg over, and crumbs of bread. Fry, broil, or bake.

POTTED FISH.

After being well cleaned cut in small pieces; soak in salt and vinegar for a few hours and drain it. Lay in a stone jar with spices and pieces of butter till all is in. Pour over good cider vinegar, a little Cayenne pepper. Cover with a crust of dough; put in a very moderate oven, or in an oven after bread has been taken out. Take off the crust and cover tight. Any kind of fresh, firm fish will answer.

OYSTER SOUP. NO. 2.

Put a nicely dressed chicken in a kettle with four quarts of water; season with pepper-corns, allspice, four blades of mace, nutmeg and salt; roll half a pound of butter in flour and put in. Keep well covered till the chicken is tender; then put in the oyster-liquor and boil five minutes; take up the chicken and strain the liquor, and pour back into the kettle, and add three pints of oysters; boil up once and serve. Dress the chicken separately or make chicken salad.

BAKED EELS.

Take eels that have been skinned and cleaned, cut in pieces; then lay in a shallow pan, setting the pieces upright; season with pepper, salt, sweet herbs, parsley cut small, and a little water. Bake till done, then stir in some flour made smooth, and serve. They should be previously boiled.

VEGETABLES.

POTATOES.

Almost every person understands cooking potatoes, nevertheless it will not be amiss to give a few hints in regard to cooking this vegetable, which has become almost the "staff of life." In the first place, care should be taken to procure the best kind; but as potatoes change so much, (in consequence of the rot,) I can not mention which would be the best—one must be guided by circumstances. In winter they should be kept where they will not freeze, and in summer in a dry place, and the sprouts should be broken off occasionally. Always have the water boiling hot when the potatoes are dropped in. If boiled with the skins on, they will be strong, except when new; give old ones an hour to boil, new ones half an hour. Potatoes are nice baked, but require a slow oven. Boiled and mashed, with cream or butter enough to moisten, with a little salt, is the best and most common way of cooking; then put them in a dish, smooth the top with a knife, and lay butter on in spots; sprinkle a little pepper over and send to the table hot. Cold ones may be warmed different ways: cut in thin slices and warmed in cream is nice. Another way is to slice and broil on a gridiron, or fry in butter, sprinkling salt and pepper over them. They can be grated and mixed with the yolk of egg and fried in butter, after being made in small cakes.

SWEET POTATOES.

The best way to cook sweet potatoes is to bake them; for a change, they can be boiled and peeled as other potatoes, or half-boiled and sliced and fried in butter.

TURNIPS.

The large English sweet turnip is the best, as they are not watery. Pare them and slice, then drop them in a kettle of boiling water and let them boil as long as potatoes; when done, drain off the water and mash with salt; put in a dish and smooth the top with a knife; put on pieces of butter and sprinkle on pepper; send to the table hot. If cooked with salt meat, cut in quarters and send to the table whole.

RUTA BAGA

is large and of a reddish color. Pare them and quarter, or cut in slices and let them remain in cold water an hour or so; then boil two hours; mash like other turnips.

ONIONS.

They should be put in a linen bag and kept in a dry cool place; when boiled they should be put in milk and water to take away the strong taste; an hour is required for boiling, but it is well to try them with a fork, for if boiled too much they will be watery. When taken up, the water should be pressed out, and seasoned with butter, salt, and pepper; it is well to throw a handful of salt in while boiling. Another way of cooking is to pare and slice them, then fry in pork gravy or butter; season well with salt and pepper; while cooking it is well to put in a little water. This is nice for a breakfast dish. They can also be baked and then seasoned.

WINTER SQUASH.

They should be kept in a dry warm place during the winter and will keep until spring. Pare them and cut out the inside; cut in strips and boil half an hour; when done, season as turnips and send to the table hot. They are better baked.

SUMMER SQUASH.

Cut off the top and end, and quarter; boil half an hour and then put them in a strainer and press out the water, then turn in a pan and season with butter and salt.

ASPARAGUS.

Cut before they grow so as to be tough; cut up in small pieces, wash and turn on water; boil until tender, (they must be cooked in tin,) then take a little flour with cream and salt, stir in, and when hot take off and send to the table hot. Another way is to tie the stalks together, heads one way, lay them in boiling water, with salt, until tender; toast bread and moisten with water, lay on a dish, then drain the asparagus and lay the heads inward, spread on the toast and pour over it melted butter.

CAULIFLOWER.

Cut off the flower and soak in cold water awhile, then tie in a cloth and drop in boiling water, or milk and water; skim well while boiling; when tender, which will be in an hour, take up and drain; send to the table with melted butter. This is nice pickled as cabbage.

CABBAGE.

This vegetable should be buried in drills during the winter season, and as a head is wanted it can be taken out, without disturbing the rest, and will be as fresh as in the fall. If put in the cellar, they will wilt. When used, they should be carefully examined, and placed in salt and water a few minutes, to draw any worms that might be in the leaves. Boil an hour with salt meat, either pork or beef, then drain and chop fine, (which can be done with a knife,) put in a piece of butter, and sprinkle pepper over the top; eat with vinegar. Another way is to cut fine, with a knife made on purpose, then put in a basin with a very little water, just enough to keep from burning on the basin; after cooking about ten minutes, wet a table-spoonful of flour with thick cream, add a little salt, stir in while boiling, then pour in vinegar, and take off; eat while hot; or you may leave out the vinegar if you like. Another method is to chop fine and turn in vinegar, with a piece of butter and salt; cook ten minutes, and eat hot; or turn on vinegar and salt, and eat cold without warming. Some prefer it in this way.

BEETS.

The young beets, when thinned out in summer, are nice for greens; take tops and all; when grown large enough to cook, wash clean with a cloth, but be careful not to break the skin, (or they will lose their flavor while cooking;) boil from two to three hours; when kept longer they require more time; when tender, take up and drop into a pan of cold water a moment, when the skin can easily be taken off; then slice them thin and sprinkle on pepper and salt, with melted butter and vinegar. They are nice cut lengthwise, and dropped in spiced vinegar until pickled. They are better baked and eaten like potatoes.

PARSNIPS.

Parsnips may be scraped and boiled tender; then mashed in a stewpan with a little cream and butter, also, salt, and sprinkle pepper on top. They may be cut lengthwise, and cooked with a few slices of pork, with just water enough to cook tender.

CARROTS.

Half-boil, then take off the skin, and slice in a stewpan. Put in a piece of butter, a tea-cupful of water, half a cupful of cream, pepper and salt; then simmer until tender, but not broken; wet up a little flour, and stir carefully in just before taking up. Another way to cook them is to boil with salt meat.

MUSHROOMS.

A person should be acquainted with the different sorts of vegetables by this name, as many persons have been poisoned by using the wrong kind. The eatable kind appears very small, of a round form, on a little stalk. They grow very fast, and the upper part and stalk are white. As they grow, the under part opens, and is of a fringy fur, of a fine salmon color; and as the mushroom grows turns to a dark brown. The skin can be easily parted from the edges and middle. Those that have white or yellow fur should be avoided.

TO STEW MUSHROOMS.

The large buttons are best, and small flaps while the fur is still red. Rub the large buttons with salt and a flannel; cut out the fur and take off the skin from the others; sprinkle with salt and put into a stewpan with some pepper-corns; simmer slowly until done, then put in a piece of butter with flour and a little cream, and take up.

TO STEW CUCUMBERS.

Slice them quite thick, strew with a little salt and pepper, with a little butter, and simmer slowly until tender, then add a little flour wet with water; onions are nice fried with them. Another way is to slice the onions and cucumbers, and flour nicely; then fry in butter, and when browned on one side, turn over and fry on the other.

TO STEW CELERY.

Strip off the outer leaves and wash clean; halve or leave whole, according to their size, cut in lengths of about three inches; stew until tender, with a little butter and water; then add a little cream, and flour seasoned with salt, nutmeg and pepper, simmer together.

VEGETABLE OYSTERS, OR SALSIFY.

This plant grows like parsnips, and when cooked, has the taste of the oyster. They should be scraped and sliced thin, then boil in water until tender, when season with pepper, salt, and stir in a little flour, after wetting in a little cold water, a large piece of butter; toast some bread and lay in a deep dish, then turn on, and eat as you would oysters. Some prefer adding a little milk to the water when boiling. The root may be partly boiled, and then chopped and made in balls, then floured and fried in butter, or dipped in batter.

SPINACH.

Pick clean, and wash; drain and put in boiling water, removing the scum as it rises. When tender, drain, and press it well; chop it fine, then put in a saucepan with a piece of butter, pepper, and salt; let it stew a few minutes, stirring all the time. It requires ten minutes to boil.

EGG PLANT.

The purple is better than the white; they must be boiled in plenty of water until tender, then take up, and take off the skins, and drain; cut them up and wash in a deep dish or pan; mix some grated bread, powdered sweet marjoram, a piece of butter, and a few pounded cloves; grate a layer of bread over the top, and brown in the oven; send to the table in the same dish. It is generally eaten at breakfast. If you fry them, slice without paring, about half an inch thick, and let them remain in cold water an hour or two, throw a little salt in to take away the strong taste; when taken out, wipe dry, and season with pepper and salt; beat the yolk of egg, and grate some bread-crumbs; have ready, in a frying-pan, some lard and butter hot; dip the plant in the egg, then in the crumbs, and fry brown; taking care to have them done through; otherwise they will be unpalatable.

PEAS.

They should be cooked as soon as shelled, or they will lose their flavor; have the water boiling, and only just enough to cook them; season with salt, pepper, and butter, or sweet cream; they will cook from a half-hour to an hour, according to age. Another method: place several leaves of lettuce in your saucepan, then put in your peas, with an ounce of butter to two quarts of peas; cover close, and place over the fire. In thirty minutes they will be done; season with pepper and salt. Another way is to take one quart of peas, one onion sliced, a head of lettuce, washed clean, a piece of butter, pepper, salt, and no more water than hangs round the lettuce from washing; stew them two hours very gently; when done, beat up an egg and stir in, or a spoonful of flour and butter.

SWEET CORN.

Is very nice boiled on the cob, and is the common method of cooking it; a handful of salt should be thrown in while boiling. It is sweeter to let part of the husk remain on until boiled.

SUCCOTASH.

Cut the corn from the cob, and boil with new shelled beans; it will require half an hour or more; season with butter or sweet cream, pepper, and salt.

CABBAGE SALAD.

Chop one head of cabbage in a chopping-bowl; then put in a pan or basin; turn on cold water with two table-spoonfuls of salt and let it remain two hours; then drain, and pour on the following mixture: Beat four eggs to a froth with a pint of good cider vinegar, and place over the fire until thick and scalding hot; be careful to stir all the time; take from the fire before it boils, and add a large spoonful of mixed mustard, two tea-spoonfuls of black pepper, a little salt, say two tea-spoonfuls, half a cup of melted butter or salad oil; it must not be mixed with the cabbage until cold. It will keep several weeks if kept in a cool place. Cream used in the place of butter is good for immediate use.

SLAW.

Melt in a sauce-pan a piece of butter or beef-drippings the size of a hen's egg; when hot, put in the cabbage, (having previously cut it in strips,) and stir it with an iron spoon until tender, which will be in about twenty minutes; season with salt and pepper, also a cup of vinegar; then take up.

GREENS.

Cowslips, dandelions, mustard, water-cresses, spinach, pig-weed, milk-weed, and young beets, tops and all, are nice for greens; they should be well looked over, and washed before using; put in clean water and boil fifteen minutes, then drain, and boil with salt meat, either pork or beef, until tender. A mixture of greens are better than all one kind; young nettles are nice, also plantain put in with other greens.

HOMINY.

Wash in cold water, and boil five hours with a quart of water to a pint of hominy; turn off all the water and add butter and salt, or the water may be dried off, as for rice.

FRENCH OR STRING BEANS.

Take off the strings and cut in pieces half an inch long; boil with a little saleratus, which not only preserves the green color, but makes them more digestible; say a quarter of a tea-spoonful to half a peck of beans; if young, they will boil in half an hour; butter after taking out of the liquor; salt should be added while boiling. A better way is to cook without saleratus, with just water enough to cook them tender, and just before taking them up, put in a tea-cupful of sweet cream, a piece of butter, pepper, and salt.

BAKED BEANS.

The small white beans are best for baking; they should be picked over and washed clean; then turn on cold water, and let them remain all night; in the morning take them out, and put in a kettle with water, also a piece of pork, and boil until nearly tender, adding a little saleratus to render them healthy; then take out and gash the pork, and place in a pan with only the rind seen; bake two hours in an oven; pepper should be sprinkled on the top, and if the pork is not sufficient to make them salt, add more before baking; some put in a few spoonfuls of molasses before baking.

OCHRA.

Take an equal quantity of young tender ochra, chopped fine, and ripe tomatoes, two onions sliced, and a small lump of butter; stew with a large spoonful of water; season with pepper and salt.

MACARONI.

Take two ounces of macaroni, one pint of water, and one of milk, add a tea-spoonful of salt; stew until tender, then cut in small pieces and butter it.

LIMA BEANS.

Wash and boil until tender, which will be about two hours; season with salt, pepper, butter, or cream; use only water sufficient. They may be kept through the winter by gathering them on a dry day, before they get hard, and packing them in a keg; put salt at the bottom, then a layer of pods, then salt, and so on until full; put a weight on and keep in a cool place; when used, soak over night in cold water, shell the next day, and soak until ready to boil; they may be shelled and dried as other beans and then soaked before using.

DRY GREEN CORN.

Gather when ready to boil; strip off the husks, and drop into boiling water; let the water boil over the ears; then take out and shell off the corn by running the prong of a fork through. This method is the best as it saves the kernel whole, and is easily done; spread on clean boards, and dry quickly, as it is apt to sour if not. When cooked, soak over night, and boil in the same water the next morning; it should be well washed before soaking; season with butter, pepper, salt, and cream. This is a nice dish in the winter; some prefer cutting it off the cobs before boiling, and drying in the oven, but I prefer the former method.

ARTICHOKES

are good cut in thin slices, with vinegar, pepper, and salt. When cooked they must be boiled until tender, keeping them closely covered; serve with melted butter, in as many cups as artichokes.

TOMATOES.

Take those that are fully ripe; turn on boiling water; let them remain a few minutes, when the skins will easily peel off; then put in a stewpan with butter, pepper, salt, and sugar; toast some bread and lay in a deep dish, pour on, or eat without the toast, with meat; they should be cooked until soft, which will be in fifteen minutes; it is much improved by turning off the water, and then seasoning; they are very nice cooked as follows. After taking off the skin, lay them in a deep dish, with alternate layers of bread-crumbs; season each layer with salt, pepper, butter, and sugar, and add cloves if liked; put a layer of bread-crumbs on top, and bake three quarters of an hour; they are nice sliced up raw, with vinegar, salt, and pepper, on them, and some like sugar; or they may be eaten with sugar and cream alone.

SEA KALE.

This is prepared on toast like asparagus.

GREEN TOMATOES.

Green tomatoes are nice sliced and fried in butter or beef-drippings, seasoned with pepper and salt, also sugar; onions or green apples may be sliced up with them if liked.

CELERIAC.

This vegetable is very much like celery, but is but little known; it is more easily cultivated. Scrape and cut in slices; boil until tender; then take out of the water, and stew a few minutes in milk, with a little salt; add butter when dished up. The roots are good boiled tender, and put into soups or meat pies.

ASPARAGUS. NO. 2.

Beat four eggs light; melt two ounces of butter, and add with pepper and salt, then pour over toasted bread; have the asparagus well cooked, and pour over the whole. Serve hot, and you will find it delicious.

BROCCOLI.

Strip off all the side shoots, leaving the top; peel off the skin of the stalk; cut close off at the bottom, and put into a pan of cold water; let it remain until you can boil some water, then throw in with salt; let it boil briskly, till tender; take up with a slice, that it may not break. It is nice served on toast, like asparagus.

BRUSSELS SPOUTS.

Trim and wash clean; then throw into cold water an hour; have some water boiling, and put in with a handful of salt; boil till tender. Drain off the water, and serve hot.

TO STEW CELERY.

Cut up in pieces; take off the green ends; stew in milk and water, till tender; thicken with a little flour; add a little butter; boil up; then add two eggs beaten, with a cup of cream, pepper, and salt.

FRIED POTATOES.

Peel uncooked potatoes; wash clean, and cut in thin slices; then fry in butter of a nice brown; lay them upon another dish, and send to the table hot.

NEW POTATOES IN BUTTER.

Scrape new potatoes, and wash clean; put in a saucepan, with a piece of butter the size of an egg; cover tight, and stew slowly. This is a nice way of doing new potatoes; and, if you like, mash them when done, and add a little salt and cream.

TO FRY POTATOES.

Pare and slice thin; fry in plenty of nice lard, and drain in a sieve; or peel large potatoes, round and round, as you would an apple, in shavings, and fry until brown; then drain in a sieve; sprinkle salt on when sent to the table. A very nice way to do them, is to take mashed potatoes, and make in little flat cakes, then dip in the beaten yolk of an egg, and then in flour or bread-crumbs, and fry in butter. They look very nice.

BAKED TOMATOES.

Take out the seeds, and fill up with bread-crumbs; then put in a square tin, and bake; eat with butter and sugar, cream if you like. Take a dozen large tomatoes; pour on boiling water to take off the skins; cut in slices in a stewpan; add a tea-cup and a half of bread-crumbs, a table-spoonful of salt, a tea-spoonful of pepper, and four spoonfuls of butter; let them stew gently four or five hours. Fifteen minutes before serving, beat up six eggs; boil up, stirring all the time.

PICKLING.

Pickles should always be made in brass, copper, or tin, and never allowed to remain in them longer than while they are warming. Cider vinegar is the best for pickling. Boil your spices with a little alum in your vinegar. I think it kills the life of the vinegar to heat it much. I prefer to scald my spices in a tin cup, with a little vinegar, and pour in. The pickles will keep longer than they will if boiled with the vinegar. If wanted for immediate use, they may be scalded. For ripe tomatoes, the vinegar should always be cold, as they will soften if put into warm vinegar. Wooden tubs, or stone jars are best for pickles. They should never be put into glazed earthenware, as it contains lead, and will combine with the vinegar, which renders them poisonous. A cloth should be kept on top, to take up the scum as it rises, then rinse it off in cold water, and put back.

Pickles should be stirred occasionally, and if any soft ones are found, they must be taken out. If the vinegar is too sharp, it will eat the pickles. If too weak, pour off and add more, putting in more alum, as that hardens them. Salt kills the life of the vinegar, and but little should be used. Any thing that has held grease will spoil pickles. If vinegar is boiled for pickles, it should not be boiled but a few minutes. Brass or copper should be perfectly cleaned before using. Never keep pickles in glazed jars. Many families have been poisoned thereby.

A NICE WAY OF PICKLING CUCUMBERS.

Pick every day from the vines; wash clean with a cloth; be careful not to bruise them, and if cut from the vines with a little stem on, they will keep better.

Make a brine of rock salt, strong enough to bear up an egg; put them in a tub, or stone jar, and cover with the brine. In twenty-four hours stir from the bottom; then pour off the brine, and scald it; then pour over them again; let stand nine days, boiling and skimming the brine every third day; then take them out and rinse in cold water, and if too salt, let them soak awhile; wash the tub or jar clean; put them in again, and pour on cold vinegar, or scald it, just as you like. If spice is added, it may be tied in a bag, and thrown in, with a little alum, and red pepper; cover tight; if a scum rises, scald, pour on again; keep a cloth on top; put in mustard.

A MORE DELICATE PICKLE.

When fresh picked, pour on boiling water, with a little salt; let them remain four or five hours; then put into cold vinegar, with alum dissolved. When you have finished collecting the cucumbers, turn the vinegar from them; scald and skim it, until clear; then scald the cucumbers, but not boil, adding ginger-root, pepper-corns, and red peppers, sufficient to spice the pickles; if scum rises on top, scald the vinegar, and pour on hot; if weak, throw away, and add more, with more alum; if any are soft, take them out. If wanted for a sweet pickle, add sugar when scalded.

TO PICKLE MUSHROOMS.

Stew in salt and water, just enough to prevent their sticking; then pour off the water, and put in cold spiced vinegar. Cork tight and keep in a cool place.

BUTTERNUTS AND BLACK WALNUTS. NO. 2.

Take them green, when a knitting-needle can easily be run through them; soak in salt water for a week, often changing the brine; then drain off the water, and wipe with a dry towel, a coarse one is best, until they become smooth. To each gallon of vinegar used, add half an ounce of allspice, the same of pepper-corns, a table-spoonful of mace, and cloves, a tea-cupful of salt; let them remain a week, then turn the vinegar off, and scald it, boiling hot, and pour on. The vinegar in which they are pickled will make nice catsup.

YELLOW PICKLE.

Take thirty ripe cucumbers, pare and split them; take the seeds out; spread them on a board; sprinkle a little salt over them; let them remain twelve hours; then put them in the sun, and let them remain until dry, turning them every day, and bringing them in at night; then wash them in vinegar; then put them in a jar, with a layer of mustard seed, horse-radish, onions, sliced, alternately. Take two quarts of vinegar, one ounce of race mustard, a few cloves, allspice, and cinnamon; let it simmer awhile; when cool, pour it on on the pickles. They will keep for years. The onions can be left out, if wished.

TOMATO PICCALILLY.

Take one peck of green tomatoes; put a half-pint of salt on them; stew them fifteen minutes; then let them stand all night; drain the water off; then slice them, and put a layer of sliced onions, alternately, with the spices. Take one quarter of a pound of ground mustard, one quarter of a pound white mustard, two ounces of black pepper, half an ounce of ground pepper, one ounce of cloves, cinnamon, and mace, each, four nutmegs. Turn good vinegar on, and let them simmer two or three hours.

GREEN TOMATOES.

Cut up green tomatoes in slices; put them in a jar, and sprinkle salt over each layer; let them stand twenty-four hours; then wash the salt off, and let them drain in a colander. Prepare your vinegar with spices, and sugar, say two pounds of sugar to one gallon of vinegar.

RIPE TOMATOES.

They should not be very ripe; wash them, and put them in a weak brine, where they must remain twenty-four hours; then rinse them off, and throw them in cold vinegar; take mustard and spices, different kinds, put them in cloths, and boil in a little vinegar, and turn in.

They will not be fit for use, quite as soon as if the vinegar was turned on hot, but will keep longer. Another way: Take one gallon ripe tomatoes, peeled; add mustard, cloves, cinnamon, red pepper, and a very little salt; grind the spices, and tie in a cloth. Cover the whole with vinegar, and let it scald, but not boil.

MELON MANGOES.

Take green melons, and pour over them a boiling hot brine, strong enough to bear up an egg, and let them stand nine days; then take them out, and cut them open on one side, and take out the seeds; scrape them clean; then take small cucumbers, green tomatoes, cabbage, chopped fine, with mustard, cloves, cinnamon, and nutmeg, also pepper. Sew them up, or tie them, and put in a jar; then pour hot spiced vinegar over them.

WALNUTS AND BUTTERNUTS.

Take butternuts, or black walnuts, when you can thrust a pin through them; put them in a weak lye, and stir them well to get the roughness off, or scald them, and rub with a flannel cloth; soak them in a brine about a week; then pierce them through with a large needle, and lay them in a jar; scald your vinegar, adding spices and mustard. They must be covered tight, and kept from the air.

CUCUMBERS.

Gather the cucumbers small, and put them in a weak brine; let them stand twenty-four hours; then scald your vinegar, with cloves, cinnamon, and pepper, and turn on. If you wish them green, add a little alum. If you wish to keep them any time, wash them, and lay them in a barrel, with a layer of salt, alternately, until your barrel is full; then put a cloth on top, lay a board over, and a stone to keep them under the brine. They will keep for years. They must be soaked several days before using; then turn on vinegar, as above.

RADISH PODS.

Radish pods may be pickled by letting them stand in salt and water a few days, and then pickle like cucumbers.

GREEN BEANS.

Boil the beans in a little salt and water, until quite tender; then take them out, and pour cold vinegar on, but scald the spices in a little water or vinegar.

MARTINOES.

Soak in salt and water, two or three days, changing the water every day, or they will grow soft; then scald them with vinegar and spices

CAULIFLOWER.

Select the nicest, and cut off the stalk; divide the flower into six or eight pieces, and scald in brine; let them remain until the next day; then rinse and dry them; lay them carefully in a jar, not to break them, and pour over them hot spiced vinegar. Asparagus and broccoli may be pickled the same way.

CABBAGE.

Chop fine and lay in a jar; scald your vinegar with spices, and turn on; scald it several times and turn on; it will make it more tender.

NASTURTIONS.

They must be gathered when ripe; wash them, and put them in cold vinegar; they require no spicing. Capers are done in the same manner.

ONIONS.

Take off the outer skin, and soak them two or three days in brine; then scald them in milk and water, and drain them; lay them in a jar and pour cold vinegar on them; scald your spices, adding a little alum; cover close.

PLUMS.

Take seven pounds of plums; three pounds of sugar; one quart of vinegar; one ounce of cinnamon; one ounce of cloves; place a layer of plums, spices, and sugar; scald your vinegar and pour over the fruit, repeating the process three times, three days in succession; then place them in a preserving-kettle, and let them come to a slow boil; they are then fit for use.

HIGDOM.

Take green melons, cucumbers, green peppers; pare the melons and cucumbers; put them in a jar, adding mustard-seed and spices; cover with vinegar; in a few weeks they will be ready to use.

EAST-INDIA PICKLE.

Take chopped cabbage, green peppers, radish pods, nasturtions, walnuts, butternuts, cherries, peaches, apricots, capers, green grapes, and butter onions; make a brine that will bear an egg; pour on boiling hot; let them stand a few days, stirring them every day; take them out and drain well; then make vinegar warm with spices added, and pour on, adding English mustard-seed; cover close and it will keep for years.

PICKLED APPLES.

Take three quarts of vinegar, one of water, three pounds of sugar, cinnamon, cloves, allspice to your taste; heat boiling hot, and turn on two or three times; peaches, pears, and plums may be pickled in the same way.

GREEN TOMATO CATSUP.

Slice green tomatoes, and sprinkle a little salt over them; boil twenty minutes in vinegar and water, with a pound of sugar; take them out and put a layer of tomatoes, then pepper, mustard, horse-radish, onions, and spices; then pour on strong vinegar to cover them; then another layer alternately, until the jar is full.

RIPE TOMATO CATSUP.

Take one gallon of ripe tomatoes; wash clean; put in six red peppers broken up; one pint of strong vinegar; let them simmer three or four hours; then strain them through a sieve; add four spoonfuls of pepper, four of salt, six of ground mustard, one of cloves, the same of allspice; add one pint more vinegar; set on the fire, and remain until the right consistency; let it cool, when you can bottle it for use. It should be made in tin.

TOMATO CATSUP.

Another way: Take ripe tomatoes; wash and strain them; then to every quart, add two ounces of black pepper, one of cinnamon, one of cloves, a little mace or nutmeg, Cayenne pepper, and salt, to suit the taste; boil slowly an hour; then add half a pint of the best cider vinegar; after which, bottle it, and seal tightly. Another way: Take one bushel of ripe tomatoes, and boil until soft; strain through a sieve; add half a gallon of vinegar, a pint and a half of salt, two ounces of cloves, two of allspice, two of Cayenne pepper, four table-spoonfuls of black pepper, four of mustard; mix together, and boil until reduced one half, then bottle tight.

MUSHROOM CATSUP.

Take the full-grown tops; wash them clean; mash them; then sprinkle salt over them, and let them remain all night; put in a stewpan, and let them stand in a hot oven ten or twelve hours; then strain through a sieve to press out all the juice; and to every gallon of liquor put half a pound of salt, one ounce of cloves, one of cinnamon, one of black pepper, an ounce of ginger; put them over the fire until reduced one half; then turn in an earthen dish to cool, when it can be bottled for use; should it not keep good, it can be heated over.

TO PICKLE GHERKINS.

Put in a strong brine until they are yellow; then in hot spiced vinegar, and keep in a warm place until they turn green; then pour off the vinegar and pour on more.

BARBERRIES AND CURRANTS.

Take bunches of currants when ripe, and put in good cider vinegar. Barberries should be preserved by drying, as they retain their color better than any other way; when used, pour on vinegar scalding hot, and let them remain until they swell out to their original size.

PEPPERS.

Take ripe peppers and cut open with a knife; take out the seed, and soak in brine eight or nine days, changing the water every day; keep in a warm place; rinse in cold water and stuff with chopped cabbage, small green tomatoes, or cucumbers, nasturtions or any thing you like; season with cloves, cinnamon, and allspice; sew them up and put in cold vinegar. The large sweet pepper is best for pickling; they are nice made into a sweet pickle; they may be soaked one day and then scalded in a weak brine, and thrown into cold vinegar, or put in cold spiced vinegar without soaking or scalding.

MARTINOES.

Take them when you can run a pin in them; put in a brine a week or ten days, changing every day; then wipe with a course towel, and pour on spiced vinegar boiling hot; in four weeks they will be ready for use.

PEPPER VINEGAR.

Take a dozen ripe pepper pods; split and boil them in three pints of vinegar, until one quart remains, then strain through a sieve; this is nice for salads, catsups, and sauces; it also imparts a nice flavor to pickles.

PICKLED PEACHES.

Take those that are not very ripe, and pour on boiling water; take out and wipe dry, in order to get off the down; take a gallon of weak vinegar, three pounds of sugar to a peck of peaches; scald it, and put in three eggs, the whites only, and they must be well beaten; skim until clear, and every time skimming take from the fire; they should be filled with cassia buds.

PICKLED APPLES. NO. 2.

Take three pounds of sugar to three pints of weak vinegar, a stick or two of cinnamon, a few cloves; pare sweet apples, and put them in whole, and boil until tender. Pears may be pickled in the same way.

PICKLED PEACHES. NO. 2.

Wipe off the down with a wet cloth; lay them in jars, and pour over them a boiling hot syrup made of one quart of vinegar, three pounds of sugar, one ounce of cinnamon, and a little allspice; four cloves should be put in the peaches before putting in the jars; let them stand a day, and pour off the pickle and scald, and pour on again; repeat this next day, and they will keep well. Other fruit may be pickled in the same way.

PLUMS AND CHERRIES.

Put them in jars, with a layer of cinnamon or cloves between each layer of fruit; dissolve half a pound of white sugar to a pound of fruit in good vinegar; then cover the whole with it, and set the jar in a pot of cold water; set the jar over the fire until they begin to boil, then take off.

FROSTING CAKE.

A quarter of a pound of white powdered sugar, to one egg, or two thirds of a tea-cupful; whip the white of the egg to a stiff froth, then add the sugar by degrees, until it becomes smooth; flavor with lemon-juice; spread it on evenly with a knife while the cake is warm, and it will soon dry; if the cake is cold when frosted, put it in a warm place till it dries. The ornamental frosting on cake is done with a syringe; have lemon-juice in the frosting to make it keep its place; then draw the frosting into the syringe, and make your figures as you press it out; it must not be put on till the frosting is hardened; sometimes a little starch may be put into frosting, but it will not require so much sugar; it is a good plan to sift a little flour over the cake before frosting it, as it will spread more evenly. Before cutting an iced cake, the icing should be cut with a penknife, for a large knife used for cutting the cake will break the frosting.

COLORING FOR ICING.

Take twenty grains of cochineal powder, the same of cream of tartar, and twenty grains of alum; add a gill of soft water, and scald it, but not boil; strain through a bit of muslin, and cork up for use. A very little of this will color icing a beautiful pink; then use white nonpareils. Rich cake that has brandy or wine in, will keep a long time. If made without milk or soda, it will keep longer. It can be made to taste almost like fresh if it becomes stale, by putting it in a basin, and setting it in a larger one with a little water in; put in a moderate oven, and cover the cake to keep in the steam; and when hot, take from the oven, and let it get cool before cutting it.

DIRECTIONS FOR MAKING CAKE.

The materials for making cake must be nice and fresh, or the cake will not be good; white sugar should always be used for delicate cake; prepare all your articles first, raisins stoned, Zante currants washed and dried, citron cut in pieces, and almonds blanched by putting them in hot water and letting them remain until the skins can be rubbed off; then dry, and pound them with a little rose-water or extract of lemon; in warm weather the eggs should be cooled before using; if frozen put in cold water to take out the frost. Frozen eggs will not make as nice cake. Butter, if washed before using, will make more delicate cake. The butter and sugar should be stirred to a cream; if milk is used, stir in gradually with half the flour; then the yolks of the eggs, with some flour; the whites next, with the remainder of the flour; soda always added last. Fruit should be rolled in flour to prevent its sticking to the bottom. The eggs will beat light sooner by beating them separate. Some cakes require a hotter oven than others; the cook will soon learn this from experience. If baking too fast on top, put a piece of paper over; when about done, try with a knife, (or a splinter kept for this purpose is best;) if it does not adhere to it, it is done.

PLUM CAKE.

Mix two quarts of flour with a pound of sifted loaf-sugar; three pounds of currants; half a pound of raisins, stoned and chopped; a quarter of an ounce of mace and cloves; a grated nutmeg; the peel of a lemon, cut fine; melt two pounds of butter in a pint and a quarter of cream, but not hot; the whites and yolks of twelve eggs beaten apart, and half a pint good yeast: beat them all together a full hour: put in citron and lemon; then butter your pans, and bake. Brown sugar will answer for this cake, and for all fruit cake.

FRUIT CAKE.

Take one pint of light dough, one tea-cupful of sugar, one of butter, three eggs, one nutmeg, one tea-spoonful of saleratus; rub the butter and sugar together, and the dough and eggs; one pound of raisins; bake one hour. It is better to stand a short time and rise before baking.

FRENCH LOAF CAKE.

Five tea-cupfuls powdered sugar, three of butter, two of milk, six eggs, ten tea-cupfuls dried sifted flour, one wine-glass of brandy, three nutmegs, a small tea-spoonful saleratus, one pound of raisins, one quarter pound of citron.

ANOTHER FRENCH LOAF CAKE.

Three tea-cups of light bread dough, two cups of white sugar, one cup of butter, three eggs, one nutmeg, one small tea-spoonful of saleratus: rub the butter and sugar together, and the eggs, and lastly the dough and fruit; put the fruit in a little flour, and it will not settle at the bottom. This will make two good-sized cakes.

LADY'S CAKE.

One pound of flour, one pound of sugar, eight ounces of butter, one pound of raisins, one gill of brandy, one gill of wine, one gill of cream, four eggs, and one nutmeg.

POUND CAKE.

Prepare a table-spoonful of cinnamon, a tea-spoonful of mace, two nutmegs grated; mix together in a wine-glass of brandy, and one of rose-water; sift a pound of flour into a broad pan, and put in a pound of white sugar; cut up a pound of butter; warm them by the fire until soft; stir them to a cream; then add the spice and liquor, a little at a time; beat ten eggs to a froth, and stir them in by degrees into the mixture, alternately with the flour; add twelve drops of oil of lemon; put in a deep tin pan with straight sides, and bake in a moderate oven from two to three hours.

FRUIT CAKE.

One cup of sugar, one cup chopped raisins, one cup sour milk, four table-spoonfuls of melted butter, one tea-spoonful of cinnamon, half a tea-spoonful of cloves, one of brandy, a little nutmeg, and saleratus.

GOLD CAKE.

One pound of flour, one pound of sugar, three quarter pounds of butter, yolks of fourteen eggs; the rind of two lemons, grated, also the juice; one tea-spoonful of sal-volatile, dissolved in hot water; just before putting in the oven, add the lemon.

SILVER CAKE.

One pound sugar, three quarters of flour, three quarters of butter, half a pound of citron, the whites of fourteen eggs.

POUND CAKE.

One pound of flour, one pound of sugar, one pound of butter, eight eggs, lemon-juice, and a very little soda.

A RICH FRUIT CAKE.

One pound of flour, browned, one pound of butter, one pound of sugar, two pounds of seeded raisins, two pounds of currants, one pound of citron, one wine-glass of brandy, one of wine, nutmeg, mace, cinnamon, cloves, allspice, ten eggs, beaten to a froth, one half tea-spoonful of soda, dissolved in hot water. This will make a very large cake.

HICKORY-NUT CAKE.

Half a teacup of sugar, half a tea-cup of cream, one tea-cup of butter, two cups of flour, and lastly one tea-cup of hickory meats, and one small tea-spoonful of soda.

SCOTCH CAKE.

Two cups of sugar, a cup and a half of butter, the juice and grated rind of a lemon, eight eggs, flour enough to make a stiff batter; bake in pans, or drop on tins two inches apart, with white sugar or sugar-

ALMOND CAKE.

Two pounds of flour, two of butter, two of white sugar, a quarter of an ounce of mace, the same of nutmeg, sixteen eggs, two pounds of currants; blanch a pound of sweet almonds, and cut them thin; half a pound of citron, a pound of candied orange, a pound of candied lemon, and an even tea-spoonful of soda.

KISSES.

Beat the whites of four eggs to a stiff froth; add the juice of a lemon, half a pound of powdered sugar, and beat with the egg; spread on white paper, laid on buttered tins. The oven should not be too hot. When the tops have become hard, take them up. Have a solution of gum arabic, and dip the lower side of the cake, and join it to another.

COOKIES.

One cup of butter, two cups of sugar, one cup of cream, one egg, any spice you like, one tea-spoonful of soda; mix soft, roll thin, and bake in a quick oven.

GINGER COOKIES.

One cup of butter, one of sugar, one of molasses, one tea-cupful of boiling water, one table-spoonful of ginger, one of saleratus; bake immediately.

TRIFLES.

One egg, one table-spoonful of white sugar, a salt-spoonful of salt, flour to make it stiff; cut in round cakes, very small, and then fried in lard. These look very nice on a table.

SOFT GINGERBREAD.

One cup of molasses, one cup of cream, one egg, a table-spoonful of ginger, a little salt, a tea-spoonful of soda; bake half an hour.

SODA CRULLERS.

Two tea-spoonfuls of cream of tartar, one tea-cup of sugar, one of milk or water, one table-spoonful of butter, one egg, one tea-spoonful of soda; fry in lard.

CRULLERS.

One pound of flour, half a pound of butter, half a pound of sugar, three eggs, nutmeg; mix well, and roll out half an inch thick, and cut in fancy shapes.

ANOTHER.

One bowl of cream, a tea-cup and a half of sugar, three eggs, nutmeg, salt, soda; mix soft, and fry as above.

DOUGHNUTS.

One quart bowl of light bread-dough, one cup of sugar, one of butter, two eggs, one tea-spoonful of soda; mix well, and let it rise. When light, cut in squares, and fry in lard.

SPONGE GINGERBREAD.

One cup of molasses, one of sour milk, half a cup of butter, two eggs, half a tea-spoonful of saleratus, one large spoonful of ginger, flour to make it stiff; put the butter, molasses, and ginger together, warm them, then add the rest.

QUEEN'S CAKE.

One cup and a half of butter, two of sugar, eight eggs, flour to make it stiff, and bake three quarters of an hour.

WEDDING CAKE.

One pound of flour, one of butter, one of sugar, twelve eggs, two pounds of raisins, two of currants, a pound of citron, nutmeg, mace, lemon; butter two pans, or one large one, and put in a layer of cake, and one citron, sliced very thin, and so on, until filled, leaving room for it to rise. The oven must not be too hot, as it will require baking from three to four hours. Let it cool gradually in the oven.

GINGER SNAPS.

Take one pint of molasses, one tea-cupful of butter, one table-spoonful of ginger, one tea-spoonful of saleratus; boil this mixture, and when nearly cold, add as much flour as is needed to roll out.

ANOTHER.

One pint of molasses, a quarter of a pound of sugar, a quarter of a pound of butter, the same of lard, two table-spoonfuls of ginger, and a quart of flour; dissolve a tea-spoonful of saleratus in a wine-glass of milk; turn into the mixture; add enough flour to roll it out very thin, and cut with a cutter, and bake in a slow oven. These are very nice, and will keep well.

COMPOSITION CAKE.

Take three quarters of a pound of butter, one pound of sugar, one tea-cup of milk, five eggs, one pound of raisins, one tea-spoonful of soda and one pound of flour.

MOCK SPONGE CAKE.

Three eggs, one cup of sugar, stirred until light; then add one and a half tea-cupfuls of flour, with a tea-spoonful of cream of tartar; lastly, half a tea-spoonful of soda.

FRUIT CAKE.

One pound of sugar, three quarters of a pound of butter, twelve eggs, one pound of flour, two pounds of raisins, half a pound of citron, four nutmegs, a table-spoonful of cinnamon, a tea-spoonful of cloves, one tea-cup of molasses, one pint of brandy, a tea-spoonful of soda. Fruit must be well rolled in flour.

COCOA-NUT CAKES.

Take one grated cocoa-cut, an equal weight of sugar, the whites of three eggs; make them the size of half a dollar, and bake on buttered tins.

DELICIOUS DROP CAKES.

One pint of cream, three eggs; thicken with rye flour, till a spoon will stand upright in it; a little salt, and soda; drop on a buttered pan, which must be hot in the oven. They may be made thinner, and baked in cups.

DELICATE CAKE.

Half a cup of butter, the whites of four eggs, one cup and a half of sugar, one half-cup of milk, two cups of flour, one tea-spoonful of cream of tartar, half a tea-spoonful of soda. Any spice you like.

GOOD COOKIES.

Take one pint of sweet milk, three tea-cups of sugar, one and a half of butter, two tea-spoons of cream of tartar, one tea-spoon of soda; add caraway seed. Use as little flour as possible to roll out, or mix and drop on buttered tins.

A RICH SODA CAKE.

Half a pound of butter, half a pound of sugar, three eggs, one tea-spoonful of carbonate of soda, one pound of flour, half a pound of raisins, half a pound of currants, nutmeg, and candied lemon-peel. Add a tea-spoonful of brandy.

LEMON CHEESE CAKES.

One pound of loaf sugar, broken small, six eggs, leaving out the whites of two, the juice of three lemons, and the rinds of two grated, and one fourth of a pound of butter. Put these ingredients into a pan, and boil them slowly, until as thick as honey; pour into a small jar, and tie down with brandy paper. One tea-spoonful is sufficient for a cheese cake. It will keep good two years.

STAR GINGER CAKES.

One tea-cup of butter, two of molasses, warm them together; add one cup of sweet milk, one egg, one table-spoonful of ginger, four cups of flour, one tea-spoonful of soda.

CREAM OF TARTAR DOUGHNUTS.

Take two tea-cupfuls of sugar, half a cup of butter, one pint of sweet milk, two tea-spoonfuls of cream of tartar, nutmeg, salt, one tea-spoonful of soda. Mix soft, and fry in lard.

CHAMPAGNE CAKE.

One egg, one cup of sugar, two table-spoonfuls of butter, two table-spoonfuls of sweet milk, one tea-spoonful of cream of tartar, half a tea-spoonful of soda. Mix as hard as cookies.

JELLY CAKE.

Half a pound of sugar, six ounces of butter, eight eggs, one lemon, one pound of flour, one tea-spoonful of soda. Bake in muffin-rings, very thin; then spread any kind of jelly between each layer of cake. Another: Take one tea-cup of butter, one of sugar, four eggs, two cups of flour, a very little saleratus. Bake as above, or if you have not the muffin-rings, bake on tins.

WONDERS.

Beat ten eggs as light as possible, half a pound of butter, half a pound of sugar, stirred to a cream, two pounds of flour. Bake in a slow oven.

CYMBALS.

Take half a pound of butter, half a pound of sugar, six eggs, two pounds of flour, nutmeg, and rose-water.

JUMBLES.

Take a cup and a half of sugar, one cup of butter, stirred to a cream; then take six eggs, beat to a froth; add nutmeg or lemon, and stir well; then roll out, and cut with a cutter, and cut out the middle with a canister-top, to leave a ring. Roll in white sugar, and bake on tins in a quick oven.

FRENCH TWIST.

One quart of lukewarm milk, one tea-spoonful of salt, a coffee-cup of yeast, flour enough to let it rise; rub in one egg, and two spoonfuls of butter; knead in flour, until stiff enough to roll out; then let it rise again, and when very light, roll it out, and cut in strips, and braid it. Then bake thirty minutes on buttered tins.

SUGAR-DROPS.

Twelve spoonfuls of butter, twenty-four of sugar, a pint of flour, half a nutmeg, three eggs; drop them on buttered tins; put sugar-plums on the top. Bake twenty minutes.

LEMON CAKE.

Take one tea-cup of butter, and three of powdered sugar, stir them to a cream, stir into them the yolks of five eggs well beaten; dissolve a tea-spoonful of soda in a tea-cup of milk; add the juice and grated peel of one lemon, and the white of five eggs; and sift in, as light as possible, four tea-cups of flour. Bake in two long tins half an hour. This cake is much improved by icing. Two tea-cupfuls of sugar will answer, but three is better.

SPONGE CAKE.

Beat well together the yolks of ten eggs, with a pound of white sugar, then stir in, the whites beaten to a stiff froth; beat the whole; then stir in gradually half a pound of sifted flour, a little nutmeg. Bake immediately.—Another: Take three eggs, and one cup of sugar, beat to a froth; add one cup of flour, one small tea-spoonful of cream of tartar, put in a table-spoonful of sweet cream, half a tea-spoonful of soda. Bake immediately.

QUEEN CAKE.

Take a pound of sifted flour, one of sugar, and three quarters of butter; rub the butter and sugar to a cream; add the beaten yolks of five eggs, one gill of brandy, one of wine, and one of cream, with part of the flour, and a pound of stoned raisins, and spice to the taste; add the whites of the eggs, beaten to a stiff froth, with the remainder of the flour.

SODA CAKE.

Half a cup of butter, two cups of sugar, four cups of flour, three eggs, one tea-spoonful of soda, dissolved in a cup of milk, two spoonfuls of cream of tartar, mixed in the cake.

SILVER CAKE.

Half a cup of butter, one and a half of sugar, half a cup of sweet milk, the whites of five eggs, one tea-spoonful of cream of tartar, one half tea-spoonful of soda.

CUP CAKE.

One coffee-cup of butter, two cups of sugar, beaten to a cream, one cup of sour cream, four cups of flour. Beat five eggs as light as possible, a grated nutmeg, and one tea-spoonful of soda. This cake is nice baked on small tins.

EXCELLENT FRUIT CAKE.

One cup of butter, one of brown sugar, one of molasses, one of sweet milk, three of flour, and four eggs, two pounds of raisins chopped fine, one nutmeg, one tea-spoonful of cream of tartar, and half a tea-spoonful of soda.

ANOTHER.

One pound of butter, one pound of sugar, one pound of flour, ten eggs, one glass of brandy, two pounds of currants, two of raisins, one and a half of citron, one ounce of cloves, one of mace, half an ounce of cinnamon, and nutmeg, a tea-spoonful of soda.

CUP CAKE.

Three cups of sugar, two cups of butter, one cup of cream, six eggs, five of flour, one nutmeg, one cup of currants, one cup of raisins, one tea-spoonful of saleratus or soda. This cake can be made of brown sugar.

PORK CAKE.

One pound of salt pork, chopped, pour on a pint of boiling water, one cup of molasses, two cups of sugar, three eggs, cinnamon, cloves, nutmeg, one pound of chopped raisins, flour to make a stiff batter, two tea-spoonfuls of soda. This will make three loaves.

SODA CAKE.

One egg, and one tea-cupful of white sugar, one tea-spoonful of soda, dissolved in a tea-cup of milk, two and a half table-spoonfuls of butter, one pint of flour, two tea-spoonfuls of cream of tartar, extract of lemon, to suit the taste.

CREAM CAKE.

Beat five eggs light as possible; take three cups of sugar, three of sour cream, one tea-spoonful of soda, and one of salt, flour enough to make a thick batter, nutmeg to suit the taste.

STRAWBERRY OR RASPBERRY CAKE.

Mix a pint of sour milk with a cup of butter, or a cup of sour cream; then stir in flour to make a thick batter; add a tea-spoonful of salt, one of soda, dissolved in a third of a cup of water. Stir well, then add more flour until stiff enough to roll out. Roll two thirds of an inch in thickness and bake quick. Split open when done, and put in a layer of strawberries or raspberries; sprinkle white sugar; put on the cover and eat while hot. If very thick, cut twice in two and spread again.

A CHEAP CAKE.

Take one cup of butter, two of sugar, one of buttermilk, four eggs, half a tea-spoonful of soda and nutmeg. Add one pound of fruit, and three cups of flour.

SOFT CAKE IN LITTLE TINS.

One cup and a half of butter, one and a half of sugar, five eggs, nutmeg, two cups of flour.

WEST-POINT CAKE.

Take one half-pound butter, one pound sugar, five eggs, one pound of flour, one cup of cream, one tea-spoonful of soda.

HONEY CAKE,

Take one cup of butter, two cups of honey, a large spoonful of ginger, nutmeg, or any other seasoning you like, and a little flour, a tea-spoonful of saleratus dissolved in a cup of water; then add flour enough to roll out and bake as gingerbread.

CRULLERS.

Take a tea-spoonful of soda, half a cup of milk, strain on to half a pint of flour, four table-spoonfuls of melted butter or lard, six of sugar that has been rolled smooth, four beaten eggs, and nutmeg. Stir well together, then add the flour and milk; and flour enough to roll out. Roll an inch in thickness, cut in strips not over an inch in width, with a jagging-iron. Twist in any fanciful form you please. Heat a pound of lard in a pot. If you wish to have your crullers very rich, omit the saleratus and milk.

FRENCH CAKE.

Take three quarters of a pound of butter, one pound of white sugar, one pound and a half of flour, twelve eggs, a gill each of wine, milk, and brandy, a pound of seeded raisins or Zante currants, a quarter of a pound of citron, the same of almonds, blanched and pounded fine; spice to the taste. Stir the butter and sugar to a cream, then stir in the eggs, flour, and spice. Mix the wine, brandy, and milk, and add the other ingredients. Stir well together; then add the fruit. When well mixed, put in buttered tins and bake.

WHISTLES.

Take a quarter of a pound of butter, half a pound of sugar, six eggs. Stir the butter and sugar to a cream, then add the eggs previously beaten, and flour to make a thick batter; flavor with rose-water, if you like. Drop the mixture on buttered paper with a large spoon, several inches apart, and spread thin. Bake them of a light brown on a board. They will bake in five minutes. Lay on a moulding-board that has white sugar sprinkled on it; roll them on a stick while warm. When cold, fill with any kind of jelly.

JELLY CAKE.

Take six ounces of butter, eight of white sugar, eight eggs, the juice and grated rind of one lemon, one pound of flour.

COCOA-NUT CAKE.

Take one cup of butter, two of white sugar, half a tea-spoonful of soda dissolved in a tea-cupful of milk, the white part of one cocoa-nut grated, half a nutmeg; add the whites of the eggs with half a pint of sifted flour. Bake as soon as the flour and whites are put in.

WAFERS.

Melt a quarter of a pound of butter, mix with half a pint of milk, a tea-spoonful of salt, a wine-glass of wine, three beaten eggs, and flour to enable you to roll out easily. Roll very thin; cut in small, round cakes, and bake in a moderate oven. Frost while warm, and sprinkle sugar-sand or comfits over it as soon as frosted.

SAVOY CAKES.

Beat the yolks of eight eggs to a froth; mix with them a pound of white sugar, the grated rind of a lemon, and half its juice. Beat the whites of the eggs and stir into the sugar and yolks; then add a pound of flour and two spoonfuls of coriander seed. Drop on buttered baking-plates, with a large spoon, several inches apart; sift sugar over them and bake in a quick oven.

VANITIES.

Beat two eggs, and add sufficient flour to make the right consistency with a little salt. Roll very thin and fry in hot lard. They may be cut in any shape you like; roll in white sugar as soon as they are taken out. If you like, fill with jelly or sweetmeats.

ANOTHER COMPOSITION CAKE.

Take one pound and a quarter of sugar, three quarters of butter, four eggs, one pint of milk, one pound and three quarters of flour, one and a half pounds of currants, one tea-spoonful of soda, and one nutmeg.

ANOTHER COCOA-NUT CAKE.

Take one nut grated, one and a half pounds butter, one pound of sugar, six eggs, and three quarters of a pound of flour. Bake in a moderate oven.

RAILROAD CAKE.

Take two cups of sugar, six eggs, beaten very light, two tea-spoonfuls of cream of tartar, one lemon; grate the peel and use the juice; four table-spoonfuls of milk, two pounds of flour, one tea-spoonful of soda.

ANOTHER MODE OF MAKING SNAPS.

One pint of molasses, one cup of sugar, one egg, one table-spoonful of ginger, one of saleratus, one of vinegar, one cup of butter, seven cups of flour. Roll thin and bake quick.

HARD GINGERBREAD.

Take one and a half cups of sugar, half a cup of butter, half a cup of sweet milk, one egg, a spoonful of ginger, one tea-spoonful of cream of tartar, half a tea-spoonful of soda.

IMPERIAL GINGERBREAD.

Rub half a pound of butter into three quarters of a pound of flour; mix six ounces of treacle with a pint of cream, carefully, lest it should turn the cream; mix in a quarter of a pound of double-refined sugar, half an ounce of ginger, and one ounce of caraway seed; stir the whole well together into a paste; cut it into shapes, and stick out candied orange or lemon-peel on the top.

ANOTHER SODA CAKE.

Take one quarter of a pound of butter, half a pound of sugar, half a pound of flour, two eggs, three quarters of a pound of currants, a quarter of a pound of candied lemon-peel, half a tea-spoonful of soda; pour in milk to make the right consistency to bake.

AN EXCELLENT GINGERBREAD.

Take one pint of molasses, one tea-cupful of butter, one tea-spoonful of soda dissolved in half a tea-cupful of hot water, half a tea-spoonful of alum dissolved in water, two table-spoonfuls of ginger. The whole mixed with flour enough to roll out and cut in cards. Bake in a quick oven.

A PLAIN SPONGE CAKE.

Take two eggs well beaten, one cup of sugar, half a cup of milk, one tea-spoonful of cream of tartar, two cups of flour, half a tea-spoonful of soda. Flavor with nutmeg or rose-water.

GINGER CRACKERS.

Take one pint of molasses, two cups of butter, one and a half of sugar, a table-spoonful of ginger, a tea-spoonful of soda, flour enough to roll out; stir the butter and sugar together; boil the molasses and pour it into the pan, and stir until the butter and sugar are melted; then put in a few handfuls of flour, and add the soda; stir well, then work in the flour, and roll very thin; bake a few minutes.

LUNCHEON CAKE.

Take half a pound of butter, and rub into a pound of flour, with two ounces of currants, the same of caraway seed, half a pound of moist sugar; beat up three eggs, one ounce of lemon-peel candied and cut thin.

Boil half a pint of milk, to which add, while boiling, a tea-spoonful of soda. Stir well and bake immediately. Bake half an hour.

A POUND CAKE MEASURED

Take one cup of butter, two of sugar, four eggs, and three cups of flour; bake in little tins twenty minutes.

SPONGE CAKE.

Take five eggs, one tumbler of sugar, beat light with the yolks, one tumbler of flour; then add the whites of the eggs, after beating light as possible, and bake in a slow oven.

SILVER CAKE. NO. 2.

Take two cups of nice white sugar, half a cup of butter; stir to a cream; then add the whites of eight eggs well beaten, two cups and a half of flour, dissolve half a tea-spoonful of soda in three quarters of a cup of milk; flavor with rose-water or vanilla; stir well together; then add a tea-spoonful of cream of tartar and nutmeg; pour into a square baking-pan, lined with white paper; bake in a quick oven; if baking too fast on the top, cover with a paper.

A LOAF CAKE WITHOUT EGGS.

Take two pounds of butter melted, two pounds of sugar stirred together thoroughly; mix half of it with two pounds of flour, together with a tumblerful of home-made yeast and one quart of warm milk. Beat well together, and let it stand in a warm place until light; say from four to six hours. Then add the remainder of the butter and sugar, also two pounds of raisins and spice. Let it stand over night in pans and bake an hour in a slow oven.

QUEEN'S CAKE—VERY RICH.

Take one pound of white sugar, three quarters of butter, one pound of flour, a pound of seeded raisins, half a pound of Zante currants, a quarter of a pound of citron, a wine-glass of wine, one of brandy, and one of milk, six eggs and a tea-spoonful of soda; after stirring the butter and sugar, put in the eggs; then add the brandy and wine, then the flour and spice; dissolve the soda in the milk, and strain in; stir well together; then add the fruit, sprinkled with flour; bake on square buttered tins from an hour to an hour and thirty minutes. This cake will keep a long time.

CUP CAKE.

Take one cup of butter, two of sugar, beat until light; add one cup of water; have measured five cups of flour, and add half; stir well with one tea-spoonful of cream of tartar; beat three eggs light; pour in, and lastly, half a tea-spoonful of soda, and nutmeg to the taste.

GOLD CAKE.

Take the yolks of eight eggs, and beat light; mix with one cup of sugar, and three quarters of a cup of butter, having previously stirred to a cream; add half a tea-spoonful of soda dissolved in half a cup of sweet milk, with two cups of flour; when well mixed, stir in a tea-spoonful of cream of tartar; flavor with lemon or nutmeg; bake in a square tin.

JELLY CAKE.

Three quarters of a cup of butter, two cups of sugar, five cups of flour, one tea-spoonful of soda dissolved in a cup of milk, three eggs; stir the sugar and butter to a cream, then beat the eggs to a froth and add with part of the flour; strain the milk with the soda into the mixture; stir the whole well together; then add two tea-spoonfuls of cream of tartar; stir several minutes and pour into buttered tins; when cool spread on marmalade or jelly on one side, and lay on more cake, until you have three or four together. Another method is, to spread each one with jelly while warm, and roll up separately; put on a plate until cold, then cut in slices.

ONE-TWO-THREE-FOUR CAKE.

Take one cup of butter, two of sugar, three of flour, and four well-beaten eggs; a pint of hickory-nut meats are an improvement to this cake; a third of a tea-spoonful of cream of tartar with one spoonful of milk, might be added, as it will insure a light cake; then it will require half as much soda to be stirred in lastly.

SODA CAKE.

Take a piece of butter the size of an egg, one cup of sugar, two tea-spoonfuls of cream of tartar dissolved in a cup of sweet milk; beat one egg light, and add two cups of flour; lastly a tea-spoonful of soda.

HARD COOKIES.

One pound of sugar, half a pound of butter, three and a half pounds of flour, and water sufficient to roll out; mould a long time, then set it away an hour or two, and repeat the moulding; add caraway seed if you like, and cut in little cakes after rolling it thin; stamp each cake with a wooden print.

SUGAR GINGERBREAD.

One tea-cupful of butter, two of sugar, two eggs, one table-spoonful of ginger, stir in two tea-cupfuls of flour, and then add a tea-spoonful of soda dissolved in half a tea-cupful of warm water; add flour sufficient to roll out; bake in a quick oven; roll thin.

LINCOLN CAKE.

One tea-cup of sugar, half a cup of butter; stir to a cream, then add half a cup of milk and one cupful of flour; stir well, and add a grated lemon, and two eggs beat to a froth, then add another cup of flour, and lastly, add half a tea-spoonful of soda.

A POUND CAKE MEASURED.

Take a tea-cupful of sugar, nearly one cup of butter; stir to a cream, then add half a tea-spoonful of cream of tartar, with a table-spoonful of milk; beat three eggs as light as possible, and add with two tea-cupfuls of flour; lastly, half as much soda as you had of cream of tartar.

UNION CAKE.

Take a piece of butter the size of a hen's egg, one cup of sugar, one cup of sweet milk, two eggs beat to a froth, two tea-spoonfuls of cream of tartar; mix well together; then stir in two and a half tea-cupfuls of sifted flour; lastly a tea-spoonful of soda; stir well, and bake in a moderate oven, and you will have a cheap and excellent cake. If you like, you can use a cup of sour milk instead of sweet; in that case no cream of tartar will be required. Add spice if you like.

BERWICK SPONGE CAKE.

Beat three eggs two minutes; add a cup and a half of sugar, then beat five minutes; add one cup of flour, one tea-spoonful of cream of tartar, beat two minutes; add a cup of cold water, half a tea-spoonful of soda, beat one minute; a cup of flour, a little salt, rose, or lemon; then bake.

COOKIES THAT WILL KEEP TWO MONTHS.

One pint of sour cream, one pint of white sugar, butter the size of an egg, one tea-spoonful of soda, two table-spoonfuls of caraway seed.

WHIGS.

Take six ounces of butter, eight of sugar stirred to a cream, beat two eggs, and add a tea-spoonful of salt, the same of cinnamon, two pounds of flour, a small cup of yeast and milk to make a stiff batter; when light, bake in small cups well buttered. They are good either hot or cold.

RUSK.

One pint of warm milk, half a pint of yeast and flour to make a thick batter; when light, add half a pound of butter, three quarters of a pound of sugar; add spice and flour to make as stiff as biscuit; let them rise, then mould in cakes the size of biscuits; put on buttered tins and bake after rising, say about thirty minutes; bake quick; mix milk with a large spoonful of egg, and rub on the top as soon as baked.

SODA JUMBLES.

One cup and a half of butter, three of sugar stirred to a cream, a tea-spoonful of soda dissolved in a tea-cupful of water. five eggs beat very light, and stirred into the sugar and cream; then stir in six cups of sifted flour with one nutmeg grated, and two tea-spoonfuls of cream of tartar; when well stirred, add the water and saleratus; drop on buttered tins and bake.

CREAM JELLY CAKE.

Stir into two cups of sweet cream flour enough to make a batter, add four well-beaten eggs, one cup of sugar, two spoonfuls of cream of tartar, and spice to the taste; when well mixed, add a tea-spoonful of soda dissolved in half a wine-glass of milk; pour into buttered tins, not over one third of an inch in thickness, and bake; when baked, put on jelly between each cake.

HARD GINGERBREAD.

One tea-cupful of shortening, one pint of molasses, a spoonful of ginger, two tea-spoonfuls of soda dissolved in a cup of water; roll out and bake.

SODA CAKE.

Stir two cups of white sugar, and one of butter to a cream, add six well-beaten eggs, four cups of flour, two spoonfuls of cream of tartar, and a grated nutmeg; dissolve a tea-spoonful of soda in a cup of milk and stir in lastly.

GINGERBREAD NUTS.

One pound and a quarter of flour, half a pound of butter, rub well together with one ounce of ginger, cinnamon, cloves, and allspice; wet the whole with one pint of molasses, and stir well; then add half a tea-spoonful of soda dissolved; take out a handful at a time and knead in little cakes, then put all together and knead a long time; cut the lump in half, and roll in thin sheets, and cut in little cakes; lay on buttered tins; bake in a moderate oven.

COFFEE CAKE.

Take a tea-cup of clear strong coffee, as made for the table, one cup of butter, one of sugar, one of molasses, or a little more than one, one egg, four of flour, one nutmeg, a tea-spoonful of cinnamon, one pound of raisins; mix your butter, sugar, spices, molasses, then add a tea-spoonful of cream of tartar, one half tea-spoonful of soda dissolved and put in last.

ELMSDALE CAKE.

Take three cups of butter, six cups of sugar; rub well together, then add two cups of buttermilk, seven eggs, ten cups of flour, one nutmeg, raisins, and one tea-spoonful of saleratus.

MOUNTAIN CAKE.

Take two cups of flour, one cup and a half of sugar, four table-spoonfuls of butter; beat light the whites of three eggs; one tea-spoonful of cream of tartar, one cup of milk, half a tea-spoonful of soda; stir the butter and sugar together, add the milk and soda, and put the eggs in last.

JAM CAKE.

Take one cup of sugar, half a cup of butter, the same of milk, two tea-spoonfuls of cream of tartar, one of soda, two eggs, two cups of flour; bake in small tins; when done, cut out a piece; fill with jam or jelly; replace the piece and ice the cakes.

CIDER CAKE.

Take one cup of butter, two of sugar, one of cider, two eggs, three cups of flour, one tea-spoonful of soda.

PILGRIM'S LOAF CAKE.

Two spoonfuls of yeast, two cups of warm milk, four cups of sugar, half a cup of butter, one egg, one pound of raisins, one fourth of a pound of citron, flour enough to make a stiff dough; put in the yeast, butter, milk, and let it rise; then add the other ingredients, and let it rise again.

CORN-STARCH CAKE.

One tea-cup of sugar, half a cup of milk, half a cup of corn-starch, one cup of flour, whites of three eggs; put in with the flour and starch, half a tea-spoonful of cream of tartar, half as much soda, also half cup of butter; when done, ice it.

PASTRY AND PIES.

For plain pastry, allow half a pound of shortening to a pound of flour, and for rich pastry, allow three quarters of a pound. Lard makes the most delicate looking crust; but if some butter is used, the crust will be nicer. Rub half the shortening with two thirds of the flour. When the flour and shortening are well rubbed together, add water sufficient to enable you to roll out. If rolled a number of times, it will be more flaky. When rolled out, put on more of the shortening with the flour; and always roll from you. It should be made as quick and as cold as possible. In cold weather it should be warmed a little, but not melted, or it will not be flaky. A plain, tender crust may be made of sour milk with soda; but it will not require so much shortening. Sweet cream and soda is still nicer. Good potatoes boiled in salted water and strained, add to the same quantity of flour, wet with sour milk, and soda, makes a very tender crust, and requires no shortening. Light bread dough, with a little butter added, and rolled thin, makes a nice crust for meat pies, and for the upper crust of fruit pies, to be made without bottom crusts.

DIRECTIONS FOR MAKING VERY NICE PASTE.

Take a quarter of a pound of shortening and rub into the flour, wet with cold water just enough to roll out. Then take the remainder and cut in very thin slices. Sprinkle a thick layer of flour on the moulding-board; lay on the flour the slices of shortening. Sprinkle on more flour and roll out in thin sheets; then roll out the paste and cover with a sheet of this. Sprinkle on more flour and fold up; then roll out again, and repeat until the shortening is used up.

PUFF PASTE.

Dissolve a little sal-volatile in cold water, then take one pound and a quarter of flour, one pound of butter; rub one third of the butter with two thirds of the flour, and add the sal-volatile with a little salt. Moisten with water to a nice paste; then cut the butter in slices as directed above. Roll out lightly about one third of an inch in thickness, and use for puffs or rim and upper crust to pies. It should be baked quick, and of a light brown; if baking too fast, put a paper on top.

QUINCE TARTS.

Take six quinces, half a pound of sugar, half a pint of cream, four eggs, and nutmeg to the taste.

COCOA-NUT PIE.

Save the milk taken out of the cocoa-nut, grate the white part and put the milk with it, say a quart; if not able to save the milk, add other milk. Simmer it together for a quarter of an hour; then take it from the fire and mix two large spoonfuls of butter, four of white sugar, a small cracker pounded fine, and half a nutmeg. When cool, add five well-beaten eggs and a wine-glass of wine. Turn into deep plates with a lining and rim of nice pastry, and bake in a quick oven. They must be eaten cold.

MARLBOROUGH TARTS.

Stew tart apples tender; strain through a fine colander. To twelve large spoonfuls of the apples, add the juice and grated rind of a lemon, three spoonfuls of melted butter, half a pint of milk or cream, a wine-glass of wine, half a nutmeg, four well-beaten eggs, and sugar to the taste. Bake with a lining and rim; ornament them with pastry cut in flowers, or any design you like. If for grapes, cut with a thimble, and for the leaves, use a pen-knife.

LEMON PIE. NO. 3.

Grate two lemons, add the juice, but leave out the white part; add two large spoonfuls of rolled crackers, one of butter, six of white sugar, and six beaten eggs. Put all into a quart of milk, and bake in deep plates with pastry on the bottom, with a rim.

A PIE-CRUST WITH VERY LITTLE BUTTER.

Take one pound of flour, and two table-spoonfuls of shortening, one tea-spoonful of carbonate of soda; dissolve half a tea-spoonful of tartaric acid in cold water, adding enough to make a paste; roll quickly. It is made better by adding an egg before the water is put in.

PASTE FOR FAMILY PIES.

Rub half a pound of shortening into a pound and a half of flour, wet with cold water sufficient to make a paste. Roll out several times.

PYRAMID PASTE.

Make a rich puff paste, and cut with different sized cake-cutters, fitting one into another; cut a bit out of each one, except the top one and bottom; bake on buttered paper laid on tins; then build them in a pyramid form, laying different preserved fruit on each one, and on the top a whole apricot with a sprig of myrtle stuck in, currants or green gages.

MINCE PIE WITHOUT MEAT.

Take four soda crackers, half a tea-cupful of water, half a cup of melted butter, half a cup of vinegar, half a cup of boiled cider, one cup of molasses, one cup of sugar, one cup of chopped raisins. Add spices.

A DELICIOUS LEMON PIE.

Take the juice and grate the rind of one lemon; take the yolks of two eggs and one cup of sugar, three table-spoonfuls of flour, with sufficient milk to fill the dish, and bake until brown. Then beat the whites of the eggs; add four table-spoonfuls of sugar, and spread over the pie.

MELON PIE.

Pare and stew the melon the same as pumpkin; to one pint of melon add one tea-spoonful of tartaric acid, or a lemon cut up fine, a small piece of butter, spice the same as for pumpkin. Bake without a crust.

A MINCE PIE WITHOUT MEAT. NO. 2.

Chop three pounds of suet very fine, three pounds of apple nicely cored, wash three pounds of currants, chop three pounds of raisins, or not, just as you like, one pound of sugar, cut twelve ounces of candied orange-peel very fine, six ounces of citron, a quarter of an ounce of nutmeg, half an ounce of cinnamon, six or eight cloves, and half pint of French brandy; cover it close and keep for use.

GROUND CHERRY PIE.

One pint ground cherries husked and washed, two table-spoonfuls of sugar, half a lemon cut in small pieces, or half a tea-spoonful of the extract; bake in a slow oven. They can be dried and kept for winter use; just before using, soak half an hour.

A DELICATE APPLE PIE.

Make a rich syrup of white sugar, boil lemon-peel to flavor it; then put in tart apples that have been nicely quartered; only put a few in at a time; take out as soon as tender, and put in your pie-plates; if not seasoned sufficiently, add more lemon; put on a nice crust.

APPLE PUFFS.

Mix a quarter of a pound of butter with a quart of sifted flour; beat two eggs, and a little salt. Rub well together with half a tea-spoonful of soda dissolved in cold water. Moisten with cold water just enough to roll it out easily. It must be rolled very thin, and cut with a tumbler; put three together, sprinkle flour between each one; put on the top a few thin slices of tart apples; sprinkle sugar and nutmeg over. Double the pastry over them so as to form a crescent; press the edges together, and fry in lard. When of a light brown, take up carefully.

GRAPE PIE.

Take green grapes, stew and strain, and sweeten to the taste. If made of whole grapes, allow a tea-cupful of sugar to each pie, or a little water.

MARINGOES OR CREAM PUFFS.

Rub half a pound of butter, three quarters of a pound of flour together; stir into a pint of boiling water while boiling. When thick, remove from the fire. When cool, stir in a small tea-spoonful of soda, ten well-beaten eggs; drop the mixture on buttered tins with a large spoon, put several inches apart; bake of a light brown, in a quick oven. When done, open on one side and fill with mock cream, which is made as follows: One quart of milk scalded, beat four eggs to a froth, one cup of sugar, one cup of flour, stir into the milk while boiling; when thick remove from the fire; flavor with lemon or vanilla. Put in the puffs when cold.

MARINGOES. NO. 2.

Take the whites of eight eggs and whisk to a froth. Stir in half a pound of white sifted sugar. Flavor with any thing you like; then sift powdered sugar over them and bake on a board in a slow oven. When done, take them up and beat the under side with a spoon to form a hollow, and dry them; fill with cream or preserved fruit; put two together, which will form an oval shape.

SNOW-BALLS.

Boil some rice until half cooked; then pare and core, but not cut, some apples; put into each a little salt and cinnamon or lemon-peel, and then put some of the rice on a cloth, and put the apples in; tie up and boil one hour. Eat with sugar and cream.

MINCE PIES

may be made by using potatoes in the place of apples. Pare and chop the potatoes fine, then soak them over night in vinegar, and they can not be told from apples. Turnips or beets may be used, though not as good as potatoes.

A PUMPKIN PIE WITHOUT STEWING THE PUMPKIN.

Pare and grate the pumpkin, and to every pint add a pint of rich milk, two eggs, spices, a little flour and salt. Squash pies may be made the same, or stewed, according to the taste. I have also made carrot pies in this way, which are rich and nice.

CUSTARD PIES.

Two eggs well beaten, a table-spoonful and a half of sugar, a table-spoonful of flour, and a pint and a half of milk, makes a good pie. But if you want it rich, take four eggs, nutmeg, and lemon; also a little salt; bake in a slow oven; be careful not to bake too much, as that will make it whey.

MOCK APPLE PIE.

One tea-cupful of light bread, two of water, one and a half of sugar, one tea-spoonful of tartaric acid, a little salt, cinnamon and lemon, if you like; boil the bread and water five minutes; then add the other ingredients.

ANOTHER.

Six crackers, one tea-cupful of water, one of sugar, one tea-spoonful tartaric acid, a piece of butter the size of a hickory-nut, and a little salt.

By using an egg and only four crackers, makes a nice pie.

RHUBARB PIE.

Pull the stalks off, (not cut them, as it injures the roots;) take the outside off, which peels easily; cut up in pieces an inch long; wash clean in cold water; have your crust ready, and put the pieces in evenly; sprinkle a little flour over them, a small piece of butter, and a tea-cupful of sugar; put on another crust, and bake in a slow oven. Sometimes a little nutmeg or lemon is an addition, but this is according to the taste.

ANOTHER.

Stew the rhubarb in a little water, and take one tea-cupful after it is stewed, one tea-cupful of sugar, and one egg, well beaten; a little butter. This makes a very nice pie.

BLACKBERRY OR RASPBERRY PIE.

Make a rich crust, and lay the berries in; sprinkle a little flour over them, a little water, and two table-spoonfuls of sugar; put on an upper crust; bake in a slow oven.

GREEN APPLE PIE.

Pare and slice the apples very thin; lay in your crust; sprinkle a little flour over them; turn in a very little water, (if the apples are juicy, they will not require so much water as those that are not;) put in sugar, according to the taste; if the apples are very sour, they require more; a piece of butter, any kind of spice you like, nutmeg or lemon, is preferable to any other.

ANOTHER.

Pare and slice the apples; put them in your crust, with a little water, but no seasoning whatever; when baked, take off the upper crust; put in sugar, butter, and spices to suit the taste. This is nice eaten warm.

Another way I have of making a green apple pie: Take off the upper crust; take out half the apple in another dish, (after spicing and seasoning it to your taste;) turn the upper crust bottom-side up; put in the apple you have taken out, and put a few spoonfuls of rich cream in; grate in a little more nutmeg. This makes a very delicious pie. I make quite a thick crust, and fill very full with apples.

Another way of making apple pies is, to stew the apples, season with sugar and spices, and put in a crust, and bake in a slow oven.

PUMPKIN PIE.

Stew the pumpkin; strain through a colander; and to two tea-cupfuls, take one and a half of rich milk, a table-spoonful of flour, one tea-spoonful of ginger, a little salt, and a little allspice; bake in a quick oven.

A PUMPKIN PIE WITH EGGS.

Stew the pumpkin down dry; strain, and to every tea-cupful and a half, add a pint of milk and one egg, a little nutmeg, cinnamon, ginger, and a little salt. This makes a rich pie.

BUTTERNUT PIE.

A tea-cupful of butter-nut meats, two eggs, a pint and a half of milk, nearly two table-spoonfuls of sugar.

A hickory pie may be made in the same way. They have a very nice flavor.

CURRANT PIE.

Take green currants; pick them clean, and wash; a single handful of flour sprinkled over the fruit, and plenty of sugar, with a little water; they are liable to run over if too much is put in. A little molasses—say half molasses and half sugar—is nice for a currant pie. One half raisins is a great improvement.

DRIED APPLE PIES.

Stew the apple, and then strain it through a colander; season according to the taste, and bake in a slow oven.

TART PIES

may be made of almost any kind of fruit which is tart; and put in a rich paste; cut strips of pastry, and twist it, and put on the top, in any shape you fancy. I have made very nice tarts of cider apple-sauce.

TARTS.

Make a rich paste; cut out with a tumbler or cake-cutter; then cut strips of paste to lay on top; press it in the middle to form deeper; then lay in sweetmeats, and bake on tins.

APPLE CUSTARD PIE.

Grate five sweet apples for every pie, a pint and a half of rich milk, two eggs, sugar, a little salt, nutmeg or lemon; bake as a custard pie.

LEMON PIE. NO. 4.

One lemon sliced very thin, one tea-cupful of sugar, one of water, one egg; bake in a slow oven. It is very good without the egg, but will require a tablespoonful of flour.

A RICE PIE.

Wash and boil the rice until nearly done; one tea-cupful after it is boiled, two eggs, a pint and a half of milk, a little salt, sugar, nutmeg; bake as a custard pie.

MINCE PIES.

Boil beef until it will slip off the bone; the head and heart are nice for pies; chop fine; take one quart of meat to two of green apples, chopped fine. A plenty of box raisins, allspice, cloves, cinnamon, nutmeg, pepper, salt, are all necessary for these pies;

also a little boiled cider, which takes the place of brandy; use either molasses or sugar; I think half of each is better, and sometimes I use a little lemon, which is an improvement. Put in all the ingredients, and put over a slow fire, and let it simmer an hour, when they can be put in the paste, and bake slowly. These pies will keep longer than any other, and are a favorite with almost every one. If you do not wish to use all your meat at once, put in the spices, and cover with molasses; then set it away in the cellar until needed, when the apples can be added, and more seasoning, if required.

COCOA-NUT PIE. NO. 2.

Grate it, and mix with milk; boil eight or ten minutes. To a pint of cocoa-nuts, add a quart of milk, and four eggs, a little sweet cream, a cracker rolled fine, and a little nutmeg; bake in a deep dish, like a custard.

TOMATO PIE.

Take green tomatoes; pare and slice them; lay in the crust; sprinkle over a little flour, sugar or molasses, part of a lemon sliced, and a little water. This makes an excellent pie.

You can use ripe tomatoes if you like, but they require an egg, and a little cream.

DRIED TOMATO PIE.

Take ripe ones; throw them in boiling water to take the skins off; then slice them; lay them on dishes; sprinkle a little sugar over them, and dry in a warm oven. They can be put in bags for winter use. Soak in a little water, and lay in the paste, with lemon, a little flour and sugar.

ELDERBERRY PIE.

This pie requires but very little sugar. A tablespoonful of vinegar or a little lemon, with a little flour sprinkled over, is an improvement. They are a juicy pie, and will need no water. Bake slowly.

A CHERRY PIE.

Stone your cherries; lay them in your paste, put in a sufficient quantity of sugar, a little water, and a handful of flour sprinkled over; then put on a nice paste. Some prefer molasses instead of sugar. They require no water, if molasses is used.

PEACH PIE.

Pare and slice the peaches; sprinkle over a little flour and sugar, then a rich crust, and bake slowly. This is a most delicious pie. Dried peaches are made the same, except the peaches must be stewed first.

ANOTHER LEMON PIE.

Grate three lemons; beat three eggs, one tea-cupful of water, three table-spoonfuls of sugar to each lemon.

GOOSEBERRY PIE.

Rub the gooseberry in a flannel cloth to take the prickles off; then wash clean, and make as a currant pie.

QUINCE PIE.

Pare six apples and one quince; stew until soft; then sweeten them, and bake in a crust.

CRANBERRY TARTS.

One pound of sugar to one quart of cranberries; put a little water on them, and stew until done. When wanted for use, put them in a rich paste.

APPLE PUFFS.

Pare the apples, and bake them slowly; when cold, season with sugar and lemon-peel grated, or cinnamon; bake them in a thin paste.

A CREAM PIE.

Make a rich crust; beat one egg, one pint and a half of rich cream, and one table-spoonful of flour, a little salt, nutmeg, or lemon. Bake as a custard.

LEMON CREAM PIE.

One raw potato grated, one cup of water, one cup of sugar, one lemon grated, and juice added; baked in pastry, top and bottom.

PUDDINGS.

DIRECTIONS FOR PUDDINGS.

For boiled puddings, a bag should be made of thick cotton cloth, or a tin basin is the best, with the cover fitting tight, and then tied on. If a cloth is used, it must be wrung out of hot water, and floured on the inside. It must have room to swell, as they swell while boiling. Put a skewer on plate in the kettle to prevent it sticking to the bottom. The water must boil when the pudding is put in, and in five minutes must be turned over, or it is apt to be heavy, if not turned. If the water boils down, more must be added, but it must be boiling hot, and not suffered to get off a boil until taken up. When taken out of the bag, dip into cold water for a minute, and it will easily slip out. Raisins or fruits should be rolled in flour to prevent their settling. Plum puddings are better if made the night before used, the eggs added in the morning.

ARROW-ROOT PUDDING.

Stir two arge spoonfuls of arrow-root, having made it smooth, into a pint of boiling milk, stir until it thickens; remove from the fire, and mix a grated nutmeg, a tea-spoonful of salt, half a cup of sugar, two spoonfuls of wine, and a pint of milk; when lukewarm, add four beaten eggs, and bake it.

POUND PUDDING.

Take one pound of suet chopped very fine, one pound of flour, one pound of sugar, one pound raisins, eight eggs; boil eight hours; eat with pudding sauce.

ALMOND PUDDING.

Beat six eggs as light as possible, add three spoonfuls of white sugar; mix with a quart of milk, three large spoonfuls of rolled crackers, four ounces of melted butter, the same of citron cut in strips. Take three quarters of a pound of sweet almonds and pour boiling water on them, and let them remain until the skins will come off, then rub with a dry cloth; when perfectly dry, pound fine, with a large spoonful of rose-water;

stir into the above mixture, and bake in a pudding-dish, with a pastry lining and rim. Bake half an hour. It is best cold.

VERMICELLI PUDDING.

Take a pint of milk and simmer, two ounces of vermicelli, the rind of a lemon and a stick of mace; when tender, remove from the fire, and mix with it a pint of cold milk, a glass of wine, salt and sugar to the taste; when cool, beat four eggs and stir in. Bake in a moderate oven.

A TRANSPARENT PUDDING.

Take tart apples, of a medium size, remove the cores without quartering and lay them in a pudding-dish, fill the holes with white sugar and a little mace; for half a dozen apples take a pound of sago, rinse in cold water, and strew around the apples in the dish, pour in water until it just covers the apples. Bake until the apples become soft, and the sago forms a jelly. They must not brown, if they do, put a plate over them. Serve up hot or cold, with white sugar and cream.

NORFOLK DUMPLINGS.

Mix a pint of milk, a pint of flour, five eggs, well beaten, a little salt; take a large spoon, and drop a spoonful at a time in boiling water. In five minutes take up and serve with pudding sauce.

TRANSPARENT PUDDING. NO. 2.

Beat eight eggs very light, and put in a saucepan with a pound of white sugar, half a pound of butter, and a little nutmeg grated; set it on the fire, and stir it until it thickens. Put a puff paste round the rim of a basin, and when cold, turn in and bake in a moderate oven. Candied orange or lemon may be added, if you like. It will cut clear.

SQUASH PUDDING.

One pint of mashed squash, four apples pared and cored, then stewed tender; add a spoonful of breadcrumbs, half a pint of milk, one spoonful of wine, and the same of rose-water, three eggs, nutmeg, salt, and sugar to the taste; beat well together, and then line a basin with puff-paste, and bake three quarters of an hour.

TAPIOCA PUDDING. NO. 1.

Put four spoonfuls of tapioca into a quart of milk, let it remain all night, then add a spoonful of brandy, lemon-peel and spice; boil gently, and add four beaten eggs, and a quarter of a pound of sugar; then bake it.

WILTSHIRE PUDDING.

A pint of milk, three beaten eggs, flour to make a stiff batter; add a little salt; stir in a large cup of currants, or any kind of fruit you like; put in a bag and boil two hours. Eat with sauce.

A RICH PUDDING.

Take four ounces of butter, the same of sugar and marmalade, also five beaten eggs; put in a stewpan and stir all one way until warm, but not boil; bake in a dish with puff-paste.

RATAFIA PUDDING.

Pound two ounces of blanched almonds, with a little rose-water, and two ounces of ratafia cakes, add the yolks of six eggs and the whites of two, two glasses of wine, a pint of thick cream, and one ounce of loaf-sugar; bake in a dish, lined with puff-paste, three quarters of an hour.

PLUM PUDDING WITHOUT EGGS.

Four ounces of finely minced suet, half a pound of grated bread, half a pound of currants, two ounces of brown sugar, a glass of brandy; mix all together with milk sufficient to make a stiff batter; boil in a cloth from four to six hours.

LEMON PUDDING.

Take half a pound of butter, the same of white sugar, put into a saucepan over the fire, and stir until it boils; then take off, and grate the rind of a large lemon into it, and let it stand until cool; then beat six eggs, and squeeze the juice of the lemon over them; mix the butter and sugar with them. Line a dish with nice pastry and fill up, then bake slowly. Add bits of candied lemon-peel. This is a very rich pudding. Fewer eggs may be used, and a little cream used, if preferred.

LEMON PUDDING. NO. 2.

Boil two lemons till quite tender, then take out the seeds, and pound the lemons to a paste; add four ounces of butter, the same of white sugar; beat to a froth the yolks of three eggs; mix well together, and bake in a puff-paste. When taken up, strew white sugar on the top.

ORANGE PUDDING.

Squeeze out the juice of three Seville oranges, and boil the skins in considerable water; when tender, pound in a mortar, and mix the yolks of nine beaten eggs, and the whites of four, three quarters of a pound of white sugar, the juice of the oranges, and half a pound of melted butter. Bake half an hour, in a dish lined with puff-paste.

CARROT PUDDING.

Scrape and boil two large carrots; mash fine, and strain through a colander; add a slice of bread, two ounces of melted butter, the same quantity of sugar, a table-spoonful of marmalade, or orange-peel minced fine, four well-beaten eggs, and nutmegs; mix well together, and bake in a dish lined with paste.

SPRING FRUIT PUDDING.

Peel and wash rhubarb; put in a stewpan with a lemon, and sugar sufficient to sweeten, set it over the fire until soft, press it through a sieve, and add the yolks of four eggs and one of whites, and a quarter of a pound of butter, a nutmeg; beat all together, and put in a puff-paste. Bake half an hour.

COCOA-NUT PUDDING.

Take four ounces of sugar, three ounces of butter; stir to a cream; add half a glass of brandy, the same of wine, beat the whites of six eggs, and stir in; then grate a quarter of a pound of grated cocoa-nut. Bake in a basin, with a lining of pastry. Grate loaf-sugar over.

FAMILY PUDDING.

One pound of flour, half a pound of suet, half a pound of stoned raisins, a little salt, milk to make a stiff batter; add two eggs, if you like, and boil five hours. Eat with sauce.

PLUM PUDDING.

One pound chopped suet, five table-spoonfuls of flour, the same of sugar, five beaten eggs, (the yolks only,) and the whites of three, a tea-spoonful of salt, and a pound of raisins. Boil six hours in a cloth. Serve with a sauce.

CITRON PUDDING.

The yolks of eggs, half a pint of cream, one spoonful of flour, two ounces of citron cut thin; sugar to the taste. Bake in a quick oven, and when done, turn out of the cups.

EVE'S PUDDING.

Half a pound of suet, half a pound of chopped apples, half a pound of sugar, half a pound of flour, half a pound of stoned raisins dredged with flour, a little salt, a glass of brandy, a grated nutmeg, lastly, five eggs, whipped to a froth.

APPLE DUMPLINGS.

Pare, and take out the core of good-sized apples; put a nice paste around them, and steam an hour and a half; then take off a piece of the top, and lay in sugar, put the paste on again, and serve with butter and cream. The apples may be filled with sugar, (where the core was taken out,) before cooking, if you like.

SOFT MUFFINS.

Take a quart of milk and two spoonfuls of butter; beat five eggs very light, and stir in; then stir in two large spoonfuls of good yeast, and a little salt, and lastly flour to make a stiff batter. Let it rise, in a warm place, which will be in about three hours; then grease your baking-iron and rings, set the iron on the rings, and bake a light brown. Do not cut them open with a knife, but pull them open with your hands.

SAGO PUDDING.

Soak six table-spoonfuls of sago two hours, in cold water, boil it in a quart of milk till soft. Stir in a little butter, add one tea-cup of white sugar, and let it cool; beat six eggs to a froth, and stir in. Season with lemon, rose-water, or nutmeg, and add currants or raisins. Flour them before putting in, or they will settle at the bottom. Stir the whole, and put in a buttered dish, and bake three quarters of an hour. It may be served cold.

BAKED INDIAN PUDDING.

Scald a quart of milk, stir in meal sufficient to make a batter. Season with molasses, allspice, and salt, to suit the taste. Then put it in a tin basin; turn a tea-cupful of rich milk on top; cut up a few pieces of butter and lay around; then put it in the oven, and bake two hours. It is equally as nice as it is with eggs.

A BOILED INDIAN PUDDING.

A quart of buttermilk, or sour milk, one tea-cupful of flour, two of meal, a litle salt, sour apples chopped up or sliced; wet your bag, and boil two hours. Serve with sugar and cream.

CORN STARCH PUDDING.

One quart of milk scalded, four table-spoonfuls of corn-starch, wet with a little cold milk, a little salt; stir it in the milk, and turn in your moulds. Eat cold, with sweetened cream.

ENGLISH PUDDING.

Two tea-cupfuls of milk, one quart of flour, two cups of molasses, three eggs, one pound of raisins, one pound of suet, two tea-spoonfuls of cream of tartar, and one tea-spoonful of soda. This can either be boiled or steamed. It is better steamed.

SUET PUDDING.

One tea-cupful of milk, one tea-cupful of molasses, three-fourths of a tea-cupful of suet chopped fine, one tea-spoonful of soda, and one of salt, half a tea-cupful of butter, half a tea-cup of raisins; stir together with flour enough to make a batter; add nutmeg or cinnamon. Steam from two to three hours. Eat with cream.

CREAM PUDDING.

Mix a pint of flour with a pint of milk; beat six eggs to a froth; mix with them three table-spoonfuls of powdered sugar, and the grated rind of a lemon; add it to the milk and flour; put in a little salt, and a pint of thick sweet cream. Bake in a tin dish.

EGG PUDDING.

One pint of milk, four eggs, four spoonfuls of flour, a little salt; boiled in a bag one hour and a half. Use a liquid sauce, with brandy, or one made of butter, sugar, and nutmeg, mashed until light. Care should always be taken in boiling puddings to have the water boiling when put in, and not stop boiling until taken out.

BREAD PUDDING.

Cut slices of bread, or broken pieces, and soak in milk until soft; then add two eggs to every quart of milk, and season with salt, cinnamon, or nutmeg, also a little butter. Bake like a custard.

A RICE PUDDING.

Boil a coffee-cup of rice, until half done; then add three pints of milk, four eggs, or two eggs will do, if you have not a quantity of them, four spoonfuls of sugar, and one tea-cupful of raisins, and a little salt. Flavor with nutmeg, and bake until thick. When half baked, take a table-spoon and stir it up, or else the raisins will settle at the bottom.

A BOILED RICE PUDDING.

Boil one pint of rice, half a pound of raisins, a tea-spoonful of salt; when soft (there should only be water enough put on to boil it tender) add a quart of milk, and a tea-cupful of cream; beat two eggs, and add four spoonfuls of sugar, and stir in, also a little nutmeg, and let it simmer five minutes. If you prefer, leave out the eggs and sugar, and eat with butter and sugar mashed, which I think is preferable. Rice, when cooking, should never be stirred.

SWEET CORN PUDDING.

Take twelve ears of sweet corn, and grate them; beat four eggs, one quart of sweet milk, a piece of butter, a little salt. Bake two hours.

PLUM PUDDING.

One pint of milk, six eggs, one pound of plums, one tea-cup of suet, one tea-cup of sugar; wet the bag, and boil three hours. Serve with sauce.

PUFF PUDDING.

Take six eggs, six spoonfuls of flour, one quart of milk. Bake twenty minutes. Serve with butter and sugar, stirred to a froth. Add nutmeg.

FLOUR PUDDING.

One quart of milk, scalded; stir a pint and a half of flour in some cold milk, just enough to wet it, and when free from lumps, stir it into the scalded milk; beat seven eggs, a little salt. It may be either baked or boiled. It takes two hours to boil, and an hour to bake. Serve with a nutmeg sauce. You could add raisins, or any kind of fruit you like.

ROLLY POOLY PUDDING.

Make a crust, as you would for a pie; roll it out, but not as thin as for pies, say half an inch thick; then strew on any kind of fruit, such as currants, raspberry, cherries, strawberry, or in the winter, dried fruit, soaked until soft, or preserves are good for this kind of pudding. Boil two hours, or according to the size of it; if large, it requires longer. It must be rolled in a cloth, and pinned at the ends, also tie a string around. Eat with a sauce, or rich cream and sugar, with nutmeg.

ENGLISH PLUM PUDDING.

Soak a pint of crackers in a quart of milk; add half a tea-cup of butter, four spoonfuls of sugar, half a pint of flour, half a wine-glass of wine, and half a grated nutmeg; beat five eggs and stir in; add a quarter of a pound of seeded raisins, the same of Zante currants, and two ounces of citron. Bake or boil two hours. Serve with a brandy sauce.

A BREAD AND BUTTER PUDDING.

Cut slices of bread; then spread them with butter and green apple sauce; lay in a bake-dish, until nearly full; then beat two eggs, one quart of milk, three spoonfuls of sugar, and pour over it. Grate in some nutmeg, or cinnamon, and bake like a custard.

LEMON DUMPLINGS.

Squeeze the juice from a lemon; chop the rind; add half a pound of suet, chopped fine, half a pound of bread-crumbs, one egg, milk sufficient to make a paste; sweeten to the taste, or not, just as you like; divide into small parts; tie in cloths; boil three quarters of an hour. Serve with wine sauce.

CRUST FOR A SAVORY PIE.

One pound of flour, one and a half pounds of butter; break in small pieces, and wash in cold water; then rub the butter and flour together, and mix in the yolks of three eggs; beat with a wooden spoon, and add a pint of ice-water; roll out, and fold three times. Leave on ice two hours before using.

BOILED RICE PUDDING.

Swell a large cup of rice in milk, till soft; then add two eggs, milk or cream, to make it sufficiently thin; butter a mould, stone some raisins, and place around the mould; add currants and sugar to the rice; fill the mould, and tie up; then boil. Add a custard, flavored with rum, when sent to the table. Good eaten cold.

MERINGUE PUDDING.

Take one pint of bread-crumbs, one quart of milk, one tea-cup of sugar, the yolks of four eggs, four ounces of butter, the rind of one lemon; mix well, and bake; then spread currant-jelly or jam on top, and over that the whites of the eggs, well beaten, with five table-spoonfuls of sugar, and the juice of the lemon. Return to the oven a few minutes.

MINUTE DUMPLING.

Beat four eggs light, mix four even table-spoonfuls of flour with one pint of milk; add the eggs; strain, and add sugar and nutmeg; then pour in buttered tea-cups, about three parts full. Bake quick. Serve with sauce.

QUAKING PUDDING.

Stir eight table-spoonfuls of flour smooth, with a little milk; then pour it into a quart of boiling milk; add two eggs, a little butter, and salt; when it comes to a boil, it is done. Eat with sauce.

A CHEAP BATTER PUDDING.

One quart of milk, one quart of flour, six eggs, a little salt; stir the flour in so that it will not be lumpy; boil one hour in a cloth. Serve with a sauce.

GOOSEBERRY PUDDING.

Stew a pint of gooseberries till soft, mash them fine, sweeten to the taste; add two ounces of butter, two of bread-crumbs, and three eggs; lay it in a puff-paste in a deep dish; bake half an hour. Apples may be used instead.

LEMONS TO KEEP FOR PUDDINGS.

Save all the rinds and throw into cold water; after a few days boil until tender, then strain, and when nearly dry, throw into a syrup of sugar and a little water; in a week or two boil till they look clear. Orange-peel may be done in the same manner.

A BOILED BREAD PUDDING.

Take a small loaf of baker's bread, soak soft; add one beaten egg, a cup of raisins, a spoonful of butter; mix well and boil one hour. Serve with sauce.

A COMPOSITION PUDDING.

Take stoned raisins, currants, minced apples, chopped suet, grated bread, and brown sugar, a tea-cupful of each; four well-beaten eggs, a little salt, a tea-spoonful of root ginger pounded fine, half a nutmeg grated, and one glass of brandy; mix well and boil in a cloth two hours. Serve with a wine sauce.

APPLE PUDDING WITH RICE.

Pare and slice nice flavored apples, and lay in a deep dish; have ready some boiled rice in milk, and seasoned with sugar; lay on a layer an inch and a half thick; pour over this, two or three eggs beaten with sugar; bake until the apples are tender; eat with cream and sugar; a little nutmeg is an addition.

FRESH FRUIT PUDDING.

Line a dish with soda biscuit, then fill up with fruit—cherries, blackberries, plums, apples, or any kind of fruit you like; sprinkle on sugar, and bake till the crust is done; eat with cream; nice for children. Another way is to put in the fruit first, and put a cover on top, then bake.

AMBER PUDDING.

Melt a pound of butter, and stir in three quarters of a pound of white sugar; then add the yolks of fifteen eggs beaten, and as much candied orange as will give it color and flavor; line a dish with paste, and lay the mixture in; lay a crust over, and bake. Eat hot or cold.

QUINCE PUDDING.

Take six large ripe quinces; pare and grate them; mix the pulp with half a pint of cream, and half a pound of white sugar; beat the yolks of seven eggs, (omitting all the whites except two,) and stir them into the mixture with one wine-glass of wine; stir the whole well together and bake in a buttered tin three quarters of an hour; grate sugar over it when cold.

BOILED APPLE PUDDING.

Pare and core as many apples as will weigh two pounds when done; put in a quarter of a pound of sugar, a little nutmeg, and one lemon, grate the peel; make a paste of suet and flour, in proportion of one pound of chopped suet to two of flour; roll it out and lay the apples in the center, and close the paste nicely over them; tie in a cloth and boil from two to three hours. Eat with cream and sugar, or butter and sugar.

A SUET PUDDING.

Take one tea-cupful of suet, chopped fine, two cupfuls of bread-crumbs; boil a quart of milk and pour on the bread; when cool, stir six eggs well beaten with the suet, into the milk, also three table-spoonfuls of flour, nuts, and cinnamon; pour it into a bag and tie firmly; boil two hours. Eat with sauce.

PUDDING IN HASTE.

Take two cups of bread-crumbs, half a tea-cupful of suet, a tea-cupful of currants, four eggs, and some grated lemon-peel, and a little ginger-root ground; make in little balls the size of an egg, and throw into boiling water; boil them about twenty minutes, or they will rise at the top when done. Eat with sauce.

A PLAIN PLUM PUDDING.

Take a pint of flour, a pint of suet, one tea-cupful of raisins, the same of currants, a glass of wine, one egg, and milk enough to wet it; add spice to your taste; boil three hours.

CREAM ALMOND PUDDING.

Beat five eggs, and take eight table-spoonfuls of flour dissolved in a little milk, one quart of cream, one quarter of a pound of almonds; add a little nutmeg and cinnamon, one table-spoonful of rose-water, and beat well together; boil an hour and a half; serve with melted butter and sugar.

SALEM PUDDING.

One cup of molasses, one of suet, one of sour milk, one of raisins, three and a half cups of flour, one tea-spoonful of cloves or any other spices you like, a tea-spoonful of soda, and a little salt; steam three hours.

SAGO PUDDING.

Soak six table-spoonfuls of sago in cold water; then boil in a quart of milk; stir in one cup of white sugar, half a tea-cup of butter, and let it cool; beat six eggs, and stir in; season with lemon or nutmeg, and add currants or raisins; lay in a buttered dish and bake three quarters of an hour. It may be served cold.

BAKED APPLE DUMPLINGS.

Take one pint of apples stewed, four eggs, four ounces of butter, nutmeg or lemon, one tea-cupful of milk, and bread-crumbs enough to make a batter; lay in a crust and bake.

GERMAN PUDDING.

Three table-spoonfuls of butter, one cup of milk, one of sugar, two eggs, two tea-spoonfuls of cream of tartar, one of soda, flour enough to make a stiff batter; bake three quarters of an hour; eat with sauce.

BOILED APPLE DUMPLINGS.

Make a paste of flour and water; roll out; put the apples in the center; close up and tie in a cloth, and boil two hours.

ANOTHER WAY.

Make in small balls and put just water enough to cover, and boil half an hour; serve with sauce; if you have a steamer, they are better steamed.

ANOTHER WAY.

Roll out the paste and spread on the apples, as you would for rolly-pooly pudding; then roll up and tie in a cloth, and boil two hours and a half.

A NICE PUDDING.

One quart of new milk scalded, one table-spoonful of corn-starch, the yolks of six eggs; season with vanilla or lemon; when cold, beat the whites with half a cup of sugar, and spread over the pudding, and brown in the oven.

BLUEBERRY PUDDING.

One cup of milk, one cup of molasses, one tea-spoonful of cream of tartar, one egg, half a tea-spoonful of soda, flour enough to make a stiff batter; stir in the berries; put in a basin, and steam it.

SWEET POTATO PUDDING.

Boil a pound of sweet potatoes very tender, and press them through a colander; add half a dozen eggs, three quarters of a pound of fine sugar, three quarters of a pound of butter, a glass of brandy, nutmeg, and lemon rind; put a paste in a dish, and bake; when done, sprinkle the top with white sugar.

A TEMPERANCE PLUM PUDDING.

Mix a pint of molasses with a pint of rich milk, eight eggs, beat light, one pound of flour, half a pound of brown sugar stirred into the milk and molasses; then add a pound of beef-suet chopped fine, a pound of seeded raisins, a pound of currants, half a pound of citron; stir until thoroughly mixed; take a cloth and dip in boiling water, and dredge it with flour; pour the mixture in, and tie, leaving room for the pudding to swell; plaster up the tying place with a little flour mixed with water; have ready a kettle of boiling water; put in and boil eight hours; keep another kettle over with water to turn in when it boils down, for should it be filled with cold water it would make the pudding heavy. Serve with cream sweetened, and nutmeg; what is left can be fried the next day.

ORANGE PUDDING.

Beat six eggs and stir into a tea-cupful of melted butter, and one tea-cupful of sugar; grate two large oranges, and squeeze out the juice, which add with a pint of cream; then lay in a rich puff-paste in a pudding-dish and bake like a custard. Lemons may be used the same.

A NICE APPLE DUMPLING.

One pint of buttermilk, half a tea-cupful of lard or butter, one egg, a little salt, and an even tea-spoonful of soda, with flour enough to make a stiff batter. Drop a table-spoonful of butter in buttered cups; put in an apple after paring, cutting, and taking out the core; then put on more batter, enough to cover the apples; put them in a steamer and cook one hour.

HASTY PUDDING.

Have your water boiling hot; put in salt sufficient, for if it lacks in this respect it is not good. Stir in Indian meal until half thickened; let it boil a few minutes; then stir in more meal, but be careful not to get it too thick, as it will boil thicker. It must boil slow for an hour.

TAPIOCA PUDDING.

To one tea-cupful of tapioca, add one pint of water; soak over night. In the morning, add three pints of milk, and add two well-beaten eggs, and bake.

FLOUR PUDDING.

Three pints scalded milk thicken to a thin batter with flour, three quarters of a pound of butter melted in the milk with a little salt, eight heaping spoonfuls of sugar, and eight eggs, beaten to a froth separately; flavor with lemon, and pour into plates lined with rich paste. Bake slowly.

WHEAT PUDDING.

Take one quart of milk, four eggs, one pint of flour, a little salt; bake quickly.

BIRD'S NEST PUDDING.

Make a batter of cream and flour, a little salt and saleratus. Pare and slice sour apples very thin; butter a tin and put some of the batter in the tin, then the apples, and cover with the remainder of the batter; bake three quarters of an hour.

INDIAN PUDDING.

Scald four cups of Indian meal, add one cup of molasses, two cups of milk, a tea-cup of milk, half a pound of raisins, four eggs—or two will do—and spice. Boil four hours.

GREEN CORN CAKE.

Take a dozen ears of sweet corn and grate it off the cob; add a little salt, one egg, a table-spoonful of sugar; stir it well; then butter a basin, pour in, and bake one hour in a hot oven. It may be eaten with butter and cream.

NIM'S PUFFS.

Boil one pint of milk with half a pound of butter, stir it into three quarters of a pound of flour, until it will not stick to the pot; let it cool; then add the yolks of nine eggs well beaten, lastly the whites; grease your tin cups and fill half full.

CRANBERRY PUDDING.

Boil a pint and a half of cranberries in a little water; add four ounces of sugar; let them boil until broken, and form a jam; make up a ball of it; cover it well with rice; then flour a piece of cloth, and tie each one up, and boil one hour. Eat with a sauce of butter and sugar stirred to a cream.

MAKING BREAD.

There is no cookery so conducive to the health and happiness of a family, as good bread, and nothing more detrimental than sour or heavy bread. There is a great difference in wheat flour; the Western flour, if pure, is preferable to any other. Winter wheat makes better flour than spring wheat, as the latter is more like wheat that has grown; but very good bread may be made from it by moulding it more, or making it harder. If wheat is grown, the flour should be scalded, and allowed to cool, before putting in the yeast, as heat kills the life of the yeast. Flour should always be sifted before using. If the directions here given are well followed, any person can make good bread. In the first place, they should supply themselves with good yeast. Many persons live near a bakery or a brewery, where they can obtain it fresh, when wanted. It is better to make home-made yeast, both for convenience and economy.

YEAST CAKES.

Take a pint of dry hops, (not over a year old, as they lose their strength;) pour on two quarts of water, and add two potatoes sliced; boil half an hour; then strain the liquor on Indian meal, sufficient to absorb all the water; stir it well, and when lukewarm, add a tea-cupful of good yeast, or one cake, previously soaked in warm water; let it rise; then add a small tea-cupful of brown sugar, a table-spoonful of ginger, and roll it out about half an inch thick; cut in small cakes, and put them on a board to dry. Be careful and turn them every day, until dry enough to put in a bag. Keep in a dry place, and they will keep good three months. When used, soak in lukewarm water a few minutes.

ANOTHER MODE.

Boil a double handful of hops in three quarts of water down to one quart; then strain into a quart of flour while boiling hot; when cool, add half a pint of yeast; let it rise, and thicken with Indian meal enough to roll out; then cut in squares, and lay them on a board; turn every day, until dry. Put in a bag, and hang up in a cool, dry place. When used, soak in warm water a few minutes.

SOFT YEAST. NO. 1.

Boil a pint of hops in three quarts of water, until reduced to three pints; strain and pour back in your kettle; make smooth one tea-cupful of flour with cold water; then stir in six middling sized potatoes, that have been boiled and mashed fine; let it stand until lukewarm; then strain it again, and add a cup of good yeast, and let it remain where it will keep warm; when light, add a table-spoonful of salt, the same of sugar, and pour into a jar; set it in a cool place. When used, take a tea-cupful for three loaves. This will not keep long without souring, when it should not be used. It will keep longer to leave out the potatoes, in which case more flour must be added.

POTATO YEAST.

Mash half a dozen peeled, boiled potatoes; make smooth a tea-cup of flour, and add with it a table-spoonful of salt. Strain through a colander, and add hot water until it is the consistency of batter; when lukewarm, add a pint of good yeast. Let it stand till it rises; then cork tight and keep in a cool place. This kind of yeast is nice; but will not keep sweet as long as hop yeast.

SOFT YEAST. NO. 2.

Pare and grate six large potatoes; boil a large handful of hops in two quarts of water; strain and pour on the potatoes while boiling hot; add one tea-cupful of brown sugar, and when sufficiently cool, put in a cupful of yeast; let it rise, and then put in a jug and cork tight; keep in a cool place. One tea-cupful, when new, is sufficient for four loaves of bread.

BAKER'S YEAST.

Two ounces of hops, with nine quarts of water, boiled an hour; when cool, add seven pounds mashed potatoes, one pound of sugar, two ounces of carbonate soda, half an ounce spirits of wine, one pound of flour, and half a pint brewer's yeast.

MILK YEAST BREAD.

Take one tea-cupful of milk, pour in two of boiling water; stir in flour enough to make a batter; if the flour is poor, put in a little saleratus. Set the vessel in a kettle of warm water, quite warm, and keep them an equal temperature, and in four or six hours they will rise. Make a hole in your flour, and pour in your wetting, which should be one third milk, the rest hot water; stir to a batter, then add the yeast. Stir up and let it remain in a warm place until it rises, (which will be about half an hour;) then knead it quickly, but not too stiff, and put it on tins. Let it rise again, and bake three quarters of an hour. It can be made without sponging, if preferred. For biscuit, use sweet cream for wetting, or butter and water; let them rise and cut out with a cutter; then rise and again bake. This yeast makes very white bread.

SALT RISING BREAD

is made in the same way, except the milk; a tea-spoonful of salt is added as a substitute. The bread must be moulded rather harder. Bran yeast may be made by making in the same manner, using wheat bran in the place of flour, and when light, strain off the water, and use as above.

WHEAT BREAD.

Make a hole in the flour, in your bread-tray or bowl, make a sponge in it of water or milk, or half and half, just as you like, and add your yeast, with a little salt. In the morning it will be risen; then mould, kneading it well—the more it is kneaded, the better will be your bread. Let it rise again, and mould only enough to put in shape; lay on tins, let it rise fifteen or twenty minutes, and bake in a moderate oven one hour. It is a good plan to put in a little soda or saleratus, when mixed in the morning, particularly if soft yeast is used, to prevent any sourness. If the flour has been scalded, or if potatoes have been added, it will require fifteen minutes longer to bake. When taken from the oven, set up on end, with a clean towel underneath; cover up with a cloth, and steam; if baked hard, it will soften the crust. Boiled, mashed potatoes, and a little sugar added, is a great improvement.

EXCELSIOR BREAD.

Have mashed potatoes for dinner the day you wish to bake, or rather the day before; save a pint, and pour boiling water on them, or use some of the potato-water, which is better, about a pint is sufficient; add a half tea-cupful of sugar, and one large yeast cake, previously soaked, or yeast; let it rise, and before going to bed, wet up your sponge with water, adding the yeast, (after straining it.) In the morning it will be light, when it must be moulded—the more, the nicer will be the bread; let it rise again; then make it into loaves, and when light, bake as above directed. Wet the top of the loaves with cold water before baking.

GRAHAM OR BROWN BREAD. NO. 1.

This is made of unbolted wheat, and should be the best kind of wheat to make good bread. It is considered more healthy than any other bread, particularly for those who are dyspeptic, or troubled with costiveness. Make as for wheat bread, only not mould so hard, and add a little molasses or sugar, and bake one to two hours.

GRAHAM BREAD. NO. 2.

Take three quarts of unbolted wheat flour, one quart of warm water, one tea-cupful of yeast, one of molasses, or without, one tea-spoonful of soda. Let it rise, and bake one hour.

RYE BREAD

must be made the same as wheat bread, only it must not be mixed so hard. It requires a longer time to rise, and must be baked longer. A few spoonfuls of shortening adds very much to rye bread.

GRAHAM BREAD. NO. 3.

One quart of sour milk, a cupful of molasses, a tea-spoonful of salt; thicken with unbolted wheat flour, and lastly add a tea-spoonful of soda; bake quick, one hour. Nice rye may be ground and unbolted like wheat, and made the same as Graham bread.

CREAM OF TARTAR BREAD.

Have a quart of lukewarm milk, make a stiff batter of wheat flour; stir in four tea-spoonfuls of cream of tartar, one of salt; add two tea-spoonfuls of soda, dissolved in half a cupful of warm water; add flour enough to mould out, quick as possible; make in two loaves, and bake. Tartaric acid is as good as cream of tartar, and only one spoonful is necessary.

POTATO BREAD.

Take mashed potatoes, and run through a colander; then add two thirds more flour than you have potatoes; wet with warm milk or water, and add a cupful of yeast or yeast cake, with a little salt. Make stiffer than common bread. Be careful it does not sour. Bake longer than the time required for wheat bread.

INDIAN BREAD. NO. 1.

Take sifted Indian meal and scald with either boiling milk or water; when lukewarm, add your yeast, and a little salt, with one third wheat flour or rye. If you like it rich, add a little molasses, and a few spoonfuls of shortening; knead quite soft, and let it rise. Bake in a slow oven two hours. If baked in a brick oven, let it remain over night.

PUMPKIN OR SQUASH BREAD

is made in the same way, only substituting stewed pumpkin or squash, instead of potato. Or it may be made with Indian meal and pumpkin, instead of flour.

APPLE BREAD.

Make a sponge as for wheat bread, and add stewed, strained apples in proportion to one part apples to two parts flour. Put on tins, and let it rise as wheat bread; then bake one hour.

CORN BREAD. NO. 2.

Take two quarts of Indian meal, a pint of bread sponge, water enough to wet it; mould in half a pint of wheat flour, a table-spoonful of salt. Let it rise, and knead a second time. Bake an hour and a half. Prize awarded for this bread.

CORN BREAD. NO. 3.

Take two quarts of corn meal, wet with three pints of warm water; add a table-spoonful of yeast, the same of salt, two of sugar; let it stand in a warm place five hours; then add one and a half tea-cupfuls of flour, and half a pint of warm water; let it rise again, an hour and a half; then pour it into a well-greased pan, and when light, bake in a hot oven. It is best cold. Prize bread.

CORN BREAD. NO. 4.

Take three tea-cupfuls of corn-meal, one of wheat flour, two table-spoonfuls of sugar, two tea-spoonfuls of cream of tartar; mix well while dry. Dissolve one tea-spoonful of soda in warm water; mix to a thin batter, and bake in a quick oven three fourths of an hour. Prize loaf.

BREAKFAST CORN BREAD.

Scald the meal at night, and when cool, add a spoonful of yeast, two of shortening, the same of molasses, a little salt. Stir well, and in the morning pour on a buttered tin, and bake.

BROWN BREAD.

Take one quart of buttermilk, one of sweet milk; thicken with half Indian meal, and half rye flour or wheat; add salt and molasses, if wished; a heaping tea-spoonful of soda.

BROWN BREAD. NO. 2.

Take one quart of corn-meal, pour on boiling water

or milk; when cool add a cup of yeast, two spoonfuls of molasses, a little salt, and one quart of rye flour, wet with milk, and stir with a spoon. Pour in tins or pans to rise. Bake slow.

CORN LOAF.

Take one pint sweet milk, half a pint buttermilk or sour milk, half a cup of butter, one of molasses, three eggs, one of wheat flour, a little salt, corn-meal to make a thick batter, one tea-spoonful of soda. Bake two hours slowly.

CURRANT BREAD.

Take some light sponge or bread-dough, enough for two loaves of bread; add half a pound of butter, one of brown sugar, one of Zante currants, and caraway seed, if you like, or a table-spoonful of allspice. Put in pans, and when light, bake one hour in a slow oven. Eat with butter.

RAISED BISCUIT. NO. 1.

Take some light bread-dough sufficient for two square tins of biscuit, mould in four ounces of butter, and let it rise again, and when light, pick up small bunches of dough and drop on buttered tins; let it rise a few minutes, then bake slowly.

RAISED BISCUIT. NO. 2.

Warm a pint of sweet milk, a piece of butter the size of an egg, a table-spoonful of sugar, two of good yeast, the white of an egg well beaten; make a hole in your flour and stir up till thick as batter. Set it where it will keep; when light, mould over and let it rise again; then pick up small pinches of the dough, and put on tins; when light, bake.

RAISED BISCUIT. NO. 3.

Make a sponge with one quart of water, one yeast-cake, a little salt; when light, add half a tea-cupful of melted butter, one egg, and knead well; but not too stiff with flour. Let it rise, and then make into biscuit, and bake on tins as directed.

RUSK. NO. 1.

Take one pint of milk lukewarm, half a cup of sugar, half a cup of butter, a pint of light sponge, two eggs or without, a little salt, and flour enough to mix. Let it rise, and follow the directions as given for biscuit.

RUSK. NO. 2.

Take one pint of warm milk, one tea-cupful of yeast or one yeast-cake; make a sponge, and when light, add half a cupful of butter, one of sugar, spice if you like, and flour to make stiff like biscuit. Let it rise, then mould into cakes the size of biscuit; put on buttered tins, and when light, bake half an hour. Mix milk with the yolk of an egg and rub on top as soon as baked.

ROLLS. NO. 1.

Take three pounds of flour, one quart of milk, six ounces of butter, warmed in the milk, a tea-cupful of yeast, or a large yeast-cake, and a little salt. Let it rise, then mould and rise again; then form into rolls and lay on tins; when light, bake them.

ROLLS. NO. 2.

Dissolve two ounces of butter in a pint of new milk, two table-spoonfuls of yeast, and the well-beaten whites of two eggs. Make a hole in the middle of the flour and mix into a sponge with a little salt; when light, work one way for fifteen minutes; then form into rolls and let them rise before baking.

BRENTFORD ROLLS.

Take two pounds of flour, four ounces of butter, two well-beaten eggs, salt, two table-spoonfuls of yeast, and two ounces of sugar; mix with sufficient milk or water to make a sponge; keep it warm until it rises; then mould and make into rolls; let it rise again, then bake.

ENGLISH ROLLS.

Take one quart of flour, four ounces of butter, two well-beaten eggs, two table-spoonfuls of sugar, two of yeast. Pour this into the center of the flour; add a pint of warm milk; beat it well with the hand until it comes off without sticking. Set it in a warm place to rise; then mould out, and put on tins; when light, bake.

FRENCH ROLLS.

Take a pint of warm water, one yeast-cake, a little salt, one well-beaten egg; make a dough of moderate stiffness. Beat it well, but do not knead it; let it rise, and bake on tins.

HARD BISCUIT.

Take two pounds of flour, rub a pound and a half of it with two ounces of butter, two well-beaten eggs, one spoonful of salt; sweet milk to wet the whole. Pound it out about half an inch thick; cut in small cakes and put on buttered tins. Bake in a moderate oven three quarters of an hour.

SALLY LUNN.

Take one pint of new milk, half a tea-cup of butter warmed together, three well-beaten eggs, half a cup of yeast and a little salt, flour sufficient to make a batter like pound cake; stir well; let it rise; then bake in a square tin, or make it stiff and bake like rolls. A few mashed potatoes may be added, if you like.

NEWPORT CAKE, OR SALLY LUNN.

One cup of sweet milk, one of sugar, two eggs, half a cup of butter, two tea-spoonfuls of cream of tartar, in one quart of flour, one tea-spoonful of soda in half a cup of milk. The butter put in last. Bake half an hour and send to the table hot. Eat with butter.

SARATOGA BREAKFAST CAKE.

One quart of sour milk, two eggs, one table-spoonful of butter, a little salt, one third wheat flour, two thirds corn-meal to a stiff batter, two table-spoons of molasses, one tea-spoon of soda. Bake in a quick oven.

INDIAN BREAKFAST CAKE,

Take two cups of corn-meal, half a cup of flour, three table-spoonfuls of molasses, one tea-spoonful of salt, five spoonfuls of melted lard; add cold water or sweet milk enough to make a batter, half a tea-spoonful of soda. Just before baking, stir in three tea-spoonfuls of vinegar.

HOE CAKE.

Scald one quart of meal to a batter with water; add two table-spoonfuls of butter, two tea-spoonfuls of salt. Bake on a board before the fire.

CORN CAKE COOKED BY STEAM.

Take a pint of sour cream, and stir in a handful of wheat flour and corn-meal; enough to make a stiff batter; add salt and one tea-spoonful of soda. Put in a basin and steam one hour or until done. Eat cream and sugar on it.

A COMMON JOHNNY CAKE.

Take one quart of rich buttermilk, one tea-cupful of flour, and sufficient Indian meal to make a stiff batter, two table-spoonfuls of molasses, a little salt, and one tea-spoonful of soda. Bake three quarters of an hour.

GREEN-CORN CAKE.

Take a dozen ears of green corn, grate it off the cob; add salt, one egg, a table-spoonful of sugar; stir well; then pour into a buttered basin; one hour in a hot oven. Eat with butter and cream. Sweet corn is the best.

CRACKERS FROM BREAD-DOUGH.

Strain a cupful of lukewarm water with a tea-spoonful of soda dissolved in it, on a quart of raised dough; add a little salt and two thirds of a tea-cupful of butter; work well together; pull in small pieces; sprinkle flour over, and mould up until it becomes stiff; then mould and roll very thin, and cut into crackers; bake on buttered tins.

BUTTER CRACKERS.

Rub four ounces butter with one pound of flour; dissolve a tea-spoonful of soda in a little milk; strain into the flour; add a little salt, and milk sufficient to roll out. Beat it well with a rolling-pin and roll out; repeat several times. Roll out thin and cut in small crackers. Bake until hard and crispy, in a moderate oven.

SODA BISCUIT.

To one quart of flour, add two tea-spoonfuls of cream of tartar, and a little salt; mix well in the flour; dissolve a tea-spoonful of soda in sufficient milk or cream to wet the flour; if milk is used instead of cream, add a piece of butter the size of an hen's egg; mix soft and bake ten minutes.

BUTTERMILK BISCUIT.

Take one quart of rich buttermilk or sour milk, a little salt, two thirds of a cupful of shortening; put in the middle of your flour and stir to a batter; then add a tea-spoonful of soda dissolved, and mix soft; roll out and cut in round cakes. Bake fifteen minutes.

CREAM BISCUIT.

Take one quart of sour cream, a little salt; stir up with flour; then add a tea-spoonful of soda, and add more flour, enough to roll out; cut in round cakes and bake.

RICE BISCUIT.

Take one and a half pints of scalding milk, half a pint of ground rice; cook a few minutes; when lukewarm, add half a yeast-cake or other yeast, half a tea-spoonful of soda, and two quarts of flour; make a sponge by adding a little lukewarm milk or water. Let it rise and mould; when raised, add a tea-cupful of butter; put in tins, and when light, bake.

STRAWBERRY SHORT CAKE.

Make a biscuit of sour cream or sour milk and butter; when baked, split open and spread on butter, strawberries, and sugar; then put together again. It should be made thin.

RYE CAKE.

Take one and a half tea-cupfuls of buttermilk, two table-spoonfuls of molasses, two table-spoonfuls of Indian meal, a little salt, one tea-spoonful of saleratus. Thicken with rye flour and bake an hour. Cream and eggs is an improvement.

A RICH JOHNNY CAKE. NO. 1.

Take one quart of buttermilk, one tea-cupful of cream, three eggs, one cup of flour, half a cup of molasses, a little salt, Indian meal to make a batter, lastly, a tea-spoonful of soda. Bake on a tin three quarters of an hour.

A RICH JOHNNY CAKE. NO. 2.

Take one quart of buttermilk, half a cup of cream, half a cup of suet, cut fine, half a cup of molasses, one egg, a little salt, one tea-spoonful of soda, to be put in last, one cup of flour, and sufficient Indian meal to thicken it. Bake as above. The suet is a great improvement.

RYE CAKE.

Take one quart of sour milk, half a tea-cup of shortening, a little salt, a tea-spoon of soda, mix soft, roll out, and cut in round cakes. Bake in a hot oven. They may be made in a stiff batter, and dropped on tins, then baked.

MUFFINS. NO. 1.

One pint of milk, flour to make a stiff batter, a table-spoonful of yeast, and a little salt; make over night, and in the morning bake in plate of rings or muffin-cups in a brisk oven.

MUFFINS. NO 2.

One quart of rich milk or cream, half a tea-cupful of yeast, five eggs; a lump of butter, the size of a hen's egg, if you do not use cream; add flour enough to make a stiff batter; add a little salt. Let it rise, and bake in rings, or on a griddle.

MUFFINS. NO. 3.

One quart of flour, two table-spoonfuls of butter, two eggs, half a cup of yeast, a little salt, lukewarm milk, sufficient to wet the whole. Let it rise, and bake in rings or cups.

MUFFINS. NO. 4.

One cup of flour, one of milk, one egg, a little salt, a

table-spoonful of butter, or if you have cream, use it instead of milk, and no butter will be required. Bake in a quick oven or in rings.

MUFFINS. NO. 5.

One quart of milk, one cup of butter warmed, four eggs, two table-spoonfuls of yeast, a little salt, flour sufficient for a batter. Mix in the morning, and bake for tea.

MUSH MUFFINS.

Take hasty pudding when cold; add one quart of milk, three eggs, salt, two table-spoonfuls of butter, flour to thicken. Bake in rings or fry on a griddle.

CRUMPETS. NO. 1.

Take a quart bowl of raised dough, a tea-cupful of butter, three eggs, a little salt, milk to make a batter. Bake in a hot buttered pan half an hour.

CRUMPETS. NO. 2.

Warm one quart of sweet milk; add half a tea-cupful of yeast, salt, stir in flour to make a batter; let it rise; then add half a tea-cupful of butter. Bake as muffins.

WAFFLES. NO. 1.

Beat two eggs; take one pint of milk, one table-spoonful of butter, or half a tea-cup of cream, a little salt, flour sufficient to make a stiff batter. Bake in waffle-irons. Eat melted butter and sugar on them. Maple syrup is very nice for these.

WAFFLES. NO. 2.

Warm one quart of sweet milk, six ounces of butter; add half a tea-cupful of yeast, a little salt, four well-beaten eggs; let it rise; when light, heat the waffle-irons, butter them, and put in some batter. When baked, put on a plate, and bake until all are baked; butter as you take out; strew with sugar, and send to the table hot.

FRITTERS. NO. 1.

Take one cupful of sour cream, a little salt, one beaten egg; stir in flour sufficient to thicken; add a little soda, dissolved, and drop a spoonful at a time into hot lard, until a nice brown. Eat with any kind of sauce you like.

FRITTERS. NO. 2.

Stir one pint of flour smooth with water; pour it into one pint of boiling water; when cool, add five eggs, beat light; a table-spoonful of butter. Fry in hot lard.

FRITTERS. NO. 3.

Make a paste as for pies, butter is preferable to lard for this purpose; roll thin, and cut out; then fill with marmalade or preserves of any kind; roll up well, and fry in hot lard.

APPLE FRITTERS.

Take a pint of milk, a table-spoonful of cream, two eggs, a little salt, pare and slice your apples, and stir into your milk, with sufficient flour to make a batter; add a little soda. Fry in lard, and serve with pudding sauce.

ANOTHER.

Make a batter of eggs and flour; pare and slice sour apples; stir in, and fry in hot lard five minutes.

FRITTERS. NO. 4.

Take one quart of milk, seven well-beaten eggs; stir in gradually flour enough to make a thick batter; beat well, and fry in boiling lard a spoonful at a time. Apples may be chopped fine, and stirred into the batter, if wished.

A NICE WAY TO PREPARE APPLES FOR FRITTERS.

Pare and slice them; put them in layers in a dish, with sugar and nutmeg strewed over; then pour on brandy enough to cover them; let them remain four or five hours.

MOCK OYSTER FRITTERS.

Grate six ears of corn; add one egg, one table-spoonful of cream or butter, one of flour, pepper and salt. Fry as directed.

OYSTER FRITTERS.

Make a batter of the oyster liquor strained, two eggs,

and flour; stir in the oysters, and fry in hot lard or butter; put one oyster in a fritter. Clam fritters made in the same way.

FRITTERS. NO. 5.

Scald a pint of milk; when cool, add three beaten eggs, a little salt; dip out with a spoon; roll in flour, and fry in lard. Eat with sauce. Stir in sufficient flour to make a batter while the milk is hot.

MOCK OYSTER FRITTERS. NO. 2.

Grate a dozen ears of sweet corn, the yolks of three eggs, the whites of four, beaten separately, one cup of milk, salt, a table-spoonful of flour; drop in hot lard as above.

RICE PUFFS.

One pint of rice-flour, and sufficient boiling water or milk to make a thick batter; beat four eggs, and when cool, mix and salt; drop this mixture into hot lard.

GRIDDLE CAKES.

BUCKWHEAT CAKES.

Take two quarts of warm water; add a yeast cake, some salt; stir in flour to make a batter. A handful of Indian meal is nice to make them brown, or a cupful of milk; bake on a griddle. Keep some in the jar to raise with after baking. If not quite light, add a cupful of buttermilk, and a tea-spoonful of soda, just before baking. Another way is to stir them up with buttermilk and saleratus; then fry as above. Half buttermilk and half water is better, but they require soda every time baking.

FLANNEL CAKES.

Put two table-spoonfuls of butter into a quart of milk; warm it until the butter is melted; add four eggs, and stir in with half a pound of flour, or sufficient to make a batter, two spoonfuls of yeast, salt. Let it rise, and bake on a griddle.

WHEAT CAKES. NO. 1.

One quart of rich milk, four eggs, a little salt, flour to make a stiff batter; grease the griddle, and put on a spoonful at a time; when brown, turn over and brown on the other side.

WHEAT CAKES. NO. 2.

Take one quart of buttermilk, half a pint of cream, a little salt and flour to make a batter, a tea-spoonful of soda. Bake as above. If you have not the cream, put in a little butter.

EXCELSIOR WHEAT CAKES.

Take one tea-cupful of sour cream, one pint of sweet milk, a little salt, and flour to make a smooth batter. Bake on a griddle.

RICE CAKES.

Boil a large cup of rice until soft; beat two eggs, two spoonfuls of butter, salt and flour to make a batter. Bake on a griddle.

BREAD CAKES.

Stale bread, soaked in cold water until soft, with two eggs, and a cupful of rich milk, a little salt; thicken with wheat flour, and fry on a griddle. Add a little soda just before baking.

RYE CAKES OR GRAHAM.

Make as buckwheat cakes, adding a little corn-meal, sour milk and soda.

POTATO CAKES.

Take mashed potatoes; mix with milk, eggs, flour, salt, and soda. They are excellent. Fry on a griddle.

CORN CAKES.

Grate ten ears of sweet corn; wash the cobs in a tea-cupful of milk; beat three eggs, and stir in with two spoonfuls of flour; add salt, and bake on a griddle.

INDIAN CAKES.

Take one pint of sour milk, one of sweet; equal parts of flour and meal, salt, and soda; two eggs may be added, if wished. Fry slowly on a griddle.

INDIAN GRIDDLE CAKES.

Scald at night half the quantity of meal you are going to use; add the rest with cold water, making it the consistency of batter; add a little salt, and set it to rise, it will require no yeast. In the morning the cakes will be light and crispy. Fry on a griddle.

CREAM CAKES.

Take one pint of cream, the yolks of three eggs beaten, flour to thicken, like pancakes; bake in the oven on a greased tin or on a griddle.

WHEAT CAKES. NO. 3.

Take a tea-cupful of Indian mush, one pint and a half of rich milk; add a little salt, and stir in wheat flour till thick enough to bake on a griddle.

FRUIT CAKES.

Make wheat cakes, and when baked, spread jelly, jam or any kind of preserves or fruit on, and roll up. Strew sugar over them, and serve hot.

ENGLISH SEED-CAKE.

Take one pint of warm milk, one tea-cupful of butter melted in the milk, one cup of yeast, two cups sugar, three eggs; make into a light sponge; when light, add one nutmeg, caraway seed, and Zante currants; mix into a stiff dough to handle on the board, then put back and let it rise again, and when very light mould into rusks, or a loaf, with sufficient flour to handle it on the board. Let it rise in the baking-pans, and bake in a moderate oven. It can be put to rise over night, and in the morning add the spices.

A CHEESE-CAKE.

Stir four ounces of butter, the same of sugar, to a cream, beat four eggs light, scald half a pint of milk; when it comes to a boil, add half the beaten eggs, and stir frequently until it becomes curd; then throw in two ounces of grated bread, and stir all together; next stir in gradually the butter and sugar, and the remaining egg; add, by degrees, a table-spoonful of mixed brandy and wine, a tea-spoonful of rose-water, cinnamon and nutmeg to the taste; sprinkle two ounces of currants with flour, and put in; mix all together, and pour the mixture into a square tin, lined with a puff-paste, which must be made first; then sprinkle two ounces more of currants with flour, and lay on top. Have a flap of paste left at each side, in the shape of a half-moon; cut slips in these flaps and turn over the top. Raisins may be used instead of currants.

MILK TOAST.

Scald a quart of rich milk, (not boil,) put in a little butter, sugar to the taste, add a little salt. Have ready in a dish eight slices of bread toasted, turn the milk on and cover it. Send to the table.

CUSTARDS, ETC.

Custards are always eaten cold, and are served up in small cups, or poured over fruit tarts or sponge cake. The flavoring may be added to suit the taste. Vanilla, lemon, orange, and nutmegs, are all nice for custards. A portion of cream makes custards nicer than all milk, and will not require as many eggs. When made as cream, and eaten raw, the whites should never be put in, but can be used for silver cake. One mode of making is to measure the number of cups which you wish to fill, and use nearly the quantity of milk; then simmer it upon the fire until beginning to boil, then add half an ounce of sugar to each cup, with lemon-peel or bay leaves; then take the yolk of an egg to each cup, beat them well, and pour in the milk; fill the cups, place in boiling water until the custard becomes firm. Custards are nicer if the eggs are strained after beating.

A PLAIN CUSTARD.

Beat four eggs until light, two table-spoonfuls of sugar, a little salt, add one quart of milk, nutmeg, and lemon; more eggs can be added, if wished. Bake in an earthen dish, and set it in a tin of water in the oven; bake slowly; try with a spoon. It must not remain in the oven longer than it sets, for if it wheys, it is not good.

A BOILED CUSTARD.

Six eggs to one quart of milk, nearly a tea-cupful of white sugar, a little salt; beat the eggs well, and stir all together; then put in a small tin pail, (which is most convenient to use for the purpose,) and set in a kettle of boiling water; let it remain until it begins to thicken, stirring it constantly, that it may not adhere to the pail; then season with vanilla or lemon, just as you like, and turn in cups.

SNOW CUSTARD.

Take eight eggs, and one quart of milk, a gill of cream, a little salt; flavor with lemon and nutmeg, and boil as above; then pour into a dish, with a whip over the whole. Serve as you would a pudding.

A RICH CUSTARD.

Boil a pint of milk with a stick of cinnamon, and lemon-peel; turn in a pint of cream, and eight eggs, well beaten; stir well together, and boil in hot water, always stiring the same way. Add the sugar before boiling.

A VERY RICH CUSTARD.

Boil one quart of rich milk, or what is better, half cream, put in a stick of cinnamon broken in small pieces; after boiling, strain, and set away to cool; then stir in gradually one tea-cup and a half of sugar, any spice you like, and the yolks of ten well-beaten eggs; then pour into cups, and place in a tin of water, put in a slow oven, and bake; when baked, grate some nutmeg on top, and add the whites of the eggs beaten to a froth, with a table-spoonful of powdered sugar, and a little essence of lemon; pile it up on top of each custard, and if you like, add a spot of red nonpareils in the middle of the pile.

A FINER BAKED CUSTARD.

Take a pint and a half of milk, and boil gently with six ounces of loaf-sugar, a little salt, the rind of a lemon; add the yolks of ten well-beaten eggs, the whites of four; strain the whole, and add a pint of cream; let it cool, and flavor with a few spoonfuls of brandy, or a little ratafia; then pour into cups, and set the cups in a tin of water in the oven, and bake very slowly.

RICE CUSTARD.

Take a pint of new milk, sweeten to the taste, then scald, and stir in ground rice till quite thick. Take off the fire, add the whites of three eggs, well beaten; put over the fire two or three minutes, stirring it, then put into cups that have lain in cold water. When cold, turn them out, and put them in the dish in which they are to be served; pour around them a custard made of the yolks of the eggs, and a little more than a pint of milk. Put on the top some currant jelly or raspberry jam.

LEMON CUSTARD.

Take three wine-glasses of lemon-juice, strain through a sieve; beat nine eggs, strain them also, and add to the lemon-juice, with one quarter of a pound of white sugar, a wine-glass of white wine, half a glass of water, with grated lemon-peel; mix all together, and boil until it begins to thicken, and then turn out and let it cool.

COLD CUSTARD, OR JUNKET.

Soak a piece of rennet in brandy, and keep it corked tight, then take one quart of milk, about as warm as when it comes from the cow, add a little salt and sugar, and stir in sufficient of the rennet to thicken the milk; then turn into cups, and grate a little nutmeg on the top. You can leave out the sugar, and use sweetened cream instead. This is very nice to serve with peaches and strawberries.

BLANC MANGE.

Take one ounce of isinglass, two quarts of milk, seasoned to your taste; the isinglass having been dissolved in boiling water over night; put on the fire and boil, stirring it all the time, then strain through a cloth until nearly cold. Flavor with lemon or any thing you like. Wet the moulds in cold water, then pour in. If it does not slip out easily, wrap a cloth wet in hot water round the moulds, then loosen with a knife, and turn into glass dishes. It may be set to cool in cups or wine-glasses.

ANOTHER BLANC MANGE.

Take an ounce of isinglass, broken in small pieces, wash well, then turn on a pint of boiling water; let it stand until morning, add one pint of cream, and one of milk, and boil, then strain through a cloth; put in two ounces of blanched almonds, pounded; sweeten to the taste, and turn into moulds. Stick thin slips of almonds all over the blanc mange, and dress around with syllabub, or whip cream.

ARROW-ROOT BLANC MANGE.

Take a tea-cupful of arrow-root, dissolved in cold water; take a pint of milk, add the grated peel of a lemon, a grated nutmeg, and boil until highly flavored; strain into a pint of cream, add one cup of sugar, and boil ten minutes; then strain hot into the arrow-root, stirring it until thick; then put into moulds.

JAUNE MANGE.

Dissolve one ounce and a half of isinglass in a pint and a half of boiling water, add one pint of white wine, the yolks of eight eggs, and the juice of three lemons; boil the peels in the liquor; beat the juice with the eggs; sweeten to your taste; boil all together; strain, and put into moulds.

JACQUE MANGE.

Take two ounces of isinglass, the rind of two lemons grated; pour on a pint of boiling water, and when it has boiled a little, pour in a pint of white wine, then the yolks of eight eggs, thoroughly beaten, the juice of two lemons, and sugar to the taste. The eggs, lemon-juice, and sugar, should be previously mixed with a little of the wine. Add the whole together and stir one way, until it boils. Strain through muslin, and pour into moulds that have been rinsed in cold water.

CHARLOTTE RUSSE.

Mix with the yolks of four eggs, a quarter of a pound of white sugar, and a pint of new milk; then put it in a kettle of hot water until it begins to thicken; then add half a pint of calves' feet jelly. Strain it; then put in a pan a pint of cream, flavored or not, just as you like; set the pan on ice, and stir the cream until it looks like float; pour the cream in a dish, and put the custard in the pan on the ice; stir it until it becomes thick like jelly; then add the cream carefully. It should look like light sponge cake before it is baked. Take sponge cake, called "ladies' fingers," and put around the sides and bottom of a round tin pan; pour the charlotte over it, and set on the ice until wanted. Then take a round dish or plate and turn out; the bottom will be at the top, and no cake at the bottom.

RASPBERRY SPONGE.

Dissolve three quarters of an ounce of isinglass in a little boiling water; add a pint of new milk, half a pint of cream, half a pint of raspberry jelly, and the juice of a lemon; whisk the whole until it looks like sponge; then put in a mould, and turn out next day.

LEMON SPONGE.

Take an ounce of isinglass, the rind of one lemon, and dissolve in boiling water; strain, and let it stand to cool, but not to set. Grate the rind of a lemon, and add the juice of the lemon, then half a pound of sugar; strain all into a bowl, and whisk them all together till they begin to stiffen. Then pour into a flat dish, and cut into squares.

APPLE, OR GOOSEBERRY SOUFFLE.

Scald the fruit and press it through a sieve; then put it in a tart dish. When cold, pour a rich custard over it; about two inches deep. Whip the whites of eggs, and lay it in rough pieces on the custard; sift white sugar over it; then put in the oven for a short time. It makes a very handsome dish.

RASPBERRY CHARLOTTE.

Take a dozen oblong sponge cakes, spread over each a layer of raspberry jam, and place them round in a glass dish. Take a pint of cream, and eight spoonfuls of raspberry jelly, and beat together and fill up the bowl. It may be made of any kind of fruit.

PLUM AND CHERRY CHARLOTTE.

Take a quart of ripe plums, cherries, peaches, or any fruit you like; take the stones out, and stew them with a pound of sugar. Cut slices of bread and butter; then lay them round the sides and bottom of a deep dish. Pour on the fruit boiling hot; cover it up and set away to cool. Serve with sweet cream.

CHARLOTTE DE RUSSE.

Take one pint of milk; add six eggs, and sugar to sweeten it. Strain into it an ounce of isinglass dissolved in boiling water. Bake it, and let it cool; then make a whip, and mix with the custard, and cool in forms. Lay in the bottom of your dish slices of sponge cake alternately, with jelly around the dish.

ICE CREAM. NO. 1.

Take one quart of sweet milk, cream is best, two eggs, one tea-cupful of white sugar, one tea-spoonful of flour, wet with a little milk; flavor with lemon, vanilla, strawberry, or orange. Put your milk in the freezer, and set in a kettle of boiling water, stirring it to prevent its burning; then when it boils, stir in the egg, sugar, and flour, also the flavoring. Pound up the ice in small pieces, and put a layer of ice and of salt in your tub alternately around it. Stir the cream and loosen from the sides of the tub with a wooden spatula.

ANOTHER MODE.

Take one quart of cream, one of milk, one pound of sugar; put into your freezer, and put in boiling water as above; add lemon-peel while boiling. Stir in four eggs. Freeze as above.

CHERRY ICE CREAM.

Take cherries, mash and squeeze out the juice; to every pint add one lemon, the juice only, and a pint of cream; freeze as above. Strawberries may be used in the same way.

WHIP CREAM.

Take a pint and a half of cream, the whites of three eggs, the juice of one lemon, sugar to your taste, flavored with the grated rind of lemon or rose-water; whip with a whisk or in a whip-churn, and as the foam rises, lay it into jelly-glasses, or the glass may be half filled with jelly, and the whip poured over it.

ANOTHER ICE CREAM.

Take one quart of sweet cream, sweeten and flavor, whip to a light froth, skim off and put into your freezer until all is whipped to a froth. It will freeze in less time, and be smoother than any other recipe.

RHENISH CREAM.

An ounce and a half of isinglass, dissolved in boiling water. Strain through a sieve; add eight eggs, half a pint of Rhenish wine or white wine, the juice and rind of two lemons grated, loaf-sugar to suit the taste. Let them boil slowly until thick; then strain through muslin into china cups.

LEMON CREAM.

Take two eggs, a pint of thick cream, a cup of sugar, and the rind of a lemon, cut thin, boil it; then stir until almost cold; put the juice of the lemon in a dish and pour the cream over it, stirring until cold. Serve in custard-cups either alone or with sweetmeats. Leave out the whites of the egg.

ICE CREAM. NO. 2.

Take four quarts of milk, one quart of cream, eight eggs well beaten, one pound and a half of sugar, four large table-spoonfuls of wheat flour, or six even spoonfuls of arrow-root. Stir the eggs and sugar together; the flour stir smooth with a little milk. Put the milk in your freezer, set it in a kettle of water and let it boil. Then stir in the eggs, sugar, and flour; beat well and let it cool. Flavor with any thing you like. Then freeze it. The patent freezer requires less ice than the other. Ice cream may be made without eggs if all cream is used, and well whisked before freezing. In that case it will not require boiling.

SWISS CREAM.

Take a pint of cream, and the peel of one lemon, set over the fire until it boils; the juice of a lemon, and a little flour beaten with it, mix with the cream, and boil a few minutes longer. Strain through a sieve. Lay your cake in the dish and pour on the cream. It should be made the day before used.

ANOTHER LEMON CREAM.

Take a large spoonful of brandy, six ounces of loaf sugar, the peel and juice of two lemons, grate the peel, mix well, and add a pint of cream and whisk it up.

ORANGE CREAM.

Take one cupful of powdered sugar, half a cup of water, two oranges, the rind grated; add four well-beaten eggs, and beat together some time. Strain through a flannel into a saucepan; set it over a gentle fire and stir it one way until scalding hot, but not boiling, or it will curdle. Serve as custard in jelly-glasses.

BLANCHED CREAM.

Take a quart of rich cream, sweeten with loaf-sugar, boil it and beat the whites of twenty eggs with a little cold cream; strain it, and when the cream is upon the boil, stir in the eggs; then strain through a hair-sieve; beat with a spoon until it is cold, then put in a dish.

SNOW RICE CREAM.

Take four ounces of rice, two ounces of loaf-sugar, two ounces of butter, six ounces of the essence of almonds, a quart of new milk. Boil fifteen or twenty minutes. Pour into a mould greased with Florence oil; turn out when cold, and serve with preserves around it.

BURNT CREAM.

Make a rich custard without sugar, put in grated lemon-peel; when cold, sift sugar over it, and burn the top with a salamander.

POMPADOUR CREAM.

Beat the whites of six eggs to a froth with one spoonful of brandy; sweeten to your taste; stir over the fire two or three minutes; pour into a dish; then melt some butter or boil cream, and cover it.

SNOW-BALLS.

Beat the whites of six eggs to a froth; sweeten to your taste; flavor with rose-water. Drop a spoonful at a time in boiling water for a minute or two. Make a cream of milk, eggs, and sugar, to float them in.

FLOATING ISLAND.

Take the white of an egg, beat to a froth; add a glass of currant-jelly; beat together until a spoon will stand up in it. Drop a spoonful at a time on a glass bowl of sweet cream.

FLOATING ISLAND. NO. 2. ANOTHER WAY.

Sweeten a pint of thick cream with loaf-sugar; add a gill of wine, the grated rind of a lemon; whisk to a froth; then pour a pint of cream in a dish, take a French roll, slice it, and lay over the cream as lightly as possible; then a layer of calves' feet jelly or currant, then whip your cream, and lay on the froth as high as you can, and what remains, pour into the bottom of the dish. Garnish the rim with sweetmeats.

ANOTHER WAY.

Beat the whites of three eggs, three table-spoonfuls of raspberry jam, or red currant-jelly. When the whole will stand in rocky forms, pour it upon apple-jelly or cream beaten up with wine, sugar, and grated lemon-peel.

TO WHIP CREAM.

Sweeten a bowl of cream, and flavor with any juicy fruit; such as orange, lemon, etc., by rubbing sugar on the peel; set another bowl near with a sieve over it; then whip the cream, and as it rises in a froth, skim it off and put in the sieve to drain; whip the cream that drains off, and when done, ornament with lemon raspings. This cream may be used before it is set, upon custard, trifle, or syllabub.

A TRIFLE.

Whip cream, as above, adding a little brandy or wine; lay in a glass dish sponge cake, ratafia cakes, and macaroons, and pour upon them as much brandy and sweet wine as they will soak; then a rich custard about two inches deep, with a little lemon-peel and grated nutmeg; then a layer of currant-jelly or raspberry jam, and upon the whole a high whip. A trifle should be made the day before used.

CAKE TRIFLE.

Cut out a rice or diet-bread cake about two inches from the edge; fill with custard, a few blanched and split almonds, and pieces of raspberry jam, and put on the whole a high whip.

PRESERVES AND SWEETMEATS.

Almost all kinds of fruit require a pound of sugar to a pound of fruit, except citron, which can be preserved with less. White sugar is more delicate for sweetmeats, and is more profitable to use than brown. It does not waste so much in clarifying, although nice brown sugar will answer very well for some kinds. The West-India sugar-house syrup is nice for preserving as it will not ferment. A preserving-kettle lined with porcelain is the best thing to preserve in, but any thing else will answer except iron; if brass is used, it should be kept perfectly clean, and the preserves poured out as soon as done. I think fruit retains its color and flavor better by boiling quick than by a slow process. Fruits should be put in the syrup when it is cold. If the syrup is rich, the fruit will be hard; take it up before they break. A wooden paddle is better for stirring than a silver spoon, which should only be used for skimming. The scum may be strained through a bit of muslin or jelly-bag, that there may be no waste, and then turned back again, the scum remaining in the bag. Fruit is nicer by being boiled a short time, but will not keep as long as if boiled longer. It is better to keep sweetmeats in small jars, just what you would use at one time; glass keeps them better than any thing else. Brown stone or earthenware will answer, but should never be used for any thing else. After they are put in, they should not be moved until cold; then wet a paper in brandy and cover the top of the sweetmeats with it, or pour on a little brandy. It will not injure the taste at all. They should be kept in a dry, cool place. Brown blotting-paper wet with the white of an egg and placed over the jars; when dry, put on another paper cover. A jelly-bag is made of a piece of flannel, half a square, and sewed on one side, the two corners together, bound with a piece of tape, and four loops sewed on to hang it by. Preserving-kettles should be broad, and the flavor of the fruit is preserved by covering the kettle.

TO CLARIFY SUGAR.

Allow the beaten white of an egg to every four pounds of sugar, and a pint of water. Put your sugar in your preserving-kettle, pour in the water and egg, set it where it will gradually warm, stirring occasionally until it boils; then skim it, and pour in a gill of cold water, and when it boils skim again. Take from the fire, and let it stand a few minutes; then put over again and boil, and continue doing so until the syrup is clear, and as often as any scum arises take off. If wanted to candy, boil until sufficiently thick, which can be ascertained by dropping some in cold water; if it is brittle and snaps, it is done. Then put in the fruit and preserve. White sugar does not require clarifying; it is therefore the least trouble as well as cheapest to use.

APPLES.

Pare them, and if very large, halve or quarter; if not, take out the core, leaving the apple whole. For six pounds of apples allow four of sugar. Make your syrup and let it cool, then add the apples and heat slowly at first; boil until they are clear and tender. When cool, add the extract of lemon, or slice up a fresh lemon, and put in a layer of lemon and a layer of apples.

BAKED APPLES.

They may be pared and the core taken out and the apples filled with sugar, and put in a tin pan with a little water in, and if you like, a bit of cinnamon, may be added. Bake until soft. They are nice baked with the skins on, and sliced up when done, and eaten with sugar and cream.

CRAB-APPLES.

Make a syrup of equal weight of apples and sugar. Simmer the apples in water until the skins come off easily; then take up and take out the core with a cutter or sharp knife. Boil in the syrup until tender; then take them up, and spread on dishes to cool; then place them in jars and pour the syrup over them.

PINE-APPLES.

Take those that are fully ripe and fresh; take off the rind, and cut in slices half an inch thick. Allow equal weights of white sugar, and make a layer of fruit, then a layer of sugar, until all are in, and let them remain until next day; then pour off the syrup and add a pint of water if four pounds are preserved; boil a few minutes, then take from the fire. When cool, put in the pine-apples, and boil until tender. Put in a deep dish and let them remain several days; then scald up the syrup and pour on the fruit while hot. When cold, put in glass jars and seal up tight. They retain their flavor better if not boiled, but are liable to ferment unless kept in a box of dry sand. They are nice canned.

PINE-APPLE MARMALADE.

Take off the rind and grate them, leaving out the core in the center; add an equal weight of sugar. When the juice begins to run so as to form a syrup, then set it on the fire and heat slowly, stirring often to prevent its burning. Let it simmer half an hour, then cool a little, and if it cuts smooth it is done.

CRAB-APPLE MARMALADE.

Boil them in just water enough to prevent their burning; keep them covered. When soft, strain and add an equal quantity of sugar. Put over a slow fire, and stir constantly until thick. Try a little by letting it cool before taking off; when done it will cut smooth.

APPLE MARMALADE.

Take twenty pounds of pared and quartered apples. Make a syrup of ten pounds of sugar, then put in the apples when the syrup is cold and boil until tender;

take them out and mash fine; cut six oranges into small slices, and boil all together, stirring all the time until done.

STRAWBERRIES.

Take ripe strawberries, but not so ripe as to be soft. Hull them and take equal quantities of sugar and berries. Put a layer of berries and a layer of sugar, and so on until all are in. Preserve only a few at a time, for if crowded they will not look well. Let them remain an hour or two to let the juice settle at the bottom; then put over a moderate fire, and when preserved put in glass or china jars, not large ones, seal tight, keep in sand; a small plate or a piece of a broken plate may be put on top to keep the fruit under the syrup. A little brandy may be put on top. They retain their natural flavor best if not cooked. This can be done by allowing a little more sugar than berries, and putting the berries in glass jars, first a layer of berries, then of sugar, and so on. Cork tight and keep in a box of sand. They are more difficult to keep in this way.

APRICOTS.

Scald them to take the skin off; cut in half and extract the stones. Boil in a little water; then take their weight in sugar and add the liquor in which they were boiled; boil gently and skim well. When it comes to a jelly, take them up. Put in jars, and cover with paper.

PEACHES.

Take those that are not fully ripe, pare them and take out the stones after halving. Take equal quantities of peaches and sugar. Put the sugar on the peaches; let it remain over night. In the morning skim out the peaches and heat the syrup; take off the scum, let it cool; then put in the peaches and heat up; when done put in jars. If you like, crack the pits and put in a few peach meats. In the course of a few days scald the syrup and turn back. When cold, put a brandy paper on top.

PEACHES IN BRANDY.

Gather them while quite hard; rub with a bit of flannel, and prick with a needle. Take half a pound of sugar to one of peaches, and make a syrup; then boil the peaches until quite tender, but not to break. Then take the peaches out of the syrup and lay on platters. Take a pint of brandy to every pint of the liquor, and turn it while hot on to the peaches. When cold, put in jars and seal up; keep in a cool place. Other kinds of fruit may be done in the same way.

PEACH JAM.

Pare and halve, then take out the stones, lay them in a pan with a layer of sugar, then of peaches, alternately, allowing three quarters of a pound to a pound of fruit. Let them remain a few hours, then put in a preserving-kettle and stew, frequently stirring to prevent their burning on the bottom; no water is necessary. They retain their flavor done in this way.

PEARS.

Pears look nice whole if not too large. Pare, leaving the stems on. Make a thin syrup and boil them tender but not to break. Let them lie in the syrup two days, then drain and add more sugar to the liquor, and boil ten minutes; skim and put in the pears, and simmer until transparent. Then take out and put a clove or a cassia bud into the end of each. Lay in a jar when cool. Then pour the warm syrup over them and add more sugar; then simmer half an hour. Weigh your sugar at first and allow three quarters of a pound to one of pears. They are very nice baked in molasses.

CURRANT MARMALADE.

Take ripe currants and squeeze out the juice of part of them; then add the same quantity of red raspberry juice. Put with the whole currants and boil gently. When they begin to boil, put in an equal weight of sugar boiled to a candy height; boil and mash them, skim as fast as any thing rises, and when thick as marmalade put in jars.

CURRANTS.

Take them when ripe, pick them over, and wash them in cold water. Let them drain well; then put equal quantities of sugar and fruit. Make a syrup, and when cool add the currants and cook gently a few minutes. After a few days, if they are not jelly, heat the liquor and pour on again. They are nice preserved green. Currants may be preserved by putting half raisins and half currants.

BRANDY PEARS.

Take pears that are ripe but not soft. Simmer in a little water until they yield to the pressure of the finger; then take them out and put in cold water. Pare them and make a syrup of three pounds of sugar to one of pears, and a cupful of water to each pound of sugar. When the syrup is clear, put in the pears while hot; boil until they look clear and the syrup is rich. Put in a glass jar and boil the syrup thick; mix a gill of brandy to one pint of syrup; pour over the fruit, and when cold put a paper on top.

QUINCES.

Select the nicest and best ones, for the inferior ones can be used for jelly or marmalade. Pare and quarter or cut in rings, taking out all the core. Boil until tender in water; then put in a jar and let them remain until the next day. Boil the skins and cores in a little water, and strain unless jelly is to be made; if it is, reserve them for that, adding a few quarters to give a better flavor. Then add the water in which they were boiled the day before, and allow a pound of sugar to each pound of quinces. (It is well to weigh the quinces before cooking them.) Let it boil a few minutes, and skim; then remove from the fire and when cool put in the quinces. If not water sufficient, add more, for if too rich they will shrink and be hard. Boil until a fork will easily go through them. Keep them covered while cooking to make them light-colored. Take them out with a skimmer, and lay in a jar. Boil down the syrup until just enough to cover them, and when cold it will be a nice jelly. They may be preserved with apples by adding one third apples, the same size as the quinces, which must be cooked in the syrup first and put in the bottom of the jar, as they will not require so much cooking as the quinces.

QUINCES WITH MOLASSES.

After paring and quartering them, boil the skins and cores in new cider, then strain them. For five pounds of quince take a pound of brown sugar, one quart of molasses, and the cider in which the skins have been boiled; add the whites of two eggs and clarify. When cool, add the quinces, and boil until tender; add more cider if necessary. Spice with orange-peel or ginger-root.

QUINCE MARMALADE.

Wash and quarter the quinces, then boil in water until perfectly soft. The parings and cores which have been left after preserving may be added; then strain and add as much sugar, pound for pound; stew gently, stirring constantly to prevent its burning. In the course of an hour take it up. If it cuts smooth when cold, it is done. Put into deep dishes that it may be cut in slices.

PLUMS.

The richest plum for preserving is the damson. Make a syrup of brown sugar, pound for pound, clarify it, and when boiling hot pour over the plums. Let them remain two days; then drain off and boil again. Skim well and pour it over them again; let them remain two more days, and then put them in the kettle and boil until rich.

TO PRESERVE PLUMS WITHOUT THE SKINS.

Pour boiling water over the large egg plum, and cover up until cold, when the skins will easily come off. Then make a syrup of a pound of sugar and a tea-cupful of water to a pound of plums; boil it and pour over and let them remain two days and boil again; then do them as in the former directions.

TO PRESERVE GREEN GAGES.

Loaf-sugar should be used for gages, pound for pound. Prick them with a large needle at the top and bottom. Make the syrup and just water enough to cover them; then boil five minutes. Put them in deep dishes and let them remain until the next day; then drain them and boil the syrup and pour on again; continue this until the fifth time, then boil the plums a few minutes and put in jars. Care must be taken not to break them.

PLUM JAM.

Boil in water until tender; then rub through a sieve, and to every pint add a pound of sugar, and make as marmalade; then put in tumblers as directed for jelly.

CHERRIES OR SMALL PLUMS.

Make a syrup, pound for pound, adding a little water, and boil the fruit a few minutes; then take out with a skimmer, and boil the syrup down rich, and pour on hot. If you wish to preserve them without the pits, take them out carefully, saving the juice. Put in small jars when cold, and seal tight.

CITRON AND WATERMELON RINDS.

Cut in squares about an inch long, boil a few minutes in alum-water, then drain after rinsing in cold water. Make a syrup of equal weight of white sugar; boil until clear. When cool, add a little essence of ginger, or what is better, when the preserves are to be used, add a little extract of lemon, or if preferred, put in the jar oil of lemon.

GRAPES.

Boil them in a syrup of an equal weight of sugar; if large, extract the seeds by halving them. If ripe, squeeze out the pulp, boil soft and strain it; add an equal weight of sugar, and boil until thick.

RASPBERRY JAM.

Allow three quarters of a pound of sugar to a pound of berries. Mix the sugar and berries; mash them and let them remain awhile; then boil, stirring all the time to prevent its burning. Another way is to add a pint of currant-juice to every five pounds of berries, and an extra pound of sugar.

TOMATOES.

Take the straw-colored, turn on boiling water to take off the skins; then weigh them and put equal quantities of sugar, and let it remain on all night. In the morning drain them and boil the syrup, removing the scum; put in the tomatoes and boil twenty minutes; take them out and boil the syrup until thick enough. When cool, slice lemon or oranges and lay between them in a jar; then pour the syrup over them and tie up.

TOMATO JAM.

Take off the skins and mash fine, adding an equal weight of sugar, and heat gradually until thick; or they may be washed clean and put in a preserving-kettle, covering it tight, and stew until soft; then strain through a colander, and add sugar; then heat on the fire, stirring constantly until done. Ginger essence or lemon may be added.

TOMATO FIGS.

After taking off the skins, weigh them and add an equal weight of sugar; let them stand two days; then boil the syrup and skim well; pour over the tomatoes and let them stand two days longer. The third time pouring on, dry them either in the sun or oven. When perfectly dry, pack them in boxes with a layer of sugar between. The syrup may be used for other purposes.

BARBERRIES

may be preserved like currants, or if preserved in molasses they will soon lose the molasses taste. The small winter grape may be preserved in the same way.

CRANBERRIES.

Allow pound for pound, equal weight; make the syrup and boil until transparent, or to a peck allow two pounds of brown sugar and half a pint of molasses; clarify and boil until transparent. For marmalade make as others, except the quantity of sugar; add a pound and a half to a pound of cranberries.

CUCUMBERS.

Take large ripe cucumbers; pare and take out the seeds, cut in pieces one inch square, put in salt and water that will bear up an egg; let them remain three days. Wash them and put into cold water with a lump of alum, and boil until tender; then drain and make a syrup, allowing equal weights of sugar and cucumbers, and when cool put in and boil until clear. They may be preserved the same as citron, and can scarcely be known from them. Flavor with any thing you like.

PRUNES.

Boil until they swell out plump; then add sugar, half a pound to a pound of prunes; cover tight while boiling; add lemon sliced up if you like. When taken from the fire add a wine-glassful of wine.

BLACK CURRANTS.

Take off the ends with a pair of scissors, and allow little over a pound of sugar to a pound of fruit; half a pint of red currant-juice to a pound is nice; put all into a preserving-kettle and boil, carefully skimming it; let it boil fifteen minutes. They are nice for tarts.

GOOSEBERRRIES.

Take off the blossoms and stems, and if not smooth roll in a cloth until they are, and for each quart take a pound of sugar and a gill of water; make a syrup and put in the fruit; boil fifteen minutes, and put in jars when cold. Keep for tarts and pies.

RHUBARB JAM.

Wipe the stalks clean, not wash them; peel off the skin, and cut up; a pound of sugar to a pound of plant must be allowed; stew until tender. It must be slowly stewed or the flavor will be lost.

TO BOTTLE FRUIT.

Take any kind of fruit and put in bottles; fill up full and put cold water in a kettle, with straw at the bottom, and while heating, cork and seal up tight. Put in a cool place and they will keep a long time. A better way is to cork up, leaving a small aperture in the cork for the heated air to escape; then seal. They should boil twenty minutes before sealing.

CANNING FRUIT.

Canning fruit is preferable to preserving, as the fruit retains its natural flavor, and does not require half the sugar. Glass cans are best, but almost any other kind will answer, tin or earthen jars. After filling they must be put into cold water in a kettle and heated gradually, leaving a hole in the top to allow the air to escape, and when boiling, fill up the aperture with a mixture of beeswax and rosin. They must be put in a cool place.

CANNING TOMATOES.

Pour on hot water to take off the skins; then cook the same as for eating, adding a little salt, and fill up your cans; if properly sealed, they will keep any length of time. Green corn, peas, or any kind of vegetables may be canned successfully.

TO CAN PEACHES.

Take half a pound of sugar to one pound of peaches. Make a syrup as directed; add half a pint of water to every pound of sugar. Pare the peaches and drop into the syrup; boil ten minutes. Put into the cans and seal up. Any other kind of fruit may be preserved in the same way. They will keep equally as well without sugar as with.

APPLE BUTTER.

Take from six to eight gallons of cider to one bushel of apples; boil down one half; then put in the apples, having them previously pared and cored, and boil down thick; add spices if you like, and sugar if the apples are tart; half sweet and half sour apples are the best. Boil the sweet ones first, as it will take longer to boil them tender. Any kind of berry may be made as well as apples, but they will not require any cider, but use half a pound of sugar to one pound of apples or berries.

PRESERVED PUMPKIN.

Cut pumpkin of a nice flavor and fully ripe; pare and cut in pieces the third of an inch thick. Take equal weight in white sugar. Allow a gill of lemon-juice to four pounds of pumpkin, or the juice of one lemon to a pound. Put the pumpkin in a pan with the sugar and juice, and let it remain all night. In the morning put into a preserving-kettle and cook till clear; be careful to skim well; then add some lemon-peel cut in small pieces. Take out and strain the syrup through a jelly-bag and pour on.

FROSTED FRUIT.

Dip any kind of fruit into the beaten whites of eggs, then in fine white sugar; put on a tin to dry, set in a warm oven. When dry, put in a dry place.

TO PRESERVE FRUIT BY DRYING.

Take strawberries, blackberries, or raspberries, and allow half a pound of sugar to a pound of berries, and dry in an oven. I think they retain their flavor better than drying in the sun. Put in jars and seal up tight. These are nice for pies or puddings in the winter when nothing else can be obtained. Any kind of fruit can be kept a long time by drying perfectly and putting in a bag and hanging in a dry place. They must be well dried or else they will breed worms, and should be immediately heated over.

TO MAKE MOLASSES CANDY.

The West-India molasses is best for this purpose. Take one quart, and half a pound of brown sugar, boil until it will crisp when cold. Care should be taken not to have it burn; when nearly done, add the juice of one lemon; do not put in too soon or the taste will boil out. When done, pour on to a buttered tin. If nut-meats are put in, they should be put in while warm. Take some out of the pan and pull with your hands until of a light color; the more it is worked the whiter it will be.

JELLY

may be made of almost any kind of fruits mashed and strained through a jelly-bag, allowing a pound of sugar to every pint of juice.

CURRANT JELLY.

Take currants, not too ripe, or the jelly will not be as good a color; just after they have turned red is the best time. Pick them over and wash them clean; then mash them, and squeeze them in a bag, or put them in a jar and set it in a kettle of cold water and put on the fire, and when hot strain through a bag. To every pint add a pound of juice, and boil ten minutes; skim well and pour into tumblers set in cold water; let it cool a few minutes before putting in or they will break. When cool, paste tissue paper on top, and set in a dry place. A more delicate jelly is made without boiling. Mash the currants and put a pound of sugar to a pint of juice. Put in glasses and paste over; then set in the sun a few days, and it will be a nice jelly.

PEACH JELLY.

Take a dozen peaches, cut in halves, take out the pits and peel them. Take a pint of clarified sugar and water, (as given before;) when it has boiled and been skimmed, put in the peaches, with the kernels broken; boil gently for ten minutes; then take out four or five of the halves for garnishing the jelly; let the rest boil a few minutes longer. Take three lemons, cut off the rinds, and squeeze the juice through a sieve into a basin; pass the syrup through with half an ounce of isinglass; run through three times. Fill your moulds half-full of jelly, and when set put in the peaches, and a little more jelly, and when that is set fill up the mould.

APPLE JELLY.

Pippins or crab-apples are best for jelly, although any tart apples will answer. Put on water sufficient to cover them; boil until tender; then strain through a bag, and make as currant jelly. They are nicer boiled with the skins on, but take out the cores. If the jelly is too pale a color, it may be colored with spinach-juice for green, or for pink use cochineal. Quince jelly may be made in the same way; add lemon-juice.

CALVES' FEET JELLY.

Take four feet, slit them in two, and wash them clean; then put them in water sufficient to cover them; boil several hours, or until reduced to two quarts. Strain it through a sieve; then let it remain until cold, when all the fat must be taken off, and the sediment at the bottom taken off. Put in a preserving-kettle and melt slowly; add the juice and grated rind of two lemons. Wash six eggs clean, and beat the whites and shells together and mix with the jelly. Sweeten to the taste with loaf-sugar; add half a pint of white wine or Madeira. Boil slowly fifteen minutes, and then strain through a jelly-bag until clear; if not clear at first, run it through again. If not sufficiently stiff, add half an ounce of isinglass. Flavor with any spices you like, or color if desired. It must be kept in a cool place or surrounded by ice. Ox-heel may be made in this way, or sheep's feet; also pigs' feet make nice jelly.

STRAWBERRY JELLY.

Put them in a pan and bruise well, adding a little water and powdered sugar; in an hour or two strain through a jelly-bag with isinglass dissolved in half a pint of cold water; mix well and pour into moulds. Raspberry, blackberry, or almost any other kind of fruit may be made in the same way. If cherries are used, they must be boiled, and the juice of lemons added.

COLORING FOR JELLIES OR CREAMS.

The juice of spinach-leaves bruised will give a green color, and saffron will make a yellow hue. For coloring pink use cochineal. Bruise it with a knife-blade; then put in a little white brandy, and let it remain awhile; then strain it. This is for immediate use. Another method is to take fifteen grains of cochineal and reduce to a powder; add a tea-spoonful of cream of tartar, and boil an hour in half a pint of water; add a bit of alum the size of a pea.

FRUIT IN JELLY.

Put half a pint of calves' foot jelly in a basin, and when it has become stiff lay in a bunch of grapes or currants, with the stems upward; put a few vines over and fill up with warm jelly; then set it away until next day, and then set the basin in hot water for a moment; then turn out carefully. It is an elegant looking dish

STRAWBERRIES FOR CREAM.

Take equal weight of sugar and berries, mash until perfectly smooth. Put in jars and paste paper over. It will keep good for several months.

STRAWBERRY TART.

Take two quarts of ripe strawberries; add a pint of wine, half a pint of clarified sugar—it must be cold—the juice of two lemons; mix these without breaking the berries, and put in a puff-paste, previously baked.

STRAWBERRIES SOUFFLE.

Pick over two quarts of ripe berries; rub them through a sieve; add a pound of white sugar and the whites of six eggs beat to a froth; mix as light as possible, and bake in a moderate oven; when done, glaze on top.

PRESERVED CURRANTS FOR PUDDINGS.

Take three pounds of brown sugar, and put in six pounds of currants well picked over and washed; just let them boil up, and then pour into a jar. Wet a paper with brandy, and when cool put on top; cover tight and set in a cool place, or they may be put on plates and dried.

STRAWBERRIES DRIED IN SUGAR.

Pick them over, and take a quarter of a pound of sugar to four of strawberries; dry in a warm oven after bread has been taken out. Any other kind of fruit may be dried in the same way.

PICKLED BLACKBERRIES.

Take seven pounds of ripe berries; add one pint of weak vinegar and three pounds of sugar. Only let them boil up once; then put in jars. They are excellent.

TO PRESERVE CURRANTS WITH THE STEMS ON.

Pick them with the stems on; melt some brown sugar in a kettle—one pound to a pailful of currants will be enough; keep the kettle on the stove, and immerse the currants in the sugar, as many as you can at a time; then take out with a skimmer and spread on a board to dry in the sun. Then place them in an oven a short time to prevent their getting wormy. Put in a bag and hang in a dry, cool place. The liquor in which they were boiled can be made into wine or jelly.

ESSENCE OF NUTMEG.

Dissolve an ounce of the essential oil of nutmeg in a pint of rectified spirits. Use for flavoring cakes and puddings.

ESSENCE OF GINGER.

Grate three ounces of race ginger and put in a quart of good brandy; take the yellow part of a fresh lemon and put in. Bottle up, and shake well every day for eight or ten days. It is nice for flavoring sweetmeats, and a little mixed with water answers for ginger tea.

EXTRACT OF LEMON AND ORANGE.

Rub the yellow part of the rind with lump-sugar, and as fast as the sugar becomes saturated with the oil put in a china bowl or jar; press down tight and cover close. A very little answers for flavoring.

ORANGE SYRUP.

Squeeze the juice through a sieve, and to every pint add a pound and a half of sugar; boil it slowly and skim well; when cold, bottle it tight. This is nice added to a butter sauce for pudding; it is also nice for custards or punch. Lemons may be done the same way. If not likely to keep, scald and skim again.

SPICE BRANDY.

Put rose-leaves into brandy, steep until the strength is obtained, then drain and squeeze the rose-leaves, and add more, and continue to do so until it is fully impregnated with the flavor; cork tight. Peach meats steeped in brandy are nice to flavor puddings, pies, etc.

BLACKBERRY SYRUP. NO. 1.

Take the high vine blackberries, as the low ones do not possess the medicinal virtues that the high ones do; set the berries on the fire and mash them, and strain through a flannel bag; to each pint put a pound of loaf-sugar, a tea-spoonful of cloves, an ounce of mace, and an ounce of cinnamon pounded fine; boil the whole together fifteen minutes; strain again, and to every pint add a glass of French brandy; cork tight in bottles and keep in a cool place. This is an excellent remedy for the bowel complaint.

BLACKBERRY SYRUP. NO. 2.

To two quarts of juice add one pound of loaf-sugar, half an ounce of nutmeg, half an ounce of cinnamon, a quarter of an ounce of cloves, the same of allspice; boil a short time, and when cold add a pint of French brandy.

ELDERBERRY SYRUP.

Wash and mash them, then squeeze out the juice; to each pint of juice put a pint of molasses; boil twenty minutes, stirring all the time; when cold, add four table-spoonfuls of brandy to each quart; bottle and cork it tight. This is an excellent remedy for a tight cough.

LEMON JELLY.

Take half a dozen lemons, squeeze out the juice, put the rinds over a slow fire with an ounce of isinglass and a pint of boiling water; when the isinglass is dissolved, add the juice and sweeten to the taste with loaf-sugar; boil a moment, then color it with any thing you like, and pass through a jelly-bag without expressing; fill your glasses and paste over. Orange jelly may be made in the same way.

WINE JELLY.

Take a pint of wine, the same of water, and boil; then add two ounces of isinglass, previously dissolved in a little water; pour in while boiling, and sweeten to the taste. Put in your glasses.

ISINGLASS JELLY.

Boil two quarts of water with a quarter of a pound of isinglass, put some lemon-peel in a basin and strain the liquor on it, with four cloves, or more if you like, and half a pound of sugar; let it remain where it will keep warm an hour or more, then take out the lemon-peel and cloves, and add two wine-glasses of brandy. This is nice for parties.

TO PRESERVE LEMON JUICE.

Squeeze and strain the juice into a dish, and add a pound of loaf-sugar to every pint of juice, and stir until dissolved, then bottle and seal up, or tie bladders over it, and keep in a cool place.

A SUBSTITUTE FOR FRESH LEMONS.

Take one ounce of the best oil of lemon, and strong rectified spirits four ounces; put in a bottle and add the spirits by degrees, until it cuts the oil. This possesses all the fragrance and flavor of the freshest lemon-peel.

LEMON PICKLE.

Take six lemons, quarter and take out the seeds, put them in a jar and sprinkle on two ounces of salt; let it remain three days, well covered, then add nutmegs sliced, cloves, mace, and mustard-seed; boil a quart of vinegar and pour over the ingredients; cork tight, and it will be fit for use in a week. It is an improvement to most sauces, particularly to fish sauce.

QUINCES PRESERVED WHITE.

Pare and core them, then strew powdered sugar over them, filling up the hole, add a small quantity of water at first, then more, and boil quickly; when tender and clear, they are done.

PUFFS OF PRESERVED FRUIT.

Roll out good puff-paste, a quarter of an inch thick, and cut in squares, about four inches; lay jam of any kind on each one, double them over, and cut in half-moons with a tin cutter; lay them on paper on a baking plate, ice them, and bake in a slow oven from fifteen to twenty minutes, taking care not to color the icing.

TO KEEP GRAPES IN BRANDY.

Take close bunches, not over ripe, put them in a jar, and sprinkle a good quantity of white sugar over them;

fill up with brandy. Tie down with a bladder, and keep in a dry place. Prick each grape before laying down.

TRANSPARENT CRUST FOR TARTS.

Take twelve ounces of butter, well washed and without salt, melted without being oiled; when cool, add one well-beaten egg, and stir into a pound of dried flour; make the paste very thin, line the patty-pans quickly, and when putting the tarts into the oven, brush them over with water and sift sugar over them.

PEACHES IN BRANDY. NO. 2.

Put them in a preserving-pan with cold water on them, let them simmer slowly; when they begin to be soft, they are done; then drain on a sieve; they will not all be done at the same time, but must be taken out one at a time; wipe dry, and when cold put in glasses, dissolve powdered sugar in brandy, and fill up.

TO CANDY FRUIT.

Make a syrup of sugar, dip in the fruit quickly, then lay on a sieve and immerse in hot water, to take off the syrup; put it on a napkin before the fire to dry, and repeat the process; sift over the fruit double-refined sugar on all sides, till quite white, then place them on the shallow part of the sieve and place in an oven to dry, turn two or three times while drying; be careful not to scorch them; do not allow them to get cold till dry.

PINE-APPLE TARTS.

Pare a large pine-apple and take out the core, cut it in strips, mix with sugar, and let it stand till there is sufficient juice to stew it, and when stewed quite soft mash it with a spoon and let it cool; then mix half a pint of cream and fill your shells with it; grate sugar on top.

PLUMS IN BRANDY.

Take plums not too ripe, twelve pounds; prick them and put in cold water over the fire; when the water boils, skim out carefully and put them in a pan of cold water; clarify three pounds of sugar; put the plums in and boil up; let them remain two days; then drain off and boil the syrup alone; then boil up the plums, and the next day drain them and put in bottles; then boil the syrup down more, and when cold add sufficient brandy to cover the fruit; stir well and strain; then pour the syrup over the plums. Cork the bottles tight.

CANDIED PLUMS.

Cut them in halves and take out the stones; lay them on a shallow dish; sprinkle sugar over them and set them into a warm oven an hour; take them out and spread on plates to dry. Other fruits may be done in this way.

TO PREPARE ANY KIND OF FRUIT FOR BRANDY.

Take the quantity desired, gathered before they are perfectly ripe; prick them and lay them in cold water and set over the fire, keeping the water nearly boiling till the fruit will give to the touch; then skim out carefully and put into cold water; drain off and add more cold water; when perfectly cold, put in bottles; if any is broken, do not put it in. Have a sufficient quantity of clarified sugar ready; put double its quantity of brandy together;. mix well and pour over the fruit. Seal up.

BLACK BUTTER.

To one pound of sugar put three pounds of any kind of fruit, currants, raspberries, cherries, etc.; stew till thick. Nice for children.

TO PREPARE FRUIT FOR CHILDREN.

Take sliced apples, plums, cherries, currants, or any kind of ripe fruit; put a layer in a stone jar with a layer of sugar; set it in a saucepan of water, and let it remain till done. Eat with bread or rice.

ICING FOR TARTS.

Beat the white of an egg till light; wash the tarts over with it, using a feather; then sift powdered sugar over.

PINE-APPLES WITHOUT PRESERVING.

Take those that are fully ripe; pare off the rind; cut in slices half an inch thick; allow a pound of sugar to every pound of apple. Put a layer in a glass jar, then a layer of sugar, and so continue until full; set the jar in a kettle of cold water with straw at the bottom, and heat up until warmed through; then cover the jar with bladder or waxed cloth, and keep in a dry, cool place.

ORANGE PRESERVES.

Take ripe oranges, and put in a kettle, with cold water enough to cover them; put over the fire till the water is scalding hot; then pour off the water, and repeat the process until the water has no bitter taste; then make a nice syrup in clear water, allowing a pound of sugar to a pound of fruit; boil the syrup until thick; put in the oranges and keep covered tight four or five days; then take out the fruit and scald the syrup; put in the oranges and give one boil; then put in jars and cover tight. Very nice to eat with ice cream.

COMPOTES OF FRUIT.

Take any kind of fruit and boil in syrup made in the proportion of one half pound of sugar to one of fruit. This mode is for immediate use. Apples flavored with lemon or oranges, and when done peel and core; then fill with marmalade. With the syrup poured over, is nice when preserves are scarce.

BAKED APPLES FOR DESSERT.

Take juicy apples; pare and core them; place in a pan and fill the holes with sugar and cinnamon; put water in the pan to prevent their burning, and bake until tender; when cold, serve with cream or boiled custard.

RICE JELLY.

Boil half a pound of whole rice with a pound of loaf-sugar in one quart of water till it becomes a glutinous mass. Strain off the jelly and cool in moulds.

ORANGE JELLY.

Boil one ounce and a quarter of isinglass in one pint of water, the rind of an orange, cut a stick of cinnamon, and three ounces of loaf-sugar, till the isinglass is dissolved; then squeeze two oranges or lemons, and enough oranges to make a pint of juice; mix all together and strain into a basin; set it in a cool place for an hour, and when it begins to congeal fill your moulds; when used, dip the mould into lukewarm water and turn on a dish; garnish with slices of orange or lemon.

RUM JELLY.

Clarify and boil to a syrup a pound of loaf-sugar; dissolve one ounce of isinglass in half a pint of water; strain it into the syrup while half warm; when nearly cold, stir in a quart of white wine; mix it well and add two table-spoonfuls of Jamaica rum; stir a few minutes and pour into glasses.

ORANGES FOR DESSERT.

Peel and slice oranges; arrange nicely in a glass dish, with powdered sugar sprinkled between each layer. If you like, add Madeira wine and more sugar when served.

APPLES FOR DESSERT.

Pare and scoop out the core; have ready a syrup flavored with cinnamon or mace; throw in and boil tender; when cold, serve.

BAKED QUINCES.

Take nice ripe quinces; bake quicker than apples; then cut them open, remove the core, sprinkle white sugar over them, adding rich cream. Eat before cold.

LEMON CUSTARD.

Strain three wine-glassfuls of lemon-juice through a sieve; beat nine eggs light; strain and add to the lemon-juice, with a quarter of a pound of loaf-sugar, a wine-glassful of white wine, half a glass of water, with a little grated lemon-peel; mix well together, and pour into a small pail; set it in a kettle of hot water, and stir until it becomes thick.

APPLES AND RICE.

Boil a coffee-cupful of rice in milk, with a stick of cinnamon; pare ten or twelve apples; scoop out the core, and fill up with raspberry jam. Border a deep dish with paste; put in the apples, leaving a space between, and fill up with the rice. Brush the whole over with the yolk of egg, and sift sugar thickly over it; form a pattern on top with sweetmeats; then bake one hour in a quick oven.

APPLE JELLY TO USE FOR OTHER FRUIT.

Take four pounds of good apples; after they are pared and cored, put them in a stewpan with a quart of cold water; stew till the fruit is broken; then strain through a jelly-bag, and to every quart of juice allow a pound and a half of sugar. This is nice to preserve other fruit in.

ORANGE CUSTARD.

Boil the rind of a Seville orange very tender; then beat it to a paste; add to it the juice of the orange, a table-spoonful of good brandy, four ounces of sugar, the yolks of four eggs. Beat all together for ten minutes. Then pour in by degrees a pint of boiling cream, and beat until cold. Put into custard-dishes; place them in a dish of hot water till set; then put preserved orange or orange-chips on top.

FRUIT ICE CREAM.

Take a pine-apple and pare off the rind; then cut the apple in slices; put a layer of apple and white sugar alternately. Let it remain until a syrup is formed; then drain off and flavor your cream. Raspberries and strawberries or any other fruit may be prepared in the same way.

BOILED CUSTARD.

Scald a quart of milk and sweeten to the taste. Mix half a pint of cold milk with five well-beaten eggs, and stir in while the milk is boiling. It is nicer to strain the eggs before putting them in. Flavor as soon as stirred in, and pour into a dish. If you wish to ornament it, beat the whites of three of the eggs with jelly, and put on top.

TO MAKE MAPLE SUGAR.

Strain the sap before putting over to boil; put it in iron kettles, and keep it constantly boiling. Have two large kettles; take out of one and put into the other to keep it boiling; fill up the one taken from with cold sap, and continue this until you sugar off, which should be done as often as you can conveniently, or every other day. This is done by straining the syrup through a bag like a jelly-bag; then put back into the kettle, and boil until nearly thick enough for sugar. Clarify as for other sugar, and skim well. If you want it white, stir well until just right to put into moulds, which should be wet with cold water to make the sugar come off easy. Shallow pans are preferable to kettles to use in boiling.

CANNING MAPLE MOLASSES.

Fill your cans with the boiling syrup, and seal as in fruit, and it will retain the flavor and keep from souring from spring to spring.

WATER-MELON SYRUP.

Take out the inside of ripe water-melons; boil them up in a little water; then strain through a cloth and boil down to a syrup. This is nice for apple butter and apple sauce.

DRIED TOMATOES.

Pour on boiling water, to take off the skins; then cook them until half cooked away; add a tea-cupful of sugar and a table-spoonful of salt to four quarts; then spread on plates, and dry in a warm oven; put in layers with paper between. When used, stew slowly in a good deal of water; then season with pepper and butter.

TO KEEP TOMATOES A YEAR.

Prepare as above, and add mace, cloves, pepper, with salt and sugar. Put in jars and run mutton suet—or lard will answer—over them.

TO DRY TOMATOES FOR PIES.

Take the skins off in the usual way, then slice thin and sprinkle sugar over them, then dry in an oven; soak a little while in cold water before using; add a little lemon.

WHITE POT.

Whip four eggs light, add a pint of cream, nutmeg and sugar, then cut very thin a few slices of bread, and lay in a dish; pour the eggs and cream over it, with a cupful of raisins and a small piece of butter, and, if required, a little milk, so that it will not be too dry when baked; bake slowly half or three quarters of an hour.

TOMATO MARMALADE.

Strain the juice, and to every pint add three fourths of a pound of sugar, with the juice and rind of a lemon; then cook until clear.

TO PRESERVE GROUND CHERRIES.

Take them from the husks when ripe, but not sufficiently ripe to leave the skins cracked; wash them clean, and add three quarters of a pound of sugar to one of cherries; put in a stewpan and stew gently until clear, then slice lemons or oranges, and put a layer in your jar as you put in your preserves. Rhubarb may be made in the same way.

TABLE OF WEIGHTS AND MEASURES.

It is sometimes more convenient to measure articles than to weigh them. I give the exact equivalents, such as I have used myself.

WEIGHTS AND MEASURES.

White sugar, one pound and a half is one quart; brown sugar, if damp, one pound and ten ounces one quart; loaf or broken sugar, one pound and six ounces one quart; Indian meal, one pound two ounces one quart; wheat flour, one pound one quart; rye flour, one pound two ounces one quart; eggs, ten eggs one pound; butter, when soft, one pound is one pint; one table-spoonful of salt is one ounce.

MAKING WINE.

Wine may be made from grapes by putting them (after sorting) in a barrel and pounding them with a pounder, but be careful not to break the seeds; then put in a coarse cloth and submit it to the pressure. A cheese or portable cider-press is good for this purpose.

When the juice is all pressed out, which is from ten to fifteen quarts per bushel, put it in a clean keg or barrel, filling within a few inches of the bung, and let it remain for a week or two, when the wine becomes clear; fill the cask full with more juice, reserved for that purpose; tighten the bung, and place in a cool place until March, when it should be racked off into jugs or bottles, and cork securely. Omit the bottling until the wine is a year old, when the bottles should be sealed hermetically. If you wish, you can add a little sugar, say one pound to each gallon, but with perfectly ripe grapes it is not necessary.

CURRANT WINE.

Press out the juice, and to every two quarts add two of water and three pounds of sugar; put in a brandy cask if one can be obtained, if not, a clean one will answer; fill up to the top, when it will run over and work itself clear; then cork tight, and let it stand six months; it will then be fit for use, but all wines improve with age. You can bottle it up.

BLACKBERRY OR RASPBERRY WINE.

Measure and bruise the berries, and to every gallon add one quart of boiling water, let it stand twenty-four hours, stirring it occasionally, then strain in a cask, and to every gallon of juice add two pounds of sugar; cork it tight, let it stand until fit for use, then bottle.

APPLE WINE.

Take nice ripe apples, press out the juice, and to every gallon add one pound of sugar; let it stand from four to six months, when you will find it preferable to almost any other wine; it can then be bottled.

TOMATO WINE.

Press out the juice, and to every quart of juice add one pint of water and one pound of sugar; set away to ferment, and skim until done fermenting; then put in a tight cask and leave until spring, when it may be bottled; add a small piece of ginger-root to each bottle. All wines are much improved by putting in brandy casks.

VINEGAR.

Every housewife should supply her family with good vinegar, and the best way to do this is to have a barrel of cider in the fall placed in the cellar, and after it has worked, draw off and put in a keg; then tack over the bung-hole a piece of gauze, and shake up as often as convenient, and in a few months you will have the best of vinegar. Keep all your cold tea, and rinsings of sweetmeat-jars, juice of fruit, etc., and pour into the barrel, and when it gets down in the keg fill up from the barrel. This is decidedly the best vinegar as well as the cheapest.

WHISKY VINEGAR.

Take five gallons of soft water, two quarts of whisky, two quarts of molasses, half a pint of good yeast; roll a sheet of white paper in molasses and put in the mixture; place in the sun, and in six weeks or two months it will be good vinegar.

MAPLE VINEGAR.

Take the sap that runs from the maple-tree in the spring and put it in a cask, roll a sheet of white paper in molasses and put in for the mother, and in a few weeks you will have good vinegar. The sap that runs after making sugar when the buds begin to come out will answer. If three barrels are boiled into one, it will be stronger.

TO MAKE BEER.

MOLASSES BEER.

Six quarts of water, two quarts of molasses, half a pint of yeast, two spoonfuls of cream of tartar; bottle after standing twelve hours.

WHITE SPRUCE BEER.

Five gallons of water, three pounds of white sugar, a cup of good yeast, with enough of the essence of spruce to give it a flavor; when fermented, bottle it up. It is a delightful beverage in warm weather.

ROOT BEER.

Take five gallons of water, a few hops, some spruce, wintergreens, sassafras, hemlock, different kinds of roots, such as burdocks, dandelions, dock, sweet-apple bark, etc.; boil and strain; add a pint of molasses and a pint of yeast; a little ginger will be an addition; let it work, and it will make a healthy drink.

HARVEST DRINK.

One gallon of water, one pint of molasses or less will do, half a pint of vinegar, a table-spoonful of ginger.

LEMONADE.

Cut the lemon in slices, press out the juice, put on water, and sweeten with loaf-sugar to suit the taste.

ELDERBERRY WINE.

To every two quarts of elderberry-juice, add two of water, one quarter of a pound ginger-root, one quarter of a pound of allspice, two ounces of stick cinnamon, two ounces of nutmeg powdered, two ounces of cloves and mace each; sixty pounds of sugar added to this quantity of spices will make forty gallons of wine. Mix well together and boil an hour; then strain and set away to cool; when milk-warm, put in your barrel; then toast a slice of bread and dip in new yeast, and put in the barrel; keep it uncorked until it has done fermenting, then cork it tight for three months; then draw carefully off and wash the barrel clean; turn back your wine, and add two pounds of raisins and from ten to fifteen pounds of sugar, also three gallons of brandy. It will be fit for use in a week, but better when older.

GINGER WINE.

Take three gallons of water and add three pounds of sugar, four ounces of race ginger well washed; boil together one hour; strain through a sieve; when lukewarm, put in a cask, adding three lemons cut in slices, and two gills of yeast. Shake it well and then cork it tight; then let it stand a week or until it becomes clear; then bottle, and it will be fit to drink in a fortnight.

SPRUCE BEER.

Boil a handful of hops and twice as much sassafras-root in ten gallons of water; then strain it and pour in while hot one gallon of molasses, two spoonfuls of the essence of spruce, two of powdered ginger, and one of pounded allspice; then put in a cask, and when sufficiently cold add half a pint of yeast; stir it well, cork it tight, and when fermented and clear, bottle it tight.

GRAPE WINE.

Bruise the grapes when ripe; to each gallon of grapes put one gallon of water, and let it remain a week without stirring; then drain off the liquor carefully, and to each gallon add three pounds of white sugar. Let it stand until fermented; then cork tight. In six months it will be fit to bottle.

CHERRY BOUNCE.

Take two quarts of the wild black cherry; pound them, in order to break the pits; then add two pounds of sugar, one gallon of good rum or apple whisky; put in a tight cask, and shake every day for three months; then run the liquor twice through a thick cloth to clear it; then put in bottles or cask. It is good for bowel complaints, and is a fine tonic.

A RICH AND PLEASANT WINE.

Take new cider, and mix as much honey as will support an egg; boil gently fifteen minutes in tin; skim well, and when cool, put in a cask, but have not quite full. In six months it will be fit to bottle; in six weeks it will be fit to drink. It will be less sweet if kept longer in the cask. This will serve for cooking purposes where sweet wine is directed.

BLACK CURRANT WINE.

Take three quarts of juice, the same of water, three pounds of sugar; put in a cask, reserving a little for filling up. Let it remain in a warm room, and it will ferment; then skim, and when the fermentation is over, fill up with the reserved liquor. When done working, add three quarts of brandy to forty quarts of wine. Bung up for nine months; then bottle, and the settlings run through a jelly-bag until clear; then bottle that. It will be good in a year, but, like all other wine, requires age.

EXCELLENT RAISIN WINE.

Take a gallon of spring-water; put eight pounds of fresh Smyrnas in a tub; stir thoroughly every day for a month; then press the raisins in a bag until dry; put the liquor in a cask, and when it has done hissing, pour in a quart of the best brandy; stop it close for twelve months; then rack off the clear and filter through a thick flannel; then add another quart of brandy. Cork it tight and keep three years; then bottle.

IMPERIAL.

Take two ounces of cream of tartar and the juice and paring of two lemons; put in a stone jar; pour seven quarts of boiling water on; stir and keep close. When cold, sweeten with loaf-sugar, and then strain and bottle it, adding half a pint of rum. This is a pleasant and wholesome drink.

MEAD.

Take three quarts of warm water, two pounds of drained honey, stirring it until the honey is dissolved; then turn into a cask, leaving the bung out; bottle as soon as fermented. Add a lemon to each gallon.

BLACK CURRANT WINE. NO. 2.

Pick the currants when fully ripe; squeeze out the juice, and to every gallon of juice add six quarts of water, and to each gallon of this mixture add three and a half pounds of brown sugar; mix well together and strain. Put into a cask till fermentation takes place; then cork well.

CIDER WINE. NO. 2.

Take a barrel of good cider; let it remain two days after coming from the press; draw off, and put in another barrel with sixty pounds of brown sugar and one pound of isinglass. After undergoing fermentation, bottle it for use.

GRAPE WINE. NO. 2.

Gather the grapes when about half ripe; pound them in a tub, and to every quart of fruit add two of water; let it remain two weeks; then draw off, and to every gallon of liquor add three pounds of sugar. When the sugar is dissolved, cask it, and when done working, cork tight. In six months it will be fit to drink, when it should be bottled.

PEACH CORDIAL.

Take a peck of ripe, juicy peaches; pare and cut them from the stones; crack about half the stones, and save the kernels; leave the other half of the stones whole, and put with the peaches, also the meats. Put the whole into a wide-mouthed demijohn, and pour on two gallons of double-rectified whisky; put in three pounds of lump-sugar; cork tightly for three months; then bottle it, and it will be fit for use. It will be clearer if strained.

BLACKBERRY CORDIAL.

Take nice ripe fruit and squeeze out the juice through a linen bag; allow a pound of loaf-sugar to every quart of juice. Put it into a preserving-kettle, and when the sugar is melted, set it on the stove and boil to a thin jelly. When cold, allow a quart of brandy to every quart of juice; stir together and bottle immediately; it is ready for use. Raspberry cordial is made the same as raspberry vinegar, except whisky is used instead of white vinegar.

RHUBARB OR PIE-PLANT WINE. NO. 1.

Mash and strain, and then add a pound of sugar to every two quarts of juice and one of water; then proceed as for currant wine. This makes a most excellent wine, and is a nice wine for the sick.

ELDER WINE. NO. 2.

Take eight quarts of berries, four of water; let it stand two days; then boil one hour; strain, and put three pounds of sugar to every gallon; add cloves, cinnamon, one ounce each, two ounces of ginger; boil again, and work with slice of toast dipped in yeast.

LEMON CORDIAL.

Pare off the rind of eight lemons cut in shreds, and put in a large bottle; add a pint of spirits of wine or brandy, a dozen bitter almonds bruised and blanched; let it remain a week. Make a syrup with a pound of lump-sugar; when cool, pour into the bottle; let stand a week longer; then filter and bottle for use.

RHUBARB WINE. NO. 2.

Cut the stalks of the rhubarb plant into small pieces; boil until tender, which will be in a few minutes; no water will be required, if washed before putting over; strain through a bag and to each gallon of juice add two of water, and four pounds of sugar. Let it remain forty-eight hours in an open vessel; then take off the scum, and add one pint of good brandy to every four gallons. Put it in a tight cask, and in six months it will be fit to bottle. Put a raisin in each bottle, and cork tight, after which seal up. This is equal to champagne.

RHUBARB VINEGAR.

Take a dozen stalks of rhubarb, about middling size; mash them fine in a tub, and then pour on five gallons of water; let it stand twenty-four hours; then strain and add nine pounds of sugar and a little brewers' yeast; let it remain where it will be warm about a month, when it must be strained and put back in the cask again until it becomes vinegar, and it will equal French vinegar.

CURRANT WINE. NO. 2.

Press out the juice, and to every two quarts add one of water and three pounds of sugar; let work as other wine; then bottle. This makes a rich wine.

SHERBET.

Boil two quarts of water, eight green stalks of rhubarb, a lemon sliced, and a quarter of a pound of raisins; boil half an hour; strain and add orange or lemon syrup to suit the taste. When cold, it will be ready to drink.

RATAFIA.

Blanch two ounces of peach and apricot kernels; bruise and put them in a bottle, and nearly fill up with brandy. Dissolve half a pound of white sugar candy in a cup of cold water; add to the mixture after it has stood a month and been strained; then filter through paper, and bottle for use.

RASPBERRY.

Pick over the fruit and put in a stone jar, and set the jar in a kettle of warm water till the juice will run; strain, and to every pint add half a pound of sugar, give one boil, and skim; when cold, add enough quantities of juice and brandy; shake well, and bottle.

CURRANT SHRUB.

To one pint of currant-juice put a pound of sugar; boil gently eight minutes; then let it cool. When almost cold, add a wine-glassful of brandy to each pint of the juice; bottle and cork it tight; keep in a cool place.

BERRY VINEGAR.

Take ripe strawberries, blackberries, or raspberries, and mix with vinegar in proportion of three quarts of berries to one of vinegar. Let it remain two or three days, then strain the whole, and to each pint put a pound of white sugar, and bottle without corking tight. This is a nice summer beverage to assuage thirst in fevers, colds, and inflammatory complaints; also for those in good health. A large spoonful mixed with a tumbler of cold water.

RASPBERRY VINEGAR. NO. 2.

Pour three pints of the best white wine vinegar on a pint and a half of fresh gathered red raspberries in a stone jar; the next day strain the liquor over the same quantity of fresh berries, and the following day the same; then strain the whole, and add a pound of white sugar to a pint of juice. When the sugar is dissolved, set in a pot of water, and boil one hour, skimming as the scum rises on top. Add to each pint a glass of brandy, and bottle tight.

LEMON WATER.

Take three pounds of white sugar, two ounces of tartaric acid, and two quarts of water; stir up and add the whites of two eggs well beaten; set in a kettle of water till it scalds but not boil; when cool, strain and add lemon sufficient to flavor it. Take two table-spoonfuls of it to two thirds of a tumbler of water. If wanted for an effervescing drink, stir in a little carbonate of soda.

GREEN GOOSEBERRY WINE.

To every pound of fruit add a quart of cold water; let it stand three days; then strain, and to every gallon of juice add three quarts sugar; to every twenty quarts of liquor, one bottle of brandy. Hang some isinglass in a bag in the cask; when it has stood a year, plup it, and if the sweetness is sufficiently gone, bottle it. The gooseberries should be green but full grown.

VINEGAR MADE FROM BEETS.

Take one bushel of the sugar beet; wash them clean; then grate them and put in a cheese or portable ciderpress; put the juice in a barrel, cover the bung with a bit of grease to keep out the flies; set it in the sun, and in two weeks it will be fit for use. One bushel will make five or six gallons of good vinegar.

GINGER BEER.

Pour a gallon of boiling water over three quarters of a pound of loaf-sugar, one ounce and a quarter of ginger, the rind of one lemon; when lukewarm, add the juice of the lemon and half a cupful of lively yeast. Make it in the evening and bottle next morning.

MEAD.

Wash your honeycomb after draining the honey, and put it in a clean barrel or keg; put in a little yeast, and when worked enough, draw off and bottle it. Lemons or oranges are a great improvement.

MILK PUNCH.

Beat up two eggs; mix them with a quart of milk; sugar, nutmeg, and lemon-peel to your taste. Boil it gently, stirring all the time, till thick enough; take it from the fire and add a quarter of a pint of rum, stirring all the time the rum is poured in.

AN EXCELLENT VINEGAR.

Take one gallon soft water; add one pint of sugar or sorghum molasses; stir till the sugar is dissolved; then put in a gallon of ripe tomatoes. In a few days you will have nice pickles and good vinegar.

SANGAREE.

Take any kind of wine; add cold water with nutmeg and sugar. Just before serving grate ice in the glasses until heaped up. Serve with cake.

HOW TO MAKE COFFEE AND TEA.

Procure the Old Java coffee; pick out the stones and bad grains; then dry well, and brown it on the stove in a spider until about the color of walnut. It must be constantly stirred, or else it will brown uneven; stir in a small piece of butter; then turn out in a box kept for the purpose, and cover tight, as it loses its flavor if left uncovered. Never grind until just before using.

In making, allow one table-spoonful to each person; have your coffee-pot well rinsed and free from grounds, as old grounds spoil the taste. For six persons take the half of the white of an egg, (as more egg prevents the strength from extracting unless boiled a long time, which injures the taste;) beat it well with the coffee, adding a little cold water; put in the coffee-pot and turn boiling water on; let it boil not longer than five minutes; pour out some and turn back to clear the spout, and then turn into an urn. Have rich cream, or scalded milk with the yolk of an egg beat stirred into it. Good sugar is also necessary to have good coffee. This is the best mode of making coffee I have ever tried.

Another way is to leech it. This can be done by having a strainer in the top of the coffee-pot, and pour on boiling water, and when the water is drained through it is ready for use. Nothing will be required to settle it. The Old Dominion coffee-pot is made for this purpose.

TEA.

Green tea should not be boiled; turn boiling water on, and after standing where it is warm five or ten minutes, fill up. Black tea should boil ten or fifteen minutes. Put a little water on at first and boil; then fill up and let it boil again. Half black and half green is generally preferred.

CHOCOLATE AND COCOA.

Take one quart of water, three spoonfuls of scraped chocolate. Let it boil fifteen or twenty minutes; then pour in one pint of rich milk, and sugar to your taste; let it boil up; then take it off and stand a few minutes, when it will settle; pour out.

Cocoa is made nearly the same, and is much used for delicate people who are out of health. Directions always come with the cocoa, on the wrapper.

MALT COFFEE.

This comes already prepared, and is a great saving, for it is almost equal to the best Java coffee. It must be boiled half an hour or longer.

SWEET POTATO COFFEE.

Wash them clean, and dry well; then put them in the oven and brown them, as coffee; grind and turn boiling water on, or boil without grinding; but they will require more boiling to extract the strength. This is a good way of using the small sweet potatoes. Parsnips scraped and browned make very good coffee.

Coffee may be nicely settled by putting in (while boiling) a small piece of codfish skin in the place of egg. Let it boil five or ten minutes; then turn in a little cold water and let it stand two or three minutes, when it will be as clear as if settled with an egg.

Rye may be washed and dried, and nicely browned about the color of coffee; then use half rye and half Java coffee, and very few persons can detect the rye. It is said that ochra, burnt like coffee, makes a beverage very much like coffee.

TO MAKE MACARONI.

Beat four eggs; strain them and add flour enough to work into a paste; work it well; cut off a small bit at a time; roll it out as thin as paper; cut it with a paste-cutter or knife into very narrow strips, twist and lay them upon a clean cloth in a dry, warm place. In a few hours they will be dry; then put them in a box with white paper top and bottom. It may be used for soup.

TO PRESERVE SWEET MARJORAM.

Beat up the white of an egg; add a little white sugar; take some marjoram and rub on a glass that is quite clean, and lay it in the form of the glass; so do it with the egg; then sear it with the sugar on it, and lay on paper to dry.

SOUR-KROUT.

Cut your cabbage fine with a knife fixed in a frame, pack tight in a clean barrel, with salt between each layer of cabbage; pound it down very tight, every layer, until full; then put a weight on top, and put the cover on tight; put in a warm cellar for three or four weeks; then take off the scum which will rise on top, and lay a clean cloth on; the juice should always stand on top. It will keep for years. Eat cold or fry in a little gravy.

FLAVORED BUTTERMILK.

Put six quarts of fresh buttermilk in a strainer; hang in a cool place two or three days, or until it drains well; then put in a dish, and add a glass of brandy or wine; sweeten with loaf-sugar; then color with raspberry jam; whisk it well together, and serve in a glass.

BUTTER AND CHEESE.

THE KEEPING OF COWS.

There is a great difference in the quality of milk; some cows gave much richer milk than others. Much depends upon the treatment of cows in the quality of butter and cheese. In the first place, farmers should endeavor to procure the best breed, not the largest and best looking, but those that produce the best quality of milk. It is not those that give the most milk that are the most profitable to keep, but the richness of the milk should be looked to. Cows must be kept well through the winter, and allowed to come in about the middle or first of April, to be good dairy cows. A few weeks before calving they should be messed as often as once a day, if not twice. The calves should be taken away within a week; the sooner the better, as they more easily learn to feed if taken away at once. Warm the milk and feed twice a day, or, if convenient, they may be fed at noon also. After the first week a little skim-milk or buttermilk may be given, the latter being the best if they will drink it. I have seen splendid calves brought up upon nothing but buttermilk, and turned into pasture. Some let them run with the cows —two calves with one cow. If the cow is healthy, the milk will be good after the seventh or eighth milking. They should always be milked in warm weather before the sun rises, so they can pasture before the heat becomes oppressive, and should be milked early at evening. Regularity should be observed, as it makes a difference in the quantity of milk. Always milk at the same hour of the day. It is well to have one cow come in the first of January, for family use, and where there are a number of cows, it is quite as profitable. They should be salted twice a week or oftener. Carrots are good for cows; turnips spoil the taste of the milk. They should never be allowed to run, as it injures the milk. When the milk is strained, it should be put in six-quart pans, only filling them half-full, as the milk will only rise so far; if more is put in, you will get but little more cream. Keep in a cool, dry cellar, not too much light, and so that the wind can not blow in, or the cream will be hard, and when churned, much of it will remain in small pieces, and you will not get as much butter. Every thing should be kept perfectly clean and sweet. Fresh meat or vegetables should never be put in a milk-cellar. An ice-house is almost indispensable to making butter, but if you have a cool cellar and cool water, very good butter may be made during the hottest weather.

DIRECTIONS FOR MAKING BUTTER.

Some people churn sweet milk, others let the milk sour, and then churn, adding a great deal of water.

But I think rich cream makes the best flavored butter, and certainly of the best color, and will keep longer than butter churned from milk. The milk should be skimmed in warm weather as soon as it is sour. Morning and evening is the best time for skimming. Put the cream in an earthen jar, and if you do not churn every day, keep a stick in it to stir occasionally. The oftener you churn, the better quality your butter will be. If you have ice, put some into a tub, well covered with flannel, to prevent its melting; this will keep your cellar cool during the warmest weather; when you churn, put a lump of ice in the churn.

In cold weather the milk should be set over the fire and warmed, when it comes from the cow; in twenty-four hours take off the cream; it will not be as thick for scalding, but will be richer, and will make more butter, and of a better color and quality. The butter will come in fifteen minutes if the cream is scalded. In warm weather, or when the milk has not been scalded, an hour is the usual time for churning. If the milk is the right temperature, the butter will be hard and yellow. The butter should be rinsed off the cover and dasher about five minutes before it gathers together; then churn slowly until it becomes solid. Take up with a wooden ladle, and wash all the buttermilk out, (or if you can work out the buttermilk without washing, the butter will be sweeter;) then salt, allowing one ounce of salt to a pound of butter; but as some people like their butter salter than others, this should be done from experience. Use no salt but rock-salt ground. It comes in sacks expressly for dairies. Work the salt in well, and let it remain a few hours, when it should again be worked, and packed; if worked too much, it will injure the taste of the butter. If put in firkins or pails, they should be soaked over night in cold water, (after being thoroughly cleaned;) wash well; then take a cloth wet with strong brine and wash again; put in your butter and pack solid. Wet a linen cloth in a solution of saltpetre, and lay on top; cover tight until another churning is put in; then repeat the process. The sooner the firkin is filled the better. If kept in firkins any length of time, put a layer of salt on the cloth; then fit the cover in tight to exclude the air; or a brine may be made in the following manner: one quart of fine salt, half a pail of water, an ounce of saltpetre, and two ounces of white sugar; boil it and skim well; when cold, pour on; this will keep it sweet a long time.

Always churn in the morning while the atmosphere is coolest; in winter, warm the cream. A little salt stirred into the cream while getting a churning, will keep it sweet, and some think the butter comes sooner.

TO PREPARE A RENNET.

Take the rennet from a healthy calf not over four weeks old; it should be kept without food for twelve hours, for the secretions of the stomach to accumulate strength, Empty the curd out, but not rinse, then rub with salt, and stretch on a hoop to dry. It is better to be a year old before using. When used, soak in a jar a gallon of water to a rennet; rub salt on, and stir often; keep more salt on than will dissolve. In three or four days the liquid is fit for use, and can be bottled and kept in a cool place. If there is any taint, do not use it, as it will spoil the cheese. Allow one gill to thirty-five gallons of milk. Stir always before using.

MAKING CHEESE.

Have every thing connected with the making of cheese well cleaned and scalded. You will require two strainers, one hoop, a basket, ladder, tub, and press. Strain your night's milk in your tub; in the morning when the cows are milked, warm it in a brass kettle or tin boiler, and turn in with the night's milk; after stirring it well, put in rennet sufficient to form the curd well in half an hour. The milk should be heated to ninety-eight degrees or one hundred of Fahrenheit. When the curd is nicely formed, take a long-bladed knife and cut it through in squares, or you may break it gently with the hands. Great care must be used, or the whey will run off milky, and the cheese will be injured. The whey should look green when it runs off. Put your ladder on another tub to catch the whey; lay on your basket, put the strainer on, and then dip out the curd carefully into the basket, occasionally lifting the ends to hasten the draining. When all is in, turn up the corners, and set a weight on to press out the whey. Every few minutes the curds should be cut up and pressed again, but must not be hurried too much. When thoroughly drained, if to be pressed the same day, it must be prepared for scalding; but if not to be pressed until another curd is made, it must be put into the cellar or some cool place, and hung up to drain.

TO SCALD THE CURD.

Cut the curd into little squares the fourth of an inch in size; put them into a strainer, and immerse it in a vessel of warm water, enough to cover it. Then heat it to the temperature of one hundred and five degrees. Stir it all the time until warmed through; then gradually add cold water until reduced to ninety degrees. Put it in your basket and drain it; then salt, allowing a quarter of a pound of salt for every ten pounds of curd, and mix carefully. Place it in a hoop, strainer and all; make it smooth, and put a cover on top, and put in the press. It must not be pressed very hard at first, but more weights put on afterwards. In two hours or three it will be ready to turn; then take another cheese-cloth wet it in a little salt and water, and turn into that, and put back into the press. In nine or ten hours turn again, and if the edges require paring, do it with a sharp knife. Let it remain two days in the press if you can. It is well to have two presses for this purpose, where a cheese is made every day. When taken from the press, rub it over with butter and keep in a dry, cool place. If they spread too much, sew a bit of cotton cloth around them when taken from the press. It is a good plan to put cayenne pepper in the butter you rub on, to prevent the flies from troubling them. They must be greased and turned every day, until fully cured. If you wish to color the cheese, boil annotto with a little lye, and put to the milk when you add the rennet. If too much rennet is put in, the cheese will be strong, and if too much salt, they will be hard. If the milk is too hot, they will be tough.

Sage cheese is made by pounding the sage, and then squeezing out the juice and straining in with the rennet. Spinach or corn leaves are also nice to add with sage.

COTTAGE OR DUTCH CHEESE.

Take half buttermilk and half sour milk after it has been skimmed, and heat over the fire until the curd settles at the bottom; then put in a cloth, sewed up at the corner like a jelly-bag, and let it drain. When drained, add salt, cream, or butter, and make in balls. This is best made fresh. It is nice eaten with cream and pepper.

BRANDY CHEESE.

Grate cheese, or the dry bits may be used for this purpose, and pack in brandy. Put a layer of cheese in a jar, pour on some brandy and pound down tight; cover well, and when eaten cut off in slices; this will keep a long time.

ANOTHER METHOD OF MAKING CHEESE.

After pressing out all the whey and scalding as for the press, pack in jars and press down closely; then put a linen cloth on top, of several folds thickness, and when saturated, remove it and place a dry one in its place. The next day add the other curd, and continue so until full. Another way is to hang it up after salting, in a strainer, and let it remain until it ripens. I have never tried either of these modes, and can not vouch for their goodness.

TO PRESERVE CHEESE FROM THE FLY.

It is the small cheese-fly that is so troublesome to cheesemakers. They lay the egg, and it soon begins to work its way into the cheese. I have sometimes put annotto into the butter before rubbing the cheese; also red peppers steeped strong and put in is a preventive; but the most successful way of keeping the insect from troubling the cheese is to rub it over with a flour paste, and then wrap a cloth round it, and one on the top and bottom. Cover over with paste, and keep in a dark, cool place.

TO RAISE CREAM.

When the milk comes in, have your pans in boiling water; strain into one and turn the other over; this will hasten the rising of the cream, and it will be of a better quality.

CHEESE CREAM.

Warm a pint of milk and a pint of cream, and put a little rennet to it; keep in a warm place till curdled; have a proper mould with holes, either of china or any other. Put the curds in to drain about an hour or less; serve with a good plain cream and sugar over it.

WELSH RABBIT. NO. 1.

Cut a slice of bread and toast it; then soak it in red wine; cut slices of cheese, and rub a little butter on the bottom of a dish; lay the cheese upon it, and pour in two or three spoonfuls of white wine and a little mustard; then put the toast on top, and set in the oven till warmed through.

WELSH RABBIT. NO. 2.

Lay slices of bread and butter in a dish, and a layer of cheese alternately, till full; then make a custard without sugar, and bake fifteen minutes.

CONFECTIONERY.

TO CANDY FRUIT.

It must be preserved and dried in a stove, that none of the syrup may remain. Sugar for candying must be prepared in the following manner. Take a pound of sugar, with half a pint of water, and set it over a fire. Take off the scum as it rises, and boil until it looks clear; take some out, and when it is cold, if it will draw a thread from the spoon, it is boiled enough for any kind of sweetmeat; then boil your syrup, and if it begins to candy around the edges of your pan, it is boiled enough, or is candy height. Sweetmeats must not be put into too rich syrup or the fruit will wither, and both the beauty and flavor will be destroyed.

TO CANDY ALL KINDS OF FRUIT.

When completed in the syrup put a layer into a new sauce, and dip it suddenly into hot water to take off the syrup that hangs about it; then put it on a napkin before the fire to drain, and then do more on the sieve. Take some refined sugar and sift over the fruit till quite white; set it on the shallow end of the sieve in a warm oven, and turn it two or three times. It must not be cold till dry. Watch it carefully, and it will be beautiful.

CARAMEL, TO ORNAMENT PASTRY.

Take syrup after it has candied high, and with a spoon drop into any kind of mould in fine threads till it is covered. The mould should be greased first, so that it will readily come off. Make a small handle of caramel or two or three small gum-paste rings, and place it over pastry of any description.

TO CANDY CITRON.

Pare them very thin and narrow, and throw them into water. Take out the inner part with great care, so as to leave only the white part. When tender, take them out and have a clarified syrup boiled to almost a candy height; then put in the rings and boil; take from the fire, and when the sugar becomes white by rubbing it with a spoon against the side of the pan, it is time to take out the rings and lay them on a sieve to drain; then cut into proper lengths and dry.

CREAM SNOW.

Take a quart of cream, the whites of three eggs, four spoonfuls of sweet wine; sugar to the taste; add a bit of lemon-peel; whip to a froth. Serve in a dish after taking out the peel.

SUGAR KISSES. NO. 2.

Stir the whites of four eggs to a stiff froth; add half a pound of white sugar, and flavor as you like. Lay in heaps on white paper, each the size and shape of half an egg, and an inch apart; place them on a board and bake in a moderate oven. When they turn a little yellow, slip them off the paper and let them cool five minutes; then take two of the kisses and join the two bottoms together; press gently and they will adhere; they look very handsome. Put currant jelly or any other kind you like between them.

LEMON DROPS.

Stir loaf-sugar into lemon-juice as thick as you can stir it; put into a basin or porcelain kettle, and stir with a wooden stick over a moderate fire five minutes; flavor with the extract of lemon, and then drop with the point of a knife on to white paper. When cold, take off.

SUGAR CANDY.

Allow half a pint of water to one pound of sugar, half a sheet of isinglass, a tea-spoonful of gum-arabic; dissolve the whole in a brass kettle or preserving-kettle; when it boils, remove from the fire and skim well; then put it on again and boil till it becomes brittle, which is ascertained by dropping a little in cold water. If made of white sugar, add a little vinegar, or it will be too brittle. Flavor with any essence you prefer; color it if you like. If nuts or cocoa-nut meats are added, put in before pouring out. Make in any shape you like.

CREAM OF ANY PRESERVED FRUIT.

Take half a pound of any preserved fruit; put in a pan, with the whites of two or three eggs; beat together half an hour; take off with a spoon, and lay on a glass dish, with other creams, or put in the middle of a basin. Raspberries will not do.

ESSENCE OF CINNAMON.

Infuse the oil in highly rectified spirits of wine in proportion of half a drachm of oil to an ounce of wine. Cloves, the oil, is made the same; the quantities are one ounce of cloves to three quarts of brandy, and four pounds of sugar dissolved in four pints of water.

LEMONS TO KEEP FOR PUDDINGS.

Put the rinds in cold water and let them remain two weeks; then boil in the same till tender; strain it, and when nearly dry, throw them into a jar of candy that you have remaining from old sweetmeats, or if you have none, make a syrup of loaf-sugar and water, and pour over them. In a week boil them till they look clear. They must be covered.

PREPARATION OF FOOD FOR THE SICK.

WATER GRUEL.

Stir three large spoonfuls of Indian meal, or oatmeal if preferred, smooth with a little water; pour into a a quart of boiling water, and let it boil fifteen or twenty minutes; season with a little salt, and if desired, a little sugar and nutmeg will render it more palatable; also a little milk or cream is nice if the patient can take it.

MILK PORRIDGE.

This is made in the same way, only use flour instead of Indian meal, and milk in the place of water.

RICE GRUEL.

Boil a little rice in water until tender; then strain off the liquor and sweeten to the taste; add a little salt and nutmeg.

BARLEY WATER.

Wash the barley and pour on cold water; let it simmer; then add a few raisins, and boil until tender; season with salt and nutmeg. Rice may be made in the same way.

PANADA.

Pour water on light bread or crackers, and season with sugar and nutmeg; add an egg, if allowed; a few raisins added with the crackers are nice. Hot water must be poured on and covered up tight until they soak.

WINE OR CIDER PANADA.

Pour boiling water on crackers, or bread toasted or not just as preferred; then add a wine-glassful of cider or wine; flavor with nutmeg. Invalids almost always relish this when they can take nothing else. A little butter should be added.

CAUDLE.

Take water gruel, rice, or barley; add a wine-glassful of wine or ale, and season with nutmeg or sugar.

BREAD JELLY.

Toast slices of stale bread; pour boiling water on and a little lemon-juice, and then boil to a jelly; strain and sweeten it; add a little nutmeg or lemon-peel to flavor. This is nice for young children.

CHICKEN JELLY.

Cut a chicken, or an old fowl will answer just as well; pound the bones and then put in a jar and cover it tight. Set the jar in a kettle of boiling water, and keep it boiling three hours; then strain off the liquor and add salt, pepper, loaf-sugar, and lemon. The fowl may be boiled again and will make as much jelly as before.

TAPIOCA JELLY.

Soak four table-spoonfuls of tapioca, in water to cover it, five hours; stir it into a pint of boiling water, and let it simmer gently; when thick and clear, mix two table-spoonfuls of lemon-juice, half a wine-glass of wine, and stir into the jelly; then turn into cups. Sago jelly may be made in the same way.

SASSAFRAS JELLY.

Take the pit of the sassafras boughs, and soak in cold water until it becomes glutinous. It is much relished by the sick, and is also nourishing.

CALVES' FEET BROTH.

Put water enough on to cover them, and boil down to half; strain the liquor, and take off the fat, season with salt and a little wine. This is very nourishing and strengthening for an invalid.

CALVES' FEET BLANC MANGE.

Split the feet and wash clean; pour on four quarts of cold water, and boil down to one; strain it and set away to cool; then remove the fat and take off the settlings at the bottom, and add a quart of new milk;

sweeten to the taste, and boil a few minutes with lemon-peel or a stick of cinnamon; then strain it through a sieve into a pitcher, and stir until cold; when milk-warm, wet the moulds with cold water, and pour in. This is nice for sick or well.

BEEF TEA.

Take a pound of fresh beef, cut it thin, and put it in a wide-mouthed bottle, with a little salt; place it in a kettle of cold water, and boil an hour; then strain it, and there will be a gill of liquid. Begin with a little at first, and give as the stomach will bear. I have sometimes added a little water when put over to boil. This has been retained on the stomach when nothing else would.

ANOTHER BEEF TEA.

Slice dried beef very thin, pour on boiling water, and cover it tight; set it in a warm place, for half an hour or so, then add a little piece of butter and pepper; crumb in a little bread, or crackers, if wished.

WHINE WHEY.

Boil half a pint of milk, and the moment it boils, pour in a glass of wine, with a little lump-sugar; the curd will soon form, then take it off and set it aside until it settles; pour the whey off and add a little hot water; sweeten to the taste.

ARROW-ROOT.

Stir a table-spoonful smooth with a little cold water, then pour on boiling water until it thickens and looks clear; season with sugar, salt, lemon or nutmeg, or eat with cream and sugar. This is nice for children when teething.

SAGO.

Take a tea-cupful of sago and let it soak three hours, then boil it with some lemon-peel until it is transparent; add a little milk, lump-sugar, and nutmeg.

CUSTARD EGG.

Beat an egg to a froth, and add a pint of new milk just from the cow; add a little sugar and nutmeg, or if wine is allowed, add a wine-glass of wine instead of the milk, and take half an hour before breakfast. This is very nourishing and strengthening for an invalid.

HOT LEMONADE.

Cut up a lemon and pour on boiling water; add a tea-cupful of lump-sugar. This is an excellent drink for colds.

BEEF, VEAL, OR CHICKEN BROTH.

Boil the meat with a little rice, until tender; season with a little salt, and put in an earthen vessel, and when wanted, warm a little at a time, and crumb in crackers.

CODFISH BROTH.

Cut salt codfish in small pieces, and put on cold water; let it boil a minute or two, then pour on more water, and add a little butter, or, if preferred, add cream instead of water; toast crackers or bread and pour on to it.

EGG FOR INVALIDS.

Break an egg in a saucer; add a small piece of butter, with a little salt; then set it on the stove, and stir until cooked sufficiently. Another way is to break the egg into boiling water, having previously salted the water; take it up as soon as the white is hard; dip a slice of toast in hot water and lay the egg on top, after buttering the toast.

FLOUR GRUEL.

Tie a pint of flour in a cotton cloth, and boil in water three hours; then take out of the cloth, and grate it when used, and pour on boiling water; add a little milk, and flavor with sugar and salt. This is good for invalids or teething children.

CREAM OF TARTAR WHEY.

Heat a pint of milk scalding hot, stir in a tea-spoonful of cream of tartar; strain it, and sweeten with lump-sugar.

SIMPLE DRINKS FOR THE SICK.

Pour boiling water on to dried tart apples, tamarinds, cranberries, currants, whortleberries, and then pour off the water and sweeten it to the taste; add a little wine, if allowed. These drinks are nice and cooling in fevers.

FLOUR COFFEE.

Take wheat flour and scorch very evenly in a spider, stirring all the time, then put some in a bowl and pour on hot water, and let it stand a few minutes, keeping it warm, and then pour off the coffee and sweeten, adding a little cream. Cocoa is very palatable and nutritious for the sick, and the directions are always given on the papers. Java coffee is sometimes used for those who can bear it, made with milk instead of water, and sweetened to the taste.

TOMATO SYRUP.

Take the juice of ripe tomatoes, and put a pound of sugar to each quart of juice; put it in bottles, and set it aside; in a few weeks it will have the flavor of pure wine, and, mixed with water, is a nice beverage for the sick.

BUTTERMILK WHEY.

Boil fresh buttermilk, and as soon as boiled pour into a bowl; add a little salt, lump-sugar to the taste, and a little nutmeg if liked; sometimes a cracker rolled fine is acceptable.

ANOTHER METHOD.

When the buttermilk is boiling, stir in an egg well beaten, and take up; add a little cream or butter, sugar, and spice.

ALUM WHEY.

Mix a little pounded alum with milk, strain it through a cloth; add nutmeg and sugar to the whey. It is good for colic and hemorrhages.

TO MAKE ALUM WHEY FOR POULTICES.

Take a pint of milk and warm it, stir in a lump of alum till it wheys, then take out the curd, and use for poultices.

EGG TEA.

Beat the yolk of an egg with a spoonful of sugar, pour boiling water on, and then stir in the white, beat en to a froth; add spice to suit the taste. When a person has taken a violent cold, get them warm in bed and give this as hot as it can be taken, and it will often effect a cure.

EGG COFFEE.

Beat the yolk of an egg with a large spoonful of sugar, then put in a cup of cold coffee; add a tea-cup of cold water and as much cream, then add the white of the egg, beaten to a stiff froth. This is much relished by invalids.

COUGH TEA.

Make a strong tea of everlasting, strain it, and to every quart add two ounces of liquorice-root, two of raisins, and boil half an hour; when taken up, add the juice of a lemon. This is an excellent remedy for a tight cough. If taken hot, care should be taken not to expose yourself after drinking it for a few hours.

THOROUGHWORT BITTERS.

Take the blossoms off, as they are apt to cause vomiting, then make a strong tea of the stalks, then strain it, and when cool, add half a pint of French brandy, the peel of two oranges cut into bits, and fennel seed; put all into a bottle and cork it tight. Take a wine-glass of the bitters and put into half a tumbler of water; sweeten it if you like. It is an excellent remedy for fever and ague and bilious colic.

FLAX-SEED JELLY.

Pour boiling water on to a quarter of a pound of flax-seed, cover up tight, and let it remain two or three hours; then strain, and add the juice of a lemon and white sugar to the taste; or it may be boiled in molasses candy and taken in that way. It is good for a cough or costiveness.

MOSS JELLY.

Steep Irish moss in cold water a few minutes, then drain off the water, and to half an ounce of moss put a quart of fresh water and a stick of cinnamon; boil it to a thick jelly, strain it, and add sugar and a glass of wine if it can be taken. It will not keep long if no wine is put in.

FOR HOARSENESS OR LOADED CHEST.

Take eight or ten drops of the balsam of copaiba and drop on a piece of loaf-sugar; take three times a day, morning, noon, and night. Try a few days, and if it does good, it will effect a cure in a week. Horse-radish, made into a tea and sweetened with honey or loaf-sugar is good; add a little vinegar. Take a tea-spoonful occasionally.

A TONIC FOR INDIGESTION.

Take twenty grains of rhubarb, gentian, carbonate of iron, and Spanish liquorice, pour a pint of boiling water on, and take from two to three table-spoonfuls three times a day. A little sugar can be added to make it more palatable if you like. Take the mixture cold.

CURE FOR A DRY COUGH.

Take half an ounce of gum-arabic, the same of liquorice, dissolve in warm water, squeeze the juice of a lemon; then add two drachms of paregoric, one of squills. Put in a bottle and shake well. Take a tea-spoonful when the cough is troublesome.

CURE FOR EARACHE.

A little sweet oil and laudanum dropped warm into the ear, and applying hot salt in a bag to keep it warm. The heart of an onion roasted is good.

STING OF A BEE.

Apply an onion cut in two, and let it remain until the pain subsides, and it is a certain remedy. Another is to apply saleratus. Wet salt is also good. Whatever is applied should be done before the part begins to swell.

TO MAKE OPODELDOC.

Dissolve an ounce of camphor in a pint of rectified spirits of wine, then dissolve four ounces of white

Spanish soap, scraped thin, in four ounces of rosemary, and mix together. Add half an ounce of origanum if you like.

TO CURE CRAMP.

A cold application to the bottom of the feet, such as iron, ice, water, or any thing cold that can be had, the colder the better. If the cramp is in the arms or upper part of the body, apply it under the arms, and it will relieve in five minutes.

TO DRY HERBS.

Gather them on a dry day, while in blossom, and before dog-days, as they are much stronger. When dry, hang up in paper bags.

A REMEDY FOR SCARLET FEVER.

Give two table-spoonfuls of yeast to an adult, and to a child two or three years old one spoonful, to be taken every two hours. For sore throat gargling yeast will give immediate relief.

IMPORTANT REMEDY FOR CANCERS.

Take an egg and break the small end to let out the white, then put in salt and mix with the yolk until a a salve is formed. Put a portion of this on a piece of leather or brown paper, and apply twice a day. This has been known to effect a perfect cure.

CURE FOR BRONCHITIS.

One drop of croton oil rubbed on the throat daily will produce an eruption of the skin, and will, if persevered in, effect a cure. Smoking is also good.

FOR A CUT.

Tie up with brown sugar and pour on spirits, then let it remain several days, wetting occasionally in spirits. When dressed apply the leaf of the fish geranium, and it will soon heal, or the leaf may be immediately applied as soon as cut. When a nail or piece of glass has been run into the foot, bind on salt pork, and if much swelled, bathe with a decoction of wormwood, then bind on more pork, and keep as quiet as possible.

Salt pork is also good for a bad cut. A poultice made of hot lye is also good, and should be kept on several hours, dipping it in lye whenever it gets cold. Slight wounds often occasion lock-jaw, and should not be neglected. Spirits of turpentine is also good. Puff-balls or spiders' webs are good to prevent bleeding. Peach leaves, or even the twigs well steeped, are said to be good to apply where a nail or glass has gone into the foot.

AN EFFECTUAL CURE FOR A FELON.

Soak the part affected in weak lye, putting it in cold, and sitting near the fire till it scalds; then take the yolk of an egg, six drops of turpentine, a few beet-leaves, a small quantity of soap, one tea-spoonful of burnt salt, and one of Indian meal. It never fails to effect a cure if applied in season. Another effectual cure, but more simple, is to apply the prickly pear, bind it on after bruising it, and change till a cure is effected.

TO CURE RINGWORM.

Get the grease from a church-bell, which forms a kind of verdigris, mix with unsalted lard, and apply a plaster twice a day. It is a certain cure. Gunpowder, applied wet on going to bed at night, and let it remain till morning, is good.

BURNS.

Many receipts are given for burns, but the best one is, to wet cotton batting with linseed oil or sweet oil; if neither are at hand, use any other, or castor oil is very good. The cotton should not be removed till the skin is healed or the new skin will adhere to it. More oil should be applied, but not opened to the air. If a very bad burn, a physician should be called to dress it, the second time. For a slight burn, spirits of turpentine is good.

CROUP.

This is a dangerous disease; medical aid should be procured as soon as possible. It is well to keep the ipecac root in the house, as that will not lose its strength like the powdered. This disease is known by a peculiar whistling sound in the breathing, and if neglected proves fatal. Steep some ipecac in warm water—it must not boil—then sweeten it, and give enough to sicken, or if they vomit it will be better. Soak the feet, put on draughts of mustard, and get the child into a perspiration, and bathe the throat with volatile liniment. This if well done will give relief. Cold water applied to the throat and chest, and then well covered with flannel to sweat it, is good, but should be carefully used. Wet the cloths in cold water as soon as they get warm.

SORE THROAT.

A gargle of salt and water, or vinegar, is good for a common sore throat. Brandy or rum and lump-sugar is also good. One large spoonful of Cayenne pepper, a tea-spoonful of salt, and a pint of boiling water, or half vinegar, is still better; pour on the water first, then add the vinegar. This is an excellent remedy for putrid sore throat. Let it settle and then gargle in the throat every half-hour. Bind on the throat a piece of salt pork cut thin, and if it is very bad, keep it on two or three days. The skin will then break out in small blisters, which will be a benefit. A mustard poultice is good and will give instant relief almost. Either of these are good for ulcerated sore throat. White oak bark made into a tea, with a small piece of alum in and used as a gargle, is good.

CANKERED MOUTH.

Touch the cankered spots with saltpetre, or burnt alum powdered is good. Red raspberry or blackberry leaves made into a tea are good for calomel sore mouth; sweeten with honey. The low blackberry should be used.

DIPHTHERIA.

This is a disease that is carrying off thousands, both young and old, because it is so rapid. The patient should be kept warm, and the throat bathed with hot salt and water, keeping it well covered in flannels, except to change the cloths. Gargle salt and water in the throat, and keep a small piece of camphor gum in the mouth, and if this is well done, and no exposure for several days, there is no danger, but there must be no delay.

TO STOP VOMITING.

Make a strong mint tea, camphor and water, or brandy and water, keeping a flannel wet in spirits on the stomach, or a mustard poultice. A little salt and water is also good. A small pill of Cayenne pepper will sometimes stop vomiting. A cloth, wet in the essence of peppermint, laid on the stomach, is sometimes a preventive. Pigeons' gizzards are good. They should be powdered and made into a tea, and when every thing else fails, a chicken boiled four minutes, and the broth given in small quantities, will stop vomiting.

MUSTARD POULTICE.

Make a paste of Indian meal scalded, and sprinkle mustard over the meal, after putting on a cloth, or you may make it of wheat flour wet with vinegar, and spread on a cloth, then sprinkle mustard on the side to be applied to the flesh.

BLEEDING AT THE NOSE.

Hold the head on a level with the rest of the body, bathe the head frequently in cold water, apply a key or something cold to the back of the neck. Grate dried salt beef, and snuff up a little.

POLYPUS.

Take bayberry and bloodroot, dry them and pulverize them, then take as snuff. Make a small swab, and dip it into the snuff and touch the diseased part as far as possible.

WARTS.

Rub them with fresh beef every day, or rub them with tobacco-juice and chalk. Strong saleratus water will soon destroy them. Lemon-juice is good, or bind on the inside of a lemon.

CHILBLAINS.

Where the skin is not broken, bathe in hot alum-water. Lime water and sweet oil are good. Rub the chilblain with it and dry before the fire, then wrap in linen. Repeat this when going to bed at night, several times. A cotton or linen stocking should be worn.

TO REMOVE PIMPLES, STIES, AND BOILS.

To remove a sty, pull out the winker where the sty commences, or apply a little spirits of turpentine every few hours, when they first make their appearance.

MORTIFICATION.

Apply poultices of boiled and mashed carrots, or yeast thickened with slippery elm, or flour. It must be applied warm, and often renewed; charcoal pounded and put in the poultice is good. Give a glass of yeast every three or four days, and tonic bitters.

SALT RHEUM.

Take a quart of vinegar and four ounces of litharge, and boil down to half a pint; when settled, pour it off; stir in two ounces of sweet oil, or more, until it forms a consistency thicker than cream. Give things for the blood.

ITCH.

Make an ointment of lard and sulphur, oint with it at night before a hot fire, and in the morning wash thoroughly, putting on clean clothes. Continue this for a week, taking a tea-spoonful of sulphur mixed with a little molasses each day.

DROPSY.

Take a pint of hickory-bark ashes, mix in a pint of wine, and take a wine-glassful three times a day.

SUMMMER COMPLAINT.

Mix two large spoonfuls of pulverized rhubarb, two of cinnamon, two of lump-sugar, the same of French brandy, and half a pint of water. Give a tea-spoonful three times every hour till the complaint is checked. Blackberry syrup is an excellent remedy. The diet should be light, such as milk porridge, toast, etc. The little weed called camp-weed, or mouse-ear, is a sure remedy. Make a tea of it, and drink as occasion requires.

BILIOUS COLIC.

Flannel wet in hot brandy, with mustard or Cayenne pepper sprinkled over, and laid on the bowels, will often give relief. A little soda and spearmint tea is good. A tea-spoonful of Cayenne pepper, one of sugar, and a very little boiling water poured on, and sip hot, will give relief. If the bowels are inactive, give injections. A pint of starch, half a pint of molasses, a pint of milk, a wine-glass of sweet oil or fresh lard, and a table-spoonful of salt. Thoroughwort bitters, as given in this book, will entirely cure this complaint if taken long enough.

CHOLERA MORBUS.

Take a tea-spooonful of soda, cinnamon cloves, pour on a pint of boiling water, and when nearly cold, add a large spoonful of brandy, and sweeten with lump-sugar. Give a large spoonful every half-hour. If much pain, give injections.

HUMORS.

Spring beer is good, putting in plenty of yellow-dock; rub a little on the face for slight eruptions, but never try to drive them away, for it is better for the health to have them come out, but diet and purify the blood. A little salt taken occasionally is good. Saffron is good to send out the humors. For boils, make a plaster of rye bread and honey, or flour and molasses if the former can not be obtained; change as often as it dries, until it comes to a head. Then make a poultice of bread and milk, and if very painful add laudanum. Epsom salts dissolved, and bathe the face where there are any eruptions, is good.

CATARRH IN THE HEAD.

Snuff fresh water every night and morning, and make a snuff of gum-arabic, gum-myrrh, and bloodroot pulverized; wash the head and neck frequently. This is a very common disease, and will end in consumption.

MEASLES.

Bathe the feet, putting a spoonful of ginger in the water; keep the patient comfortably warm; give cooling drinks. It is a mistaken notion to give hot drinks when a person has the measles. Something is required to allay inflammation, not increase it.

MUMPS.

Bathe the swelling with volatile ointment, and wrap in cotton, being careful not to take cold. Perspiration kept up by warm drinks, and the bowels kept regular.

SPINAL DIFFICULTIES.

Bathe in tepid salt and water is good, keeping very quiet, not using the arms much.

WORMS IN CHILDREN.

Sage, powdered fine and mixed with molasses, is good, adding a very little saleratus. Salt and water is good to prevent fits.

TO REMOVE PROUD FLESH.

Loaf-sugar pulverized very fine, and apply to the part. It is said to remove it without pain. Burnt alum is good, but causes it to smart.

AGUE IN THE FACE.

Make a poultice of Indian meal and poppy leaves, which should always be dried and put in a paper bag for use. Hops are also good, mustard or ginger poultices. A bag of salt heated very hot is good.

TOOTHACHE.

Hop water is very good to hold hot in the mouth, and is not injurious to the teeth. Red pepper and camphor, laudanum, peppermint, salt, and many other things put in the cavity of the tooth will stop toothache. Burnt alum is good, but the best thing is to have the tooth extracted, as bad teeth injure the health. An onion cut in two and placed upon each foot will give relief.

HEADACHE.

This is a very prevalent complaint, and arises from different causes. If owing to acidity in the stomach, a little soda will do it good. Hop tea, camomile, sage, Cayenne pepper, is good for nervous headache; a few drops of camphor or hartshorn will sometimes give relief; bathing the feet in warm, and the head in cold water, putting mustard poultices on the feet, and the back part of the neck, is good. If it proceeds from a deficiency of acid in the stomach, a lemon, or a few drops of nitric acid, will relieve; tie the head with a bandage very tight, applying a brown paper wet with salt and vinegar. If subject to the headache, it is advisable to die

NEURALGIA.

Bathing in cold water, particularly where the pain is located. A tea made of hops, valerian, motherwort, or sage, will quiet the nerves, and often afford relief. Camphor and water are good.

RHEUMATISM.

This is very much like neuralgia, and must be treated almost in the same way. Bathing well with cold water, and rubbing with a flannel to get up a circulation, is good; hop tea or brisk cider with ginger is good. Lemons are excellent for rheumatism.

HYDROPHOBIA.

Wash and cleanse the wound, then apply the nitrate of silver to every part of it. It should be done immediately.

STIFF JOINTS.

For stiff joints, take strong salt and water, beef's gall, one gill each, the yolk of four eggs beat up; mix well together, and apply three times a day.

QUINSY.

Inhale the steam of hops, or wormwood and vinegar, and bind some on the throat, is good. Gargle the throat with weak lye, and if much swelled, apply a slippery elm or flax-seed poultice made with weak lye.

TREATMENT OF COLDS.

If feverish, bathe the feet in warm water, take some hot herb tea, or hot lemonade, but use no spirits, as this will only increase the fever. Get up a perspiration, and be careful about exposure the next day.

ASTHMA.

Dissolve a pint of saltpetre in a pint of water, dip sheets of fine brown paper in till they become saturated, then dry the paper. Burn a strip of it in a close room, having the patient exhaling the flames of it.

FOR RHEUMATISM.

Take two drachms of camphor, gum guiacum one ounce, nitre one ounce, two drachms of balsam tolu, one quart of spirits; mix well, and take half a teaspoonful three times a day in a little water.

ANOTHER.

One pint of the best brandy, one ounce of guiacum powdered fine; take as much at a time as you can bear.

FOR A SPRAINED ANKLE.

Wash the ankle in cold salt and water, and keep the feet cool as possible, to prevent inflammation, and have it elevated on a cushion. Live on a low diet, and take some cooling medicine every day.

HOARHOUND CANDY.

Take fresh hoarhound as green as you can get it; cut up stalks and all; scald a pitcher, then put in the hoarhound, pressing it down with your hands. It should be two thirds full. Fill up with boiling water; cover perfectly tight, to prevent any of the strength escaping with the steam; set it close to the fire until it comes to a hard boil, then strain it and mix loaf-sugar to make a paste. Put it over the fire and boil until sufficiently hard. Try some in water; if crispy, it is done; then make into sticks.

SPITTING BLOOD.

Take three spoonfuls of sage juice in a little honey, or two spoonfuls of nettle juice. Alum dissolved in water is good.

TO PREVENT NAILS GROWING DOWN INTO THE TOES.

This is a very troublesome disease, but easily cured if managed rightly; take a sharp-pointed knife, and cut a furrow all along the top of the nail lengthwise; when it fills up, scrape it out again. This will cause the nail to contract at the top, and will loosen its hold from the flesh.

A CURE FOR BARBER'S ITCH.

Take corrosive sublimate, and add oil of almonds, apply to the face occasionally, and a cure will soon be effected.

CAMPHOR SPIRITS.

Every family should prepare the liquid camphor for convenience and economy. Buy three ounces of camphor gum and a quart of alcohol; break up the gum and put in a bottle; then pour on the alcohol, and cork closely. It is best to take some out for use, and keep the larger bottle well corked. For bathing it should have half whisky and half alcohol put on, the alcohol first to cut the gum, then add the whisky. For faintness or nervous pains, pour a few drops into a wine-glass of water and swallow it. Peppermint should be likewise prepared for family use. Purchase the oil, and pour on alcohol to cut it. It is much cheaper than to get it at the druggist's. It is said that a cranberry bound on a corn will soon cure it.

FOR WEAK EYES.

Take rose leaves and steep till the strength is out; then bottle and use as a wash. It is well to dry the leaves and keep in a paper bag. Cold tea is very good for weak eyes. Milk and water is also good. Twenty drops of laudanum and five of brandy in a wine-glassful of water is good; apply three times a day, hot.

A DRESSING FOR A BLISTER.

Pure hog's lard, three quarters of a pound, two ounces of white wax; melt in an earthen vessel; stir till cold, and keep covered up close.

TO PREVENT THE RECURRENCE OF BOILS.

Take a table-spoonful of yeast in a glass of water twice a day. The leaven of gingerbread is good to put on a boil.

CORNS.

Roast an onion in the ashes, and apply until cured. Dip a linen cloth in sweet oil, or, what is better, castor oil, and keep the part wrapped in it until a permanent cure is effected. This is also good for chilblains.

CURE FOR A COUGH.

Take half an ounce of gum-arabic, the same of liquorice-juice; dissolve the gum in warm water; squeeze in the juice of a lemon; add two drachms of paregoric, one drachm of squills. Cork it in a bottle and shake well. Take one tea-spoonful when the cough is troublesome.

MEDICAL EFFECTS OF HOT WATER.

In bruises, hot water is good to prevent stiffness and discoloration; also for removing pain. It should be applied as soon as possible, and as hot as it can be borne. Insertion in hot water will cure a whitlow, if done in season.

FOR CHAPPED HANDS.

Mix a quarter of a pound of unsalted hog's lard, which has been washed in cold water, and then rose-water, with the yolks of two eggs, and a large spoonful of honey; add as much fine oatmeal or almond paste as will work into a proper consistency, and rub in well before going to bed. Almond paste is very nice for the skin.

THE NAUSEOUS TASTE OF MEDICINE PREVENTED.

Chew a little orange or lemon-peel, a clove, or any spice you like before taking medicine; a peppermint lozenge is good, or a lump of sugar with a drop or two of peppermint put on. You will scarcely taste the medicine.

TO PURIFY THE AIR OF A SICK-ROOM.

Take six drachms of powdered nitre, and the same quantity of the oil of vitriol; mix together by adding to the nitre one drachm of the vitriol at a time, placing the vessel in which you are mixing it on a hot hearth or plate of heated iron; stir with a tobacco-pipe or glass rod; then place the vessel in the contaminated room. Dr. J. C. Smith obtained £5000 from the English Parliament for this recipe. Onions are good placed in a sick-room, although the smell is bad. Chloride of lime is good to cleanse a room.

STIES IN THE EYE.

Sties are little abscesses which form in the roots of the eyelashes, and are rarely larger than a pea. Bathe them frequently with warm water; when they break, use an ointment composed of one part citron ointment, and four of spermaceti well rubbed together, and apply along the edges of the eyelid.

LUMBAGO, OR STIFF NECK.

Dip a piece of flannel in scalding hot water; sprinkle some turpentine on and apply to the part affected by the pain; repeat this several times, and it will afford relief. One third hartshorn to two thirds oil, and rub with the bare hand, is also good.

TO MAKE PAREGORIC.

Take opium one drachm, flowers of benzoin one drachm, camphor two scruples, oil of anise one drachm, liquorice one ounce, spirits of wine one quart. Dose, a tea-spoonful for an adult.

GODFREY'S CORDIAL.

Dissolve half an ounce of opium, one drachm of the oil of sassafras in two ounces of spirits of wine. Mix four pounds of treacle with one gallon of boiling water, and when cold mix together. This is the celebrated cordial so much used for children.

A SYRUP FOR PURIFYING THE BLOOD.

Take six pounds of sarsaparilla, three ounces of gum-guiacum, two pounds of the bark of sassafras root, two pounds of elder-flowers, two pounds of burdock root; add one gallon of spirits and one gallon of water; boil and pour off the liquor till all the strength is obtained; boil down to six quarts; add fifteen pounds of sugar. The spirit should not be added till boiled down to two quarts. Yellow dock and sweet-apple tree bark should be added also. Put a tea-spoonful of saleratus to each bottle. Take a wine-glassful three times a day.

SPIRITS OF TURPENTINE will cure freezing if applied at once. It is also good for burns.

A TEA-SPOONFUL of castor oil and a table-spoonful of molasses mixed together, is a good remedy for hooping-cough; take daily.

FOR SCARLET FEVER, bathe the patient all over in weak lye.

AS MUCH Cayenne pepper, taken hot, as you can bear, is a sure remedy for sea-sickness.

ONE DROP of the oil of cinnamon will cure the hiccough.

TO TAKE OUT THORNS AND SPLINTERS.

Make a plaster of turpentine and tallow; spread on leather, and apply it. A decoction of the pine tree, sweetened with loaf-sugar, is an excellent remedy for a cold.

WHITLOW.

Steep in distilled vinegar, as hot as you can bear it, four or five times a day, for two days, then moisten a tobacco-leaf in the vinegar and bind round the part, and a cure follows.

IMPROVED METHOD OF TAKING SENNA.

When steeped, put in allspice or any other kind, and steep with it, and it will prevent the griping for which senna is noted.

FOR MEASLES, SMALL-POX, AND SCARLET FEVER.

Take elderblows, one lemon, a tea-spoonful of cream of tartar; pour on boiling water, and when cold, strain, and give a cupful every two hours.

FOR RHEUMATISM AND NEURALGIA.

Make a liniment of the tincture of belladonna one ounce, aconite half an ounce, chloroform half an ounce.

WALNUTS FOR MEDICINE.

Take when fit for pickling; lay them in a stone jar with plenty of moist sugar; place the jar in a kettle of boiling water, and simmer some time; the sugar when dissolved should cover the walnuts. In six months it will be fit for use; if older, it will be still better. One walnut is sufficient for a child six years old, as a purgative. These should always be prepared where there are children.

HUSK BEDS.

Select the inner husks; clip the ends, but not the butts; put them in the tick; do not split them; once in two years separate all the fine husks, dust, and pieces, and replenish with new ones. They are preferable for under-beds to straw.

DANDELION BEER.

Take two ounces or more of dandelion roots; after being well washed, boil in six quarts of water for thirty minutes; strain and add a pint of molasses, half a teacupful of yeast; let it ferment twelve hours. To be drank every morning and evening.

A FEW PRACTICAL HINTS ON GARDENING.

Every house, if possible, should have attached to it a good vegetable garden, it is so conducive to the health, happiness, and comfort of a family. A garden well managed will supply, with a little expense and trouble, a variety of nutritious and luxurious food the year round. Neither should the flower or fruit garden be forgotten or neglected. Every house can have a few trailing vines, some shrubbery and plants to adorn and beautify it, with little or no expense. Rose-bushes, lilacs, snowballs, syringa, and others are easily cultivated, and with their beauty and fragrance will contribute much to the enjoyment of home.

TOMATOES.

They should be sown in a hot-bed, and the last of May can be transplanted about four feet apart in rich ground. The great secret of transplanting is to do it in such a way as not to impede their growth. A hole made in the ground, and water poured in; then set the plant and press the dirt around well, shading it for a few days, is a very good way of doing it. When the tomato begins to set, cut off the top vines, and the tomatoes will be larger and better flavored.

CELERY

should be sowed in a hot-bed, and transplanted in rich compost and earth about six inches apart, in a deep trench, and as they grow, draw the earth around them, but not to touch the central part. It is a saline plant, and should be watered with salt and water. In the fall cover them up with earth and straw for winter use, or take them up carefully, so as not to break or bruise them, else they will rot. Lay them upright in a box of dry sand, and keep in the cellar.

CAULIFLOWER AND BROCCOLI.

These vegetables are cultivated like the common species of cabbage; grow in rich soil and occasionally sprinkle salt over them, the same as cabbage. Vegetable oysters are raised the same as other spindle-shaped roots.

ASPARAGUS.

If this is raised from the seed, it will take two or three years to bring it to maturity. The soil should be made rich; in the fall and in the spring the earth should be hoed two or three inches over the beds, and the compost mixed in; the weeds must be kept out, and when the tops are cut off, take them close to the surface. This plant is saline, and is benefited by sprinkling salt and water over.

RHUBARB.

This may be raised from the seed, but will take so long to bring to perfection that they should be started from the roots. It requires rich soil and good cultivation. The leaves are poison; the root is used for medicine.

EGG-PLANT

must be raised in a hot-bed, and transplanted in June, about two feet apart. Pepper-grass may be sown in drills with lettuce or alone. Nasturtions are very pretty as a flower, and are used for pickle. They require a frame-work.

MARTINOES

are easily cultivated; pour boiling water on the seeds; then plant in hills like cucumbers. When a pin will run through easily, they must be pickled.

PEPPERS.

There are many varieties of peppers, but the large red sweet pepper is best for pickling. They should be started in a hot-bed.

SHRUBS.

Give them a rich soil, and protect the tender ones in winter by covering with straw. Shrubs are generally obtained from cuttings, suckers, or buds. The suckers are young plants that shoot up around a shrub, which can be separated in autumn or spring, and transplanted. If cuttings are taken, they should be of last year's growth, and planted four or six inches from the end of the stem, or cut off the top of the stem, which is better. Rose-bushes should be pruned after they have done flowering; cut out the old wood, shorten shoots that have a good bud and are healthy. If insects are troublesome, steep tobacco leaves in water and sprinkle with it; examine the bushes, and if any worms are found, kill them; soot is good also. Never water plants when the sun shines; morning and evening is best, except when just transplanted, when they should be kept shaded. Fall is the best time to set out plants or shrubbery. Honeysuckles are increased by turning the ends downward into the ground.

TO OBTAIN DIFFERENT FLOWERS FROM THE SAME STEM.

Split a small twig of elder-bush lengthwise; scoop out the pith; fill with flower-seeds of different sorts, but which blossom about the same time; surround with mould; tie together, and plant the whole in the earth.

TO RESTORE FLOWERS.

Take a bouquet which has begun to fade, and immerse the ends in scalding water, deep enough to cover one third of the length of the stem; let them remain till the water is cold; then cut off the ends and put them in cold water.

TO HASTEN THE BLOWING OF FLOWERS.

Take sulphate or nitrate of ammonia four ounces, nitrate of potash two ounces, sugar one ounce, a pint of hot water, dissolve and keep in a bottle; for plants in pots, add a few drops in the water when watered.

GOOSEBERRIES.

It must be well trimmed every spring, never allowing two branches to rub against each other. Dig around it, and enrich the soil; sprinkle soap-suds from the wah-tub on and around it till it blossoms.

The currant should be cultivated in the same way, and the fruit will be larger and better flavored. Ashes applied to the roots are good.

RASPBERRIES.

The white and the large English raspberry are the best to cultivate. Set them in a moist soil, partly shaded, and they will produce large and well-flavored berries; keep them well trimmed and supported with frames.

BLACKBERRIES.

The Lawton and the white are the best flavored, and are easily cultivated. Set them in rich soil and keep trimmed.

STRAWBERRIES.

Set in a rich soil, with plenty of charcoal dust sprinkled and hoed in; keep out the runners, and you will have plenty of nice large berries. Hovey's Seedling, and Wilson's are the most acceptable to raise.

DAHLIAS.

These can be raised from the seed, but are better raised from the root. When they are done flowering, cut off the tops and let them ripen; if in any danger from frost, cover with earth five or six days; then dig up and lay in a box of dry sand; keep in the cellar if not too damp. They must not be kept too dry nor too damp. Take them out in April or earlier, and put them in light earth to sprout. About the last of May set out in beds well prepared with rich compost; place a stake near, and fasten with twine, that the wind may not blow them over.

GERANIUMS

are easily propagated from slips; in the summer may be placed out-doors; in the winter must be potted, and the ground kept moist. They do not require much sun.

CALLAS, OR ETHIOPIAN LILY.

This requires much watering, except while in blossom; give it plenty of air and light. It is best propagated by suckers.

MONTHLY ROSES.

Water them in proportion as they receive it. They need plenty of sun and air. They can be hardened to remain out-doors in winter.

THE CACTUS.

The cactus should have rich soil, kept moist, particularly about the time of blossoming, when they require more moisture.

DIRECTIONS FOR WASHING CALICOES.

Black calicoes are very apt to fade, and great care should be used in washing them. They should either be washed in water where potatoes have been boiled, or a starch-water made by scraping two or three potatoes. Pour boiling water on wheat-bran, then strain it, and when lukewarm wash them in that, using no soap. If there are any grease-spots on calicoes, a little hard soap should be rubbed on before going into the water, as the spots can not be seen after wetting them. They should not be washed in very hot water, as they are more liable to fade. Old soft soap a year old, will answer as well to wash with as hard soap; but new soap should never be used except for yellow. All colors should be rinsed well in clear water and dried in the shade. Alum is good to set the color of green; a little salt put in the rinsing water where blue, black or green are washed, will prevent the colors running into each other. As little soap as possible should be put into the water, and when calicoes fade, beef's gall should be put in. They should be rinsed the moment they are washed, and then hung up to dry—never allowed to remain wet any time.

DIRECTIONS FOR WASHING WOOLENS.

Take clear soft water, have it cold, and put a little soap in; if very dirty, make quite a suds, using hard soap, or old soft soap. Wash them perfectly clean, and rinse in cold water and hang up to dry. A little indigo in the rinsing-water makes them look nicer. Colored flannels that are inclined to fade, should be washed in beef's gall before washing in suds. Press them before they are dry. If woolens are washed in warm water, they should be dried in a heated room.

DIRECTIONS FOR WASHING WHITE CLOTHES.

Table-cloths or napkins that have fruit-stains or coffee on them, should have boiling water poured on, and let them remain until cold, then wash out the stains before putting into the suds, as soap will set them. If put into milk before washing, the stains will come out.

Clothes wash much easier in soft water than in hard, and do not require as much soap. If the water is hard, it can be softened by putting in a little bag of ashes while the water is heating, or a little sal-soda. It is a great saving of labor to use a pounding-barrel; have a hot suds and pound the clothes, then wring them out and wash in a tub. If any streaks are left in, soap them and put into cold water and boil. Then take them out, and pour on cold water sufficient to put the hands in, suds well and rinse with a little blueing put in the water; if blueing is put in the water while boiling, the clothes will look clearer, and they will not require as much in the rinsing-water. A little sal-soda will take the dirt out while boiling, but I think it injures the texture of the cloth, and should be well rinsed out; besides, it is not good to wash calicoes.

I have sometimes put a table-spoonful of spirits of turpentine in while boiling. It makes clothes look clear, but is not healthy to use in that way, and I think the best way is to use only soap and water. The suds should be saved to put on shrubbery, or to harden walks or yards, when graveled.

TO CLEAN WOOLEN AND SILK SHAWLS.

Pare and grate raw potatoes; pour on cold water, and let it remain half a day; then strain it through a sieve, and let the strained water settle again. Put a clean sheet on a table, and spread the shawl on smooth, pinning the corners down; take a clean sponge and dip in the potato-water; then wash it all over, and rinse in clear water with salt in it. Spread out to dry—if hung up, the colors will spread. Fold it quite damp, and put a heavy weight on, and let it remain to dry.

TO CLEAN SILKS AND RIBBONS.

Take equal quantities of soft soap and alcohol and molasses; mix well and lay the silk on a table, and rub over with the mixture, using a flannel cloth; rinse in cold water and hang up to dry; iron on the wrong side before it gets dry. Deer's horn sawed in small pieces, and boiled several hours in water, and then strained, is nice to dress silk with. It gives a stiffness and lustre almost like new. Camphene will extract grease, but will sometimes change the color. They should be dried in the open air, and ironed before they are entirely dry.

TO EXTRACT GREASE FROM MERINOS, SILKS, ETC.

Spread on magnesia or powdered chalk, and let it remain a few hours; then blow off and put on more, and continue this until the grease is removed.

TO RESTORE VELVETS.

Steam them by holding them over a kettle of boiling water, then pass the under side of the velvet over a warm smoothing-iron. The best way for doing this is for one person to hold the velvet tight, and another pass the iron over on the wrong side, then spread the velvet out, and pass a soft brush over the right side.

TO WASH RIGOLETTES, WOOLEN SHAWLS, AND ZEPHYR WOOL.

Put into warm water, and let it remain until nearly cold; then squeeze it with white soap, lay it in a colander and set it over a pan of boiling water, and let it remain until cool; then squeeze it out and shake it well; then place it over another pan of boiling water, rinsing it up and down until the soap is rinsed off, then shake it well and dry fast.

TO REMOVE MILDEW FROM LINEN.

Rub it over with soap; then scrape fine chalk or whitening, and rub on. Lay it in the sun, and wet it from time to time; if not removed, repeat the process. Lemon-juice and salt is also good.

TO REMOVE INK OR IRON-RUST.

Wet the place with sorrel or lemon-juice, and rub on hard white soap. As it is the acid which extracts, vinegar or any other acid will answer. It should be exposed to the heat. Colored cotton goods that have ink spilled on them, should be soaked in milk, either sour or sweet skim-milk, before wetting in water. Iron-rust can be taken out by applying lemon-juice and salt, and exposing it to the sun. A few crystals of oxalic acid on the spot, pour on a little warm water to dissolve it. It should be used with care, as it is poisonous.

TO REMOVE SPOTS OF PITCH OR TAR.

Scrape off all the pitch or tar you can, and then warm some lard, or any kind of oil will do; rub it well, and let remain in a warm place two hours; then rub on soap and wash in suds.

STAINS FROM BROADCLOTH.

Grind an ounce of pipe-clay fine, and mix twelve drops of turpentine, the same of alcohol; rub a small portion of this mixture with alcohol; then rub the spots, and let it remain until dry; then rub with a flannel cloth.

STAINS FROM SILKS.

Salts of ammonia mixed with lime, will take out stains of wine from silk. It is also good to renew the color if there are any spots.

STAINS FROM THE HANDS.

Mix equal proportions of oxalic acid and cream of tartar, and keep in a covered box; when used, dip the fingers in warm water, and rub on a little of the powder; when the stains disappear, wash with soap. This is poison, and should be kept out of the reach of children. Lemon juice, or any acid is good to take stains out.

TO TAKE STAINS FROM BLACK WOOLEN GARMENTS OR SILKS.

Wet the stain thoroughly with strong hartshorn, and if the color is not restored, repeat again next day. Should this also fail, wet with black ink, two successive days. Any dark silk can be done the same. Flowered silk may be cleaned by rubbing crumbs of bread on, and then brushing them off.

TO WASH A BLACK LACE VAIL.

Mix beef's gall with sufficient hot water to make it as warm as you can bear your hand in. Do not rub the vail, but squeeze it through; then rinse in two cold waters, the last adding a little indigo, and dry it. Pour water on a small piece of glue, put the vail in to stiffen it, squeeze it out and clap it; lay it on a linen cloth, and make perfectly smooth, then iron on the wrong side.

HEAT MARKS FROM MAHOGANY.

Pour lamp-oil on the spots, and rub with a soft flannel cloth; then pour on alcohol, and rub them with a clean soft cloth until dry. Ink may be taken out by putting on oxalic acid; after letting it remain a few minutes, rub with a cloth wet in warm water. Colored paint, carpets, or mahogany will require rubbing with hartshorn to restore the original color.

TO EXTRACT PAINT FROM CLOTHING.

Saturate the spots with spirits of turpentine, let it remain a few hours; then rub it between the hands, and wash with suds and rinse.

STARCH.

Starch may be made of potatoes, by grating them and then washing the pulp in several waters and straining it through a sieve, then allowing it to settle until morning; then pour off the water, and dry the starch on plates. Very nice starch can be made of corn in the same way. The white corn is the best. Poland starch is most used. Clothes that are not worn should never be put away in the starch, as it will rot things that are not exposed to the air.

TO MAKE STARCH.

Flour-starch is made by mixing the flour smooth with cold water, and then pour on boiling water, stirring all the time; boil five or six minutes, then strain through a cloth or bag, kept for the purpose. Poland starch is made in the same way as flour, but a small piece of spermaceti or lard will give a glossy appearance. The best way is to dissolve an ounce of gum-arabic in water, and bottle it up, and when starch is made, add a spoonful, and it will make linen look almost like those that are done up in cities.

RICE PASTE.

Mix rice-flour smooth with water to a thick paste; then pour on more water and boil until it is thick like starch, stirring all the time. When cool, it is nice to paste fine paper or pasteboard ornaments.

FRENCH POLISH.

Take a quarter of an ounce of gum-copal, gum-arabic, and one ounce of shell-lac; bruise them well, and put into a pint of spirits of wine; put in a bottle and cork; then shake well, and put in a warm place. In a few days they will be dissolved; then strain through a piece of muslin, and keep it corked for use.

TO MAKE HENS LAY IN WINTER.

Keep them in a warm place, with sand to roll in, and plenty of fresh water. They should have fresh meat occasionally, when they can not procure worms, and a change of food—buckwheat, corn, oats, etc. It is well to give them a hot mess every other day; such as hot potatoes, turnips, or meal scalded; add Cayenne pepper or ginger. All kinds of vegetables are good chopped raw, such as cabbage, carrots, turnips or potatoes. A little lime or bones burnt and pounded fine, and clam-shells, are good to form the shell. A box of ashes should always be put in their coop, or they will become filthy with lice. This will prevent it. Glass eggs, or wooden eggs painted white, should be put in the nest in the winter, for nest-eggs, as the hens will eat the eggs if left in the nests. When the chickens are hatched, the hen should be cooped in a garden, and allow the chickens to roam. They are of great service in a garden. Feed them on Indian meal, or pieces of bread soaked in water. They will almost get their own living in a garden. Give them plenty of fresh water, and buttermilk. Chickens will never have the gapes if not allowed to run where there is stagnant water. I have kept fowls over twenty years, and have never lost a chicken with the gapes. It is said that vinegar that has stood in iron, is a preventive, by putting a little in their food every day. Some say it is caused by worms in the throat, and that they may be reached and taken out with the end of a feather. No poultry should be kept longer than three years. They are best for laying the second year.

TO POLISH MAHOGANY FURNITURE.

Rub it with cold-drawn linseed oil, and polish with a dry, soft cloth. Do this once a week, and you will have a fine polish. The oil fills the pores, and hardens when exposed to the air, and the surface becomes much like glass.

TO CLEAN PAINT.

Put a little saleratus in the suds, and wash with a flannel cloth, then rinse and wipe with a linen cloth.

TO CLEAN PAPER WALLS.

Sweep down all the dust, and then rub with breadcrumbs, beginning at the top and rub down. The best way is to take a piece of bread.

TO REMOVE PAINT AND PUTTY FROM WINDOW-GLASS.

Rub on a little spirits of turpentine, until well saturated, then wash off and rub with a woolen cloth, or put saleratus in hot water, to make a strong solution; then let it remain until nearly dry; then rub with a flannel cloth.

CARPETS.

Carpets should be shook often to have them wear well, as the dust underneath collects and wears them out very fast. Straw put under a carpet makes it wear longer, and it will not require shaking so often. If there is any danger of moth, sprinkle tobacco on before putting down the carpet. Tea-grounds sprinkled on a carpet before sweeping, make it look nice. Grated raw potatoes will answer, but the tea-grounds should always be saved for this purpose. If there are any grease-spots, rub camphene on them. Chalk, grated and rubbed on, with a brown paper over, and then place a warm smoothing-iron on. When the paper is soaked with grease, apply another till all is extracted.

TO CLEAN BEDS AND MATTRESSES.

When feather beds become soiled, shake all the feathers down into one end of the tick, and wash; then shake the feathers back again, and wash the other end, in soap-suds. Take care to rinse well. Hang on a line to dry. Shake well two or three times a day, bringing in at night. Pillows may be washed by rubbing them with a soft brush dipped in warm suds; then rinse well, and lay on boards to dry, shaking well, and turning over occasionally. Hair-mattresses that have become hard and dirty, should be ripped up, and the ticks washed clean. Pick the bunches out of the hair and put it in a dry place for a number of days; then put back in the tick, and tack it.

TO WASH CARPETS.

Shake them well, and then tack them firmly down, and clean with a flannel cloth; add one quart ox-gall to three quarts of soft cold water. If there are any grease-spots, rub some of the gall on them, and then wash clean with a clean cloth. If very dirty, it may be washed with a broom and strong soap-suds; then rinsed well and hung up to dry.

CEMENT FOR GLASS.

Take ten ounces of isinglass, and dissolve it in a wine-glass of gin, before the fire. It should be warmed when applied, and put on with a camel's hair brush; the pieces joined and then bound together with strips of cloth.

CEMENT FOR CHINA.

Tie some lime powdered very fine, and sifted through a bit of muslin, on to the broken part; wet first with the white of an egg, and then join together.

CEMENT TO FASTEN THE HANDLES OF KNIVES AND FORKS.

Take brickdust and resin; melt together in a pipkin.

TO GILD OR SILVER LEATHER.

To ornament leather, powder some resin, and dust over the surface of the leather; then lay on the leaf and apply hot the letters or impression you wish to transfer; then dust off the loose metal with a cloth.

A CEMENT FOR EARTHENWARE

White lead, boiled in linseed oil, is good for common crockery or earthenware. Apply some on each broken piece, and join together. Let it remain till dry It is a good plan to keep this prepared. Boiling crockery in milk will cement it. As soon as broken, tie together and put into cold skim-milk and boil an hour; then take from the fire and let it remain till the milk becomes cold, when it can be taken out, and put away for two or three weeks before using.

CEMENT FOR IRONWARE.

Beat the whites of eggs to a froth, and stir lime into them till thick; then add iron filings. Fill the cracks with this, and let it remain a number of weeks without using it. Ashes and common salt made into a paste is good.

TO CLEAN VIALS OR BOTTLES.

Fill a large pot with water, and immerse the vials in it; put in a shovelful of ashes, and boil an hour gradually; then take from the fire, and when partly cool, take one by one and wash in clean suds, and rinse in cold water. If any thing is left in that will not come out, put in a little shot and shake around, and then rinse.

TO TEMPER EARTHENWARE OR IRON.

Before using earthenware, put it into cold water and heat slowly till the water boils; then take from the fire and let it remain till cold. Iron cooking utensils should be heated gradually and cooled slowly before using. New flat-irons, stoves, or any kind of iron, should be treated in the same manner.

CEMENT FOR BOTTLES OR CANS.

Mix together a quarter of a pound of sealing-wax, the same of resin, and a couple of ounces of beeswax. When it froths, stir with a tallow candle. As soon as it melts, use it by covering the corks.

TO POLISH SILVER, BRASS OR BRITANNIA.

Whiting or chalk should be used for silverware. Wet first with a little water, and rub with the chalk; then take a dry, fine cloth and rub dry. If stained, soak in soap-leys for two hours; then cover with chalk wet with vinegar, and let it dry on; then rub off, and rub over with dry bran. Rotten-stone and spirits are best for brass. Britannia ware should be rubbed with a flannel rag, dipped in oil; then washed in soap-suds and wiped dry. Rub with a dry flannel and chalk or whiting.

TO REMOVE RUST FROM CUTLERY.

Rub on a little sweet oil and let them remain a few days; then rub with a flannel cloth and Bristol brick. New knives and forks are very apt to rust, and great care should be taken to have them wiped dry before putting away, and if not used constantly they should be rubbed with sweet oil, and wrapped each one in brown paper. Ivory handles should never be wet, but wiped with a wet cloth, or the ivory will turn yellow.

TO KEEP CIDER SWEET.

Put a gill of white mustard in a barrel of cider; or a pint of clean wheat will keep it sweet for some time; but the most effectual way is to smoke the barrels before using with brimstone; then rinse well and put in your cider. It will not taste nor smell of the brimstone. When you bottle cider, put in a few raisins to make it brisk.

TO PRESERVE FURS AND FLANNELS.

Pack in a tight box, with camphor-gum or tobacco. A tallow candle is also a preventive. Woolen yarn, to be kept any time, should never be scoured, and the moths will never touch it. If moths get into a carpet, it is hard getting rid of them, as the eggs will hatch out, and the best way is to lay a wet cloth on the carpet, and iron over it. The heat and steam will destroy the eggs and not injure the carpet.

TO STAIN BEECH THE COLOR OF MAHOGANY.

Take a pound of logwood, and boil in four quarts of water, and add a double handful of walnut peelings; take out the chips, and put in a pint of good vinegar, and it is fit for use.

TO CLEAN MIRRORS AND GILT FRAMES.

Take a piece of sponge and wash clean; then dip in alcohol or spirits of wine, and rub over the glass, with whiting sifted on; then take a clean cloth, and rub well; then polish with a silk handkerchief. Be very careful not to touch the frame. If the frames are gilt, rub over with cotton wool. This will take off the dust without injuring the gilding. If the frames are varnished, rub with spirits of wine.

TO STAIN HORN TO IMITATE TORTOISE-SHELL.

Take an equal quantity of quicklime and red lead; mix with strong lye, and lay on the horn with a small brush; when dry repeat several times.

TO PREVENT WATER SOAKING

through boots and shoes, and making them wear as long as two pair. Take one pound of tallow, half a pound of resin, and melt together; warm the boots and apply until they will take no more. If a polish is wanted, let them dry, and then dissolve an ounce of beeswax, a tea-spoonful of lampblack, and an ounce of turpentine. Rub the boots over with this, but not near the fire.

LIQUID BLACKING.

Take a quarter of a pound of ivory-black, six gills of vinegar, and a table-spoonful of sweet oil, and two of molasses. Stir well together, and it is fit for use.

INK FOR MARKING LINEN WITH TYPE.

Dissolve one part of asphaltum in four parts of oil of turpentine; add lamp-black in sufficient quantity to render it of proper consistency to print with type.

INK FOR MARKING LINEN.

Dissolve two drachms of lunar caustic, half an ounce of gum-arabic in a gill of rain water. Wet the article to be marked in saleratus water, and dry; then pass a hot flat over, to make it smooth; then mark, and pass a hot flat over again. It should be corked tight and kept in the dark.

ANOTHER.

Take four drachms of lunar caustic, four ounces of water, sixty drops of nutgalls made strong by being pulverized and steeped in water.

FOR MAKING BLACK INK.

Take four ounces of nutgalls, two of copperas, one of gum-arabic; put the galls in a quart of water; soak eight or nine days where it will be warm, shaking it often; then add the copperas and gum, also half an ounce of alum well dissolved in warm water. It will be fit for use in a few days.

TO PRESERVE GRASSES.

Make a solution of alum water, a piece of alum the size of a hen's egg to a quart of water. Dip the grasses in, and then sprinkle with flour; they look quite pretty in the winter season, put in a vase with a few everlastings. Fruit and flowers may be preserved by dipping them into a solution of gum-arabic two or three times, allowing them to dry each time. They must be entirely immersed or they will not keep; tie a string to them and let into the liquid.

BLUE INK.

Dissolve a little indigo in oil of vitriol; dissolve a little gum-arabic in water, and add to it.

RED INK.

Boil an ounce of Brazil wood in half a pint of water for a quarter of an hour; add an ounce of alum and three drachms of gum-arabic.

Scarlet ink is made by dissolving vermilion in a solution of gum-arabic. Green ink may be made by mixing two ounces of verdigris, one ounce of cream of tartar, half a pint of water; boil until reduced one half; then filter.

TO MAKE PLASTER OF PARIS FIGURES LOOK LIKE ALABASTER.

Dip the figures in a strong solution of alum water

TO KEEP AWAY HOUSEHOLD VERMIN.

Sage put around where ants frequent is a preventive. It is said that the rattles of a rattlesnake will keep them away. Hellebore rubbed with molasses, and put in places where cockroaches frequent will soon destroy them. Flies can be thinned by putting strong soap-suds in a tumbler, and then put a piece of board on top with a hole in the middle, and a little molasses on the under side. The molasses will draw the flies, and they will fall into the water.

To KEEP AWAY mosquitoes, attach a piece of flannel to the top of the bedstead, wet with camphorated spirits, and they will leave the room.

FOR BED-BUGS, get a sixpence worth of corrosive sublimate; put it in a bottle, and add a gill of whisky; shake it up well, and then take a feather and put it around the bedstead twice a year, and you will never be troubled with bugs. Red peppers boiled in water and the bedstead washed in the water is good, but I have never tried any thing so effectual as the corrosive sublimate; the bottle should be marked poison. Spearmint put around places where mice infest will drive them away, as they have a great aversion to it.

GRAFTING.

Melt beeswax and tallow together, stirring in a little chalk, if handy. While hot, dip in some strips of rags, and put on so as to prevent the escape of the sap or the introduction of water.

TO MAKE COURT-PLASTER.

Suspend black silk or white on a frame; then dissolve isinglass and apply with a brush; let it dry, and then repeat it; then cover with a strong tincture of balsum of Peru. This is the real English court-plaster. The more common is covered with the white of an egg.

TO MAKE BLACKING.

One pound of ivory-black, well pulverized, half a pound of loaf-sugar, half an ounce of oil of vitriol, six ounces of sweet oil, one gallon of vinegar; stir it well, and it produces a fine polish.

OIL OF FLOWERS.

Take thin pieces of cotton wadding and dip in pure Florence oil or sweet oil, and lay in a china dish; cover it thick with rose-leaves, or any flowers from which you wish to get perfume. Lay on another layer steeped in oil, and continue this until full; cover it closely, and set in the sun a week. Take out the leaves and squeeze the oil in vials.

A DELICATE CEMENT FOR GLASS OR CHINA.

One ounce of mastic put in as much spirits of wine as will dissolve it; soak an ounce of isinglass in water until soft; then dissolve in rum or alcohol till it forms a glue; add a quarter of an ounce of gum ammonia, well rubbed and mixed. Put the two mixtures together over a gentle heat until united; then keep in a vial well corked. When used, place in a kettle of warm water; warm the articles to be mended; apply the cement and put tight together for several hours, and it will be scarcely perceptible.

WASHING RECIPE.

Mix a gill of alcohol with a gallon of soft soap; mix well, and apply the soap in the usual way, letting them remain several hours in the suds; then wash in the usual way and boil; they will require very little rubbing.

ANOTHER.

Take four ounces of borax; pour four quarts of boiling water on, and when dissolved, add three pints of soft soap. Use as above.

ANOTHER.

One ounce of borax, eight quarts of water, one pint of soap; boil all together twenty minutes; when partly cool, soak the clothes over night in some of it. Wash the next morning; boil and rinse.

ANOTHER.

Pour two quarts of boiling water on half a pound of soda; then take half a pound of hard soap cut fine; put on the fire with two quarts of cold water; when dissolved, add the soda; mix well, and let it stand till cold. Soak your clothes, rubbing the seams and dirtiest parts some; let them remain until morning; then wring them out, or boil in the same water if you like, but add a pint of the soda liquid, and boil twenty minutes; then rinse, and the clothes will look well. A little spirits of turpentine put into clothes while boiling makes them look clear.

TRANSPARENT JAPAN VARNISH.

Eight ounces of oil of turpentine, six ounces of oil of lavender, one drachm camphor, two ounces bruised copal; dissolve the whole. To be used for tin-ware.

TO REMOVE MILDEW.

Pour a quart of boiling water on two ounces of chloride of lime; then add three quarts of cold water, and soak the linen in it twelve hours. This is preferable to any other recipe that I have seen.

TO CLEAN WHITE FEATHERS.

Wash them in soft water with white soap, and blue; rub them through white paper, and beat them on paper; then shake them before the fire; dry them in the air, and curl them.

TO CURL FEATHERS.

Heat them gently before the fire; then with the back of a knife applied to the feather they will curl quickly.

TO CLEAN KID GLOVES.

Take a little camphene and a small piece of camphor and rub on with a piece of sponge, having the glove on the hand; wet it as little as possible; then lay on a clean towel, and wipe with a dry cloth; blow in the fingers, and hang up to dry, or keep on the hands till dry. Sometimes a crust of stale bread will clean, if not too dirty. If greasy, a little magnesia is good. A piece of India rubber is good to keep them clean.

TO BLEACH WOOL, SILK, AND STRAW.

Take a barrel and put a small kettle or basin in, with pounded brimstone in it; take live coals and put in, or it is best to put the coals in first, then the brimstone on top. Hang the straw on a stick and put across the barrel, and cover tight. Flannels that you wish to bleach, put on top; continue this till they are bleached white; let them lie loose. The straw should be soaked in pearlash water until yellow before putting in. Brimstone will take stains out of cotton or linen goods by holding them over.

TO DYE GLOVES.

Put them on the hands and take a soft brush; dip into any dye you wish to color them, wetting them as little as possible. For a York tan, steep saffron several hours in hot water, and wet with either a soft brush or sponge.

KNIVES AND FORKS.

Clean ebony handles with a soft cloth dipped in sweet oil; after laying awhile, wipe with a clean towel. Ivory handles should be washed with a flannel, soaped, using warm water; then wipe dry with a towel; soak occasionally in alum water to preserve their whiteness; the water must be cold; let them lie an hour in it; then take them out and brush them. Wet a towel in cold water, squeeze out, and wrap around the handles, leaving them in to dry gradually; if dried too fast out of the alum water, they will be injured. This will make them very white.

A CHEAP PAINT.

Take one bushel of unslacked lime and slack with cold water; add twenty pounds of Spanish whiting, seventeen pounds of salt, and twelve pounds of sugar; strain through a wire sieve, and it will be fit for use after reducing with cold water. This is for outside buildings. Put two coats on wood and three on brick; let each coat dry before putting on another. For painting inside, use only five pounds of salt and three of sugar. Make it any color you please; for green, use chrome green; for lead and slate, use lampblack; for yellow, ochre and chrome yellow.

TO MAKE A SIMPLE WHITE PAINT.

Skim-milk, two quarts, eight ounces of unslacked lime, six ounces of oil, white Burgundy pitch two ounces, Spanish white three pounds; the lime to be slacked in water exposed to the air; mix in about one fourth of the milk; the oil, in which the pitch is to be previously dissolved, must be added a little at a time; then the rest of the milk, and afterward the Spanish white. This quantity will cover twenty yards, two coats, and the expense will not be more than tenpence.

FOR SCOURING BOARDS.

Use three parts of sand and one of lime; no soap is required.

WHITEWASH OF THE PRESIDENT'S HOUSE IMPROVED.

Take half a bushel of unslacked lime and slack it with boiling water; cover it tight; strain it and add a peck of salt dissolved in warm water; three pounds of ground rice boiled to a thin paste; put in boiling hot half a pound of Spanish whiting, and a pound of clear glue, dissolved in warm water; mix, and let it stand several days; then put it in a kettle and heat it hot, and put on with a brush.

A SIMPLE WHITEWASH.

Take unslacked lime and slack by pouring on boiling water; cover tight, and when cool enough, put on with a brush. A handful of salt will make it look nice, but it is more liable to scale off. A little skim-milk is good to thin it with. If your walls are very smoky, put in a little ashes for the first coat. A little blueing in the second coat looks well.

TO SEPARATE BEESWAX FROM THE COMB.

Put it in a pan with holes in the bottom, and set it in the oven or a grate; put another pan under, half-full of water; the wax will melt and drop in the water, when it can be taken out.

ANOTHER.

Tie it in a bag and put it in a kettle of water, with a weight on top. The wax will rise to the top, when it can be taken off.

POISONS.

Every person should endeavor to inform themselves of the nature and antidotes of poison. It is generally so sudden that a few hours' waiting for medical aid might prove fatal, as it will admit of no delay. The first thing is to find out what has been taken; the next is to use remedies, and if one fails, try others.

ANTIDOTE FOR ACIDS.

Acids cause great heat and a burning sensation in the mouth and stomach, an inclination to vomit, hiccough, a burning thirst, great pain in the bowels, and soreness. Give an ounce of magnesia in a pint of water, a wine-glassful every two minutes. Soda or saleratus, dissolved in plenty of water, is also good, but the magnesia is better. Flax-seed tea, rice water, or water alone is good. An ounce of soap dissolved in a pint of water, and given, a wine-glassful every two minutes, is good. No nourishment should be taken but sweetened rice-water for several days.

ALKALIES.

They are the reverse of acids, and acids are given as a remedy; two table-spoonfuls of vinegar or lemon-juice in water; then drink large quantities of soap and water.

ARSENIC.

Symptoms: vomiting and convulsions. Give ipecac or something to assist vomiting—large doses of cold water and sugar. Hydrated peroxide of iron, charcoal, magnesia, chalk, lime-water, and whites of eggs are also good.

TARTAR EMETIC.

Peruvian bark or white oak.

OPIUM OR LAUDANUM.

Dash cold water on the head; give strong tea or coffee, and acid drinks; give a dose of Cayenne pepper or mustard and water alone, and keep the patient in motion. Sometimes a table-spoonful of vinegar will relieve.

PRUSSIC ACID.

Hot brandy and water, hartshorn, soda, or turpentine. It is said that immersing the patient in cold water will neutralize this poison.

MUSHROOMS.

Mix three grains of tartar emetic, twenty-five of ipecac, and an ounce of salts dissolved in a glass of water. Give by degrees till it vomits the patient; then give vinegar and water.

SALTPETRE.

Give emetics and plenty of rice-water, flax-seed tea, milk and water.

CORROSIVE SUBLIMATE.

Give whites of eggs mixed with water, or soap and water freely.

SNAKE BITES, OR MAD DOG.

Apply a ligature above the part bitten; then apply a cupping-glass, or it is better to cut out the bite, and then burn with caustic; put in a piece of cotton saturated with it. As soon as it is cut take off the ligature. A decoction of Spanish flies and turpentine should be applied to the skin around the wound to excite inflammation and suppuration. Keep up the discharge of matter some time. Charcoal made into a paste with hog's lard is a good antidote for the bite of snakes; so is the bark of yellow poplar; bruise it; then make a poultice of it and apply to the wound; bathe all around the part that is bitten with a strong decoction of the same, and drink a pint every hour.

ALCOHOL.

Give an emetic and dash cold water on the head; give ammonia.

VERDIGRIS.

Give white of egg and plenty of water.

CHARCOAL.

Many persons are killed by sleeping in apartments where coal is burnt, on account of the carbonic gas.

Remedy: remove the patient to the open air; dash cold water on the head and body; stimulate the lungs and nostrils by hartshorn; at the same time rub the chest briskly.

NITRATE OF SILVER.

Give a strong solution of common salt, and then emetics.

TOBACCO.

Give an emetic; then strong dose of tea.

LEAD.

Give Epsom salts or some carthartic; if the symptoms continue, do as directed for acid. In almost all cases of poison, emetics should be administered the first, and whatever you have on hand; ground mustard stirred up in warm water, may be given every few minutes, until the patient vomits freely.

VARNISH TO MAKE WOOD LOOK LIKE IVORY.

Take half an ounce of isinglass; boil gently in half a pint of water; when dissolved, strain it and add flake powder till it becomes white as cream; give the wood three or four coats of this, letting each coat dry before putting the other on; then smooth it with a damp rag. If when mixed it looks too white, add a few grains of carmine white or chrome yellow.

CEMENT FOR GLASS OR WOOD.

Dissolve common glue, and add to it finely-sifted wood ashes till quite thick; then apply while hot, and press the sides firmly together. This is said to be very adhesive to wood.

CEMENT FOR GLASS.

Boil one ounce of isinglass in two wine-glassfuls of spirits of wine.

FOR ROSE-BUSHES.

Take the soot from the chimney, and pour on water; let it remain until the strength is entirely out; then sprinkle your bushes with the liquor, and it will prevent the worm from injuring them. As soon as the worm makes its appearance, the leaves should be carefully examined, and every worm destroyed, or they will in a short time destroy the bush.

TO MAKE CABBAGES OR ASPARAGUS GROW.

Sprinkle salt over cabbage occasionally while heading, and the heads will be firmer and much larger. It is also a great improvement to asparagus. Old brine which has been used for other purposes is good.

CEMENT FOR WOOD.

Take beeswax and resin, equal quantities; melt them and add powdered chalk, until sufficiently thick. A strong solution of glue and whiting makes a good cement for ivory.

TO COLOR GOLD.

Make a solution of two ounces of saltpetre, two of alum, and one of sal-ammoniac, and dip the article in to be colored.

TO WASH DELAINES OR CALICOES THAT FADE.

Pour boiling water on wheat bran, and let it remain until nearly cold; then strain, and it is ready for use. You will require no soap. It will make delaines look like new.

SUBSTITUTE FOR COURT-PLASTER.

Clean hogs' feet as for cooking; boil to a jelly; then spread on silk, and it will be equal to any adhesive plaster used.

TO PREVENT INSECTS FROM DESTROYING ROSE-BUSHES.

Take one peck of soot, one quart of unslacked lime, three gallons of water, and let it remain twenty-four hours; when the soot rises to the surface, skim it off. Use a syringe for applying the water.

MAKING SOAP.

Take a barrel without a bottom; set it on a large flat stone or plank, with a channel cut for the lye to run. Or, what is still better, have a pine tub made at the cooper's, larger at the top than at the bottom.

Have a large hole bored about two inches from the bottom, with a plug to fit in. Put in the bottom straw, then a peck of lime, and fill up with good wood-ashes. (Any hard green wood makes good ashes.) If you have a tub made, it will last many years, and is much more convenient than a barrel. If the ashes are wet while packing in the tub, it will get to running much sooner. Make a hole in the middle of the tub and pour on water. Hot water will get the strength out sooner than cold. Five bushels of good ashes will make a barrel of soap. When they have been well soaked, take out the plug and the lye will run off clear; if not, pour back on the leach until it does. It must bear up an egg plump, or it will not make soap. Use the first to eat up the grease; the weaker will answer to fill up.

Put all your grease in a large iron kettle, and make a slow fire under it; stir with a stick constantly, until it is warmed through; then pour in your strongest lye; a pailful first, and stir well. Watch it carefully or it will boil over; if it does, add more lye, and continue this until the grease is entirely eaten up. Strain it into a barrel while hot, and fill up as fast as you draw off your lye, and you will have good soap. Should your lye be too strong to make it come soap, add a pail of water. Another way is to cleanse all your grease and put it in a barrel and pour on your lye; in a few weeks you will have nice white soap. Another method is to have half a barrel of lye, and put in your grease through the year, and at the end you will have a barrel of soap without any trouble.

To cleanse grease, put in a little strong lye, and boil it thoroughly; then fill up with cold water and the grease will float; then skim off.

POTASH SOAP.

Take twenty-five pounds of grease melted, eighteen pounds of potash dissolved in four pails of water; boil till dissolved; put the grease and two pails of hot lye in a barrel, the next day two more, and the next two more; then fill up the barrel—a pailful of hot water each day—stirring it well, and it will be good soap. The sediment of the potash is not good.

HARD SOAP.

Put to a pail of nice soft soap, one pint of salt; boil it, and then take it off and stand until cold; when hard, take from the lye and heat slowly. If you wish to have it yellow, add palm-oil, and pour in wooden vessels. When cold, separate it again from the lye, and cut in bars. Let them stand in the sun to dry.

ANOTHER METHOD.

Take sixteen pounds of soft soap, boil two hours with twelve pounds of salt, and it will make ten pounds of hard soap. When melted over as the above recipe, add a little resin. Scent it with fragrant oil if you like.

BAYBERRY AND MYRTLE SOAP.

Dissolve two pounds and a quarter of white potash in five quarts of water. Boil over a slow fire ten pounds of bayberry, tallow or myrtle wax, with it; then add a tea-cup of cold water, and boil ten minutes; scent with any fragrant oil, and turn in moulds to dry. Let it remain a week or more; then remove it. This is good for chapped hands; also for shaving.

CASTILE SOAP

Is made by boiling common soft soap three hours and a half in lamp-oil.

WINDSOR SOAP.

Slice the best white soap and melt it over a slow fire; when melted take off, and when lukewarm add oil of caraway, or any other fragrant oil. Turn into moulds and let it remain in a dry place a week.

TRANSPARENT SOAP.

Take equal parts tallow soap, made perfectly dry, and spirits of wine; put into a copper still, and plunge into a water-bath furnished with its capital and refrigeratory. The heat applied to effect the solution, should be as slight as possible, to avoid evaporating too much of the alcohol. The solution being effected, it must settle, and after a few hours the clear liquid is drawn off into tin frames, into forms desired for the cakes of soap. It will not be transparent until several weeks' exposure to dry air. It is colored with strong alcoholic salution of ochre for the rose tint, and turmeric for the yellow.

NICE SHAVING SOAP.

Take one pound of old Windsor soap, a quarter of a pound of Castile soap, a gill of lavender-water, a gill of cologne, and a very little alcohol. Boil until thoroughly mixed.

TO CLEAN SILK.

Take a quarter of a pound of soft soap, a tea-spoonful of brandy, and a pint of gin; with a sponge wash each side; then wash in two or three waters, and iron on the wrong side.

WASH-BALLS.

Take three quarters of a pound of Castile soap, cut thin, two ounces of alcohol, one ounce of borax, half a pound of Indian meal; mix and dissolve by gentle heat; add any perfume you like, and make into balls. This is excellent for the skin.

DRESSING SKINS WITH THE FUR ON.

As soon as the skin comes from the animal, stretch it on a board, flesh side out; then apply an equal mixture of salt and alum, pulverized together. Let them remain some time; then wash in warm soapsuds; dry moderately; rub soft with the hands.

HONEY SOAP.

Take a quarter of a pound of honey, a quarter of a pound of the otto of citronella, and twenty-five pounds of melted bar soap. It should be put in an iron vessel, and set into another of hot water, to be melted. This is very nice for the skin.

ALMOND SOAP.

Take a quarter of a pound of the otto of almonds, and twenty-five pounds of melted bar soap. A very small quantity of water should be added while melting; stir with a stick until it becomes smooth; then it may be perfumed or colored; then pour into bars, cut in squares and stamped. Vermilion dyes soap pink, and smalt a blue color.

ROSEMARY SOAP.

Take one and a half pounds of the essential oil of rosemary, and sixty pounds of melted soap; proceed as for almond soap.

HARD SOAP. NO. 2.

Take three fourths of a pound of fresh slacked lime, one gallon of water; dissolve one pound of sal-soda in another gallon of water, and boil all together fifteen minutes; then let it settle. A white precipitate of chalk will fall at the bottom of the vessel, and the clear liquid will be a caustic lye; pour this off, and boil your grease till it becomes soap, then pour into moulds, and when cold it will be hard soap. The secret of making soap is to have an alkaline lye of sufficient strength, and continue boiling until the chemical union of the grease and alkali is effected.

Resin is used for common hard soaps, as it unites with alkalies and tends to make soap harder than grease alone. White soap should be made of tallow. Any family may prepare their own fancy soap by melting good bar soap in a tin vessel, placed in a kettle of water, and adding any of the essential oils, at the rate of one ounce of oil to five pounds of soap. Whenever the oil is mixed with the melted soap, it must be cooled quickly or the perfume will evaporate. Otto of roses, musk, lavender, bergamot, or almost any kind, may be used.

FOR DYEING.

Light colors should be colored in brass or tin; dark colors in iron. Materials should be clean and free from grease. Wet them so that they will not spot, and rinse well, that they may be free from suds.

COCHINEAL TO COLOR WOOLEN OR SILK.

Pound two ounces of cochineal fine, and pour on cold water sufficient to wet two pounds of cloth, (for it will color that quantity;) let it boil up in brass or tin; then add four ounces of muriate of tin, one of cream of tartar; wet your clothes in warm water, and put in; stir well and take out, and dry in the shade, and you will have a beautiful color.

TO COLOR YELLOW ON COTTON.

For six pounds of cotton goods, use nine ounces of sugar of lead, six of bichromate of potash; wet the goods thoroughly in cold water, dissolve the potash in a tin vessel with four quarts of cold water, the sugar of lead in as much, but keep them separate. Dip the goods into the sugar of lead, and wring out then in the potash, and you will have a splendid color. If required deeper, dip in the sugar of lead again, then in the potash, several times alternately; then dry in the shade.

TO COLOR ORANGE.

Make a strong lime-water as for whitewashing. It should be made the day before wanted. Let it settle, for if there is any settles it will not color. The stronger the lime water the better color you will have. Put some in an iron kettle, and when it boils dip in the yellow which you have just colored, while wet; stir well with a stick, and take out; hang up to dry. It must be done very quickly or it will be spotted.

TO COLOR COTTON LEMON COLOR.

To two pounds of cloth take six ounces of sugar of lead dissolved in a pailful of hot water; four ounces of bichromate of potash in a pailful of cold water. Dip your cloth in the lead water first, then in the potash water, several times back and forth. Dry in the shade.

TO COLOR GREEN COTTON GOODS.

Color yellow by the recipe below, and dip in the chemical blue, and hang up to dry in the shade. These colors must all be cold, and they will not fade.

TO COLOR BLUE COTTON GOODS.

Use the chemical boxes of blueing. No certain rule can be given, as some boxes are much better than others. Use cold water, and dip your goods in cold water first, then in the blue, and if not deep enough add more blue; wring out and dry in the shade. It will not color woolen.

TO DYE BLACK.

To each pound of goods to be dyed allow a pound of logwood chips, or a quarter of a pound of extract of logwood, a small bit of copperas, and sufficient vinegar to wet the goods. If the chips are used, put in a bag, and soak over night in an iron vessel; then heat it next day and add the vinegar and copperas. Wet the goods in hot water and put in; let them steep all day; take out two or three times and air, or they may remain another day; wash until the dye will not come off.

ANOTHER.

Take the common horse sorrel, and steep in an iron kettle two or three hours; then put in half a pound of the extract of logwood, and have your goods perfectly clean; dip in a strong soapsuds before putting in; then let them steep all day; take out and air several times; then wash as above. This will color three pounds of woolen goods.

SLATE COLOR.

One paper of ink-powder, one quart of vinegar, and water enough to wet the goods. It must be done in brass. This makes a beautiful slate color. Sugar-loaf paper boiled in water and set with alum, makes a purple slate color; but it is difficult to obtain now, as sugar does not come in loaf at the present time. Tea-grounds boiled in iron and set with copperas, will make a slate, both for cotton and woolen. Birch bark, or black walnut bark, boiled in brass, and set with copperas, makes a nice color. Set with alum, the birch bark will make a bright nankeen color.

ROYAL PURPLE.

Soak logwood chips in soft water until the strength is out; then add alum—a tea-spoonful to a quart of the liquor. If not bright enough, add more alum. Rinse and dry. When the dye is exhausted, it will color a fine lilac.

BLUE OR GREEN PER POUND.

Take one ounce and a half of the oil of vitriol, a quarter of an ounce of Spanish indigo, which will answer just as well as the East-India indigo, which is much higher. Stir well together, and add a lump of pearlash of the size of a pea. As soon as the fermentation ceases, bottle it, and it will be fit to use the next day. Be careful not to let it get on cotton cloths, or it will eat them. Chromic blue is made in the same way, only using half the quantity of vitriol. This dye will only answer for silk and woolen goods. For blue, have your water warm, and add some of the mixture; put in your cloth without crowding, and let it remain till colored, keeping it warm but not boiling. Do not wring them, but drain; then hang up to dry in a shady place. When dry, wash them in lukewarm suds to prevent the vitriol from injuring them. For green, mix the above mixture with yellow dye, but do not let it boil. It must be used with care, as it is poison.

A NANKEEN COLOR.

A pailful of lye, with a piece of copperas as big as a hen's egg boiled in it, will produce a nankeen color that will not fade.

YELLOW DYES.

Take equal parts of common potash and annotto; boil in soft water. When dissolved, take it from the fire, let it cool, and put in the goods; set them by the fire, and let them remain until the right color. To dye an orange color, tie annotto in a bag, and squeeze it in soapsuds; put in your goods and boil until the proper shade; drain them, but not wring, and dry in the shade. When dry, wash in soapsuds. Fustic colors a nice yellow; hickory bark, peach leaves or saffron, set with alum, make a good yellow color.

TO COLOR MADDER.

Prepare a brass kettle with two gallons of water; bring it to a steady heat; then add three ounces of alum, and one ounce of cream of tartar; put in your cloth, and steep two hours; then take out and rinse in cold water. Empty your kettle, and fill with as much water as before; then add your madder, and rub well before putting in your cloth. When the dye is as warm as you can bear your hand in, put in the cloth, and let it remain an hour, and keep a steady heat; keep it in motion constantly; then boil fifteen minutes; air and rinse it. This will color one pound.

SCARLET.

Dip the cloth in a solution of alkaline or metallic salt, then in a cochineal dye, and let it remain some time, and it will come out permanently colored.

ANOTHER WAY.

Half a pound of madder, half an ounce of cream of tartar, one ounce of marine acid to one pound of cloth. Put all together, and bring the dye to a scalding heat. Put in your cloth, and it will color in ten minutes. The dye must only be scalding hot. Rinse in cold water.

CINNAMON.

For twenty-four yards of woolen cloth, take three pounds of ground camwood, three pecks of butternut bark; put your water in a kettle, and let it boil to extract the strength; put in your cloths, and simmer slowly one hour; stir often; take it out and air it; then put back, and let it remain as long again. If not dark enough, dissolve a little copperas and put in. Boil a few minutes, and rinse in cold water. Butternut bark, or the bark off the nut, makes a very pretty color, set with alum. The color is very much like Scotch snuff.

TO COLOR CARPET RAGS ALL ONE COLOR.

Take dark woolen rags, and boil, or simmer rather, in a dye of redwood and madder, half and half; soak the madder in vinegar over night, and set the color with alum; boil in brass. After taking out the woolen rags, put in the calicoes and boil. If not deep enough, add more redwood.

TAN.

Put the cloth in the vats, and let it remain four or five days; then dip in a strong limewater, and rinse in cold water and dry, or you may get some of the tanner's liquid, and heat boiling hot, and put in your cloth and color in a day.

FOR THE TOILET.

FOR REMOVING FRECKLES.

Take one ounce of rectified spirits of wine, a teaspoonful of muriatic acid, applied with a camel's hair brush, two or three times a day.

ANOTHER.

Use burnt alum and lemon-juice.

ANOTHER.

One ounce of bitter almonds, the same of barley flour; mix with honey, and anoint at night, wash off in the morning.

CHAPPED LIPS.

By the frequent use of honey-water, and protecting the lips from the cold, they will be speedily cured. This is also good for chapped hands. Apply it at night, upon retiring to bed, and put on kid gloves.

LIP SALVE.

To a pint of white vinegar, put an ounce of lavender flowers; add the rind of a lemon cut thin; steep twenty-four hours in a stone jar; then filter, and put in a bottle, corking tight.

LEMON CREAM FOR SUNBURN AND FRECKLES.

Put two spoonfuls of fresh cream into half a pint of milk; squeeze in the juice of a lemon, half a glass of brandy, a little alum and loaf-sugar; boil the whole, and skim well, and when cool it is fit for use.

LOTIONS FOR WRINKLES.

Take a weak barley-water, one pint; strain it, and add twelve drops of balm of Mecca; shake it well together, till the water assumes a whitish appearance. Wash the face in soft water, and then apply once a day. It will beautify the face, preserve the freshness of youth, and give a brilliancy to the skin.

TO IMPROVE THE SKIN OF THE HANDS AND ARMS.

Take equal weights of Venice soap and lemon-juice; when dissolved, add one ounce of the oil of bitter almonds, and an ounce of the oil of tartar. Mix well till it has acquired the consistency of soap.

TO DARKEN THE HAIR.

Wash the head in spring water, and comb the hair in the sun, having dipped the comb in oil of tartar. Do this three times a day for a fortnight.

OIL FOR THE HAIR.

One half sweet oil and half brandy is very nice for the hair, or alcohol and castor oil is also good. The castor oil should be boiled before using. Scent with any thing you like.

MACASSAR OIL FOR THE HAIR.

Take half an ounce of alkanet root, and divide into four parts; tie up each part in a bit of clean thin muslin; put them in a large tumbler or earthen vessel, and pour on half a pint of the best fresh olive oil; cover up tight, and let it remain a week. Then take out the little bags carefully, and lay them in a saucer. The oil will be colored a beautiful crimson. Put into a bottle any perfumery you like, such as oil of roses, oil of pink, extract of violets. The pungent oils are not good for hair, and should not be used for scenting Macassar oil. After filling your bottle or vials, tie a bit of white leather over the corks. Do not shake it when used, but pour a little in a saucer, and with the finger rub into the roots of the hair. The bags of alkanet will answer to use again.

MACASSAR OIL—ANOTHER WAY.

Take   quarts of common oil, half a pint of spirits of wine, three ounces of cinnamon powder, two ounces of bergamot. Heat them together in an earthen vessel; then remove from the fire, and add four small pieces of alkanet root; keep it closely covered for several hours; then filter and put in vials, with white leather tied over the corks.

TO MAKE SOFT POMATUM.

Beat half a pound of fresh lard in water; then soak it in rose-water; drain it, and beat with two spoonfuls of brandy; drain it from this, and add any scent you like.

ANOTHER WAY.

Soak half a pound of beef's marrow, and a pound of fresh lard in water two or three days, changing and beating it every day; put it to drain, and when dry, put into a jar, and set it in a kettle of water. When melted, pour it into a basin, and add two spoonfuls of brandy; beat it well; then pour off the brandy, and add lemon or any scent you like.

HARD POMATUM.

Prepare equal quantities of beef marrow, and mutton tallow suet, in cold water as above; then brandy to preserve it, and scent with any thing you like. Put into moulds or vials the size you want, and when cold, break the vials, and put paper around.

POMADE DIVINE.

Take a pound and a half of beef marrow; put it into a vessel of spring-water, and let it remain ten days, changing the water every day, night and morning; then steep it in rose-water twenty-four hours; drain it in a cloth till dry; then take an ounce of storax, gum-benjamin, odoriferous cypress-powder, or of Florence, each an ounce, half an ounce of cinnamon, two drachms of cloves, two of nutmegs, all finely powdered; mix with the marrow, and put into a pewter pot that holds three pints. Make a paste of the white of egg and flour; put on a cloth; then put over another cloth, to make it thick; fasten on the pot tightly that none of the steam may escape; set it into a brass or copper kettle with water in, and boil four hours without ceasing. Have hot water in another kettle to fill up as fast as it boils out. Do not let it come up to the top to wet the cloth; strain it through a linen cloth, and put into small pots; when cold, cover them. Don't touch it with any thing but silver.

POT POURRI.

Put into a china vessel the following things in layers, with bay salt between each layer: two pecks of damask roses, part in buds and part in blossom, violets, orange flowers, jasmine, a handful of each, orris root sliced, benjamin and storax, two ounces of each, a quarter of an ounce of musk, a quarter of a pound of angelica roots sliced, a quart of the red parts of clove gilliflowers, two handfuls of lavender flowers, half a handful of rosemary flowers, bay and laurel leaves, half a handful of each, three Seville oranges, stuck full of cloves, dried in a cool oven, half a handful of knotted marjoram, and two handfuls of balm of Gilead dried. Cover close, and when the pot is uncovered the perfume is beautiful.

TO MAKE ROSE-WATER.

Take rose leaves and place them on a napkin, tied over a basin filled with hot water; put a dish of cold water on top; keep the lower basin hot, and as often as the upper water warms, put on more cold. By this process you will obtain the essential oil.

OIL OF ROSES.

Olive oil one quart, one drachm of otto of roses, the same of oil of rosemary; mix together. Color with alkanet root steeped in the oil, before scenting it.

FOR SUNBURN, AND TO PREVENT THE SKIN FROM CRACKING.

Melt two ounces of spermaceti in a pipkin; then add two ounces of oil of almonds, and when they are well mixed, add a table-spoonful of honey; stir until well mixed; then put in a jar. Apply on going to bed at night.

FOR PIMPLES ON THE FACE.

Boil together a handful of the herbs of patience and pimpernel, each in water, and wash every day.

CREAM OF ROSES.

Take eight ounces of rose-water, the same of oil of almonds, half an ounce of white wax, the same of spermaceti; proceed as for cold cream; then add ten drops of neroli, eight drops of otto of roses; when cold, put into pots. This is preferred to cold cream.

TOOTH POWDER.

Mix equal parts of powdered chalk and charcoal; add a small quantity of Castile soap. This will keep the teeth beautifully white.

ANOTHER.

Take equal parts of myrrh, chalk and orris powder.

MIXED TOOTH POWDER.

Finely prepared chalk four ounces, pure starch four ounces, myrrh three ounces, ginger one ounce, cream of tartar six ounces, sugar and flower of lavender at pleasure; mix well together.

WASH FOR THE HAIR.

One drachm of rosemary, half an ounce of olive oil, two drachms of hartshorn, half a pint of rose-water. Add the rose-water by degrees, or it will not amalgamate.

TO PREVENT THE HAIR FROM FALLING OFF.

Make a decoction of white-oak bark, and use freely. Make it fresh every two weeks.

GOWLAND'S LOTION.

Take one and a quarter grains of bichloride of mercury, one ounce of emulsion of bitter almonds; mix well. The mercury is a poison. This is one of the best cosmetics for imparting a delicate complexion, and is useful in ringworms and sun-blistering, or for hard dry skin.

MILK OF ALMONDS.

Bruise sweet almonds in a mortar; add water by degrees, in proportion of a pint to twenty or thirty almonds; put in a lump of sugar to prevent the separation of the oil from the water, rubbing constantly. Pass the whole through a flannel, and perfume with orange-flower water. This is used to bathe the face.

TO REMOVE SUPERFLUOUS HAIR.

Two ounces of lime, four ounces of carbonate of potash, two drachms of charcoal powder. Make into a paste with warm water, and apply to the part, which must be previously shaved. When completely dry, wash off with warm water.

WASH FOR SUNBURN.

Take two drachms of borax, one of Roman alum, one of camphor, half an ounce of sugar-candy, one pound of ox-gall; mix and stir well together three or four times a day, until transparent; then strain through filtering paper, and bottle up close.

LAVENDER WATER.

Take rectified spirits of wine half a pint, essential oil of lavender two drachms, five drops of otto of roses; mix well and cork tight.

ANOTHER.

One ounce of English oil of lavender, the same of bergamot, one pint of rectified spirits of wine, four cloves. Shake well together, and let it remain a month well corked; then add two ounces of distilled water, and then distill the whole.

AROMATIC VINEGAR.

Take four ounces of dried tops of rosemary, four ounces of dried leaves of sage, four ounces of dried flowers of lavender, half an ounce of cloves, three drachms of camphor, six pints of distilled vinegar. Let it remain in a warm place two weeks, and then filter.

ROSE-WATER.

Put some roses in water, and add a few drops of vitriolic acid; the water will assume both the color and perfume of the rose.

HOW TO MAKE LAVENDER WATER.

Take four handfuls of dried lavender leaves; sprinkle on them one quart of brandy, the same quantity of white wine, and rose-water. Leave a week in a large bottle well corked; then distill, and bottle tight. Bergamot may be made in the same way, only using bergamot leaves.

BRITISH OTTO OF ROSES.

Take any convenient quantity of the petals of fragrant-scented flowers, roses, jasmine, and others of the same season, a small quantity of mignonnette, and sweet-brier, more rose leaves than any thing else. Spread them on thin layers of cotton, and a layer of flowers alternately, until a glass jar is filled. The cotton must be dipped in Florence or Lucca oil first. Tie a bladder over the top to keep tight; then place the vessel where it will have the heat of the sun for two weeks. Then open and squeeze out the mass, and a fragrant oil will be expressed nearly equal to the high-priced otto of roses.

A NICE WASH FOR THE HAIR.

Take one ounce of borax, half an ounce of camphor; powder fine, and dissolve in one quart of boiling water; when cool, wash the head with a piece of sponge, rubbing the roots of the hair well; afterward wipe with a dry towel. It should be done at night before retiring to bed. In the morning use oil or pomatum. This wash cleanses the hair and stimulates its growth; the oil is required to soften and maintain its gloss.

TOOTH POWDER.

Charcoal two ounces, Peruvian bark one ounce, powdered orris root half an ounce, the same of prepared chalk, oil of lavender or bergamot twenty drops; work in a mortar until thoroughly incorporated. This is preferable to other tooth powders, because it gives an odorous breath, cleanses and purifies the gums, and preserves the enamel.

CAMPHOR CERATE FOR CHAPPED HANDS.

Take one ounce and a half of spermaceti, half an ounce of white wax, six drachms of camphor, and four table-spoonfuls of olive oil; put in an earthen vessel, and let it stand before the fire till it dissolves; stir it well when liquid; rub the hands thoroughly with a little of the cerate, and then wash them as usual. It is better to put on at night. Keep it well covered, or it will evaporate. For perspiration of the hands, use a little wheat bran.

TO WHITEN THE HANDS.

Take a wine-glass of eau de Cologne, and another of lemon-juice; then scrape two cakes of brown Windsor soap, or pure white soap, and mix well in a mould. When hard, use for whiting the hands.

TO MAKE EAU DE COLOGNE.

Take two quarts of spirits of wine; add three fourths of an ounce of bergamot, three eighths of an ounce of oil of cedra, the same of lemon-peel and orange flowers each, sixteenth of an ounce of oil of rosemary, and four grains of camphor. Shake the whole a quarter of an hour; then let it remain a fortnight without agitation; then filter through white blotting-paper, and bottle.

ANOTHER.

Take a pint of alcohol, and put in thirty drops of the oil of lemon, thirty of bergamot; shake well, and then add half a gill of water. Bottle tight.

ODOR DELECTABILIS.

Take four ounces of distilled rose-water, four ounces of orange-flower water, one drachm of oil of cloves, one of English oil of lavender, two drachms of oil of bergamot, two grains of musk, one pint of spirits of wine; macerate thoroughly, and add one drachm of essence of musk.

PALMA CHRISTI OIL.

Take one ounce of palma christi oil; add oil of bergamot or lavender to scent it; brush it well into the hair twice a day for two or three months. It will make the hair luxuriant.

BANDOLINE FOR THE HAIR.

Put one ounce of quince seed to a quart of water; let it simmer half an hour; then strain it, and when cold add any scent you like. Linseed or gum-arabic are good done in the same manner.

ANOTHER.

Take an ounce and a half of isinglass, two thirds of a pint of water; pour the water over the isinglass, and cover it; let it remain all night. The next day put where it will warm till dissolved; then add two wine-glasses of spirits of wine; scent with any oil you like, but mix with the spirits before adding.

TO MAKE WASH-BALLS.

Shave two pounds of new white soap in a tea-cupful of rose-water; then pour as much boiling water on as will soften it; put a pint of sweet oil into a brass pan; four ounces of oil of almonds, half a pound of spermaceti; set it over the fire till dissolved, then add the soap, and half an ounce of camphor reduced to a powder, by adding a little spirits of wine or lavender-water. Boil ten minutes, then pour into a basin, and stir till thick enough to make into balls, which must be done as quick as possible. If essence is used, stir in quick after taking off the fire.

THE NAILS.

To give a fine color to the nails they must be washed in fine soap; then rub with equal parts of cinnabar and emery, and afterward with oil of bitter almonds. Lemon-juice is good to wash them in. They should never be scraped.

COLD CREAM.

Take oil of almonds two ounces, white wax and spermaceti each one drachm; melt in an earthen vessel, and while warm add rose-water two ounces, half an ounce of orange flower.

TO CLEAN HAIR-BRUSHES.

Dissolve a table-spoonful of saleratus in a pint of boiling water; wash your brush in this with a soft cloth or sponge, but do not wet the backs or handles; when well washed rinse in clear hot water; then wipe with a dry towel. Wash them in one third ammonia and two thirds water is nice, and will stiffen the bristles.

COLD CREAM. NO. 2.

Take one drachm of pulverized borax, one ounce of spermaceti, hog's lard four ounces; add rose-water enough to boil up thick as cream; keep air-tight.

FOR THE HAIR.

Take four ounces of castor-oil; boil it; then add by degrees one pint of bay-rum, a little borax pulverized, and two drachms of the tincture of cantharides; perfume with any thing you like; shake well and apply to the hair as occasion requires.

TO MAKE LEATHER WATER-PROOF.

Take one ounce of the balsam of copaiba, and one ounce of beeswax; melt together and apply warm. It improves the leather, and is good for sore or chapped hands.

FOR PIMPLES ON THE FACE. NO. 2.

Dissolve ten grains of corrosive sublimate, fifteen grains of muriate of ammonia, in two ounces of Cologne and two of rose-water; bathe the parts affected.

INVISIBLE CEMENT.

Dissolve isinglass in hot alcohol, and it will stick firmly broken crockery or glass.

TO DARKEN THE HAIR.

Take two ounces of lac sulphur, half an ounce of sugar of lead, half an ounce of sulphate of iron; perfume with any thing you like; moisten the hair at night and comb out in the morning.

POMATUM FOR THE COMPLEXION.

Take one ounce of oil of sweet almonds, half an ounce of white wax and spermaceti each, with a little balm; melt these ingredients slowly over a fire; then pour into a marble mortar, and stir until smooth and cold; then add gradually an ounce of rose-water; stir till it resembles cream. This renders the skin soft and smooth. Keep it tied with a bladder.

LIP SALVE. NO. 2.

Take half a pound of fresh lard, an ounce and a half of white wax; set it on the fire till melted; then take a small tin dish, fill with water, and a few chips of alkanet root; let the water boil till it becomes red; strain and mix with the other ingredients; scent with any agreeable extract, and pour into small jars.

INDEX.

AILMENTS, DISEASES, ETC.:
Ague in the Face, 231; Ankle, Sprained, 233; Asthma, 233; Barber's Itch, Cure for, 234; Bleeding at the Nose, 228; Boils, to prevent, 234; Bronchitis, 225; Burns, 226; Cancers, Remedy, 225; Cankered Mouth, 227; Catarrh in the Head, 230; Chapped Hands, 235; Chilblains, 228; Cholera Morbus, 230; Colds, Treatment of, 232; Colic, Bilious, 230; Cough, Cure for, 224, 235; Corns, 235; Cramp, to cure, 225; Croup, 226; Cut, for a, 225; Diphtheria, 227; Dressing for a Blister, 234; Dropsy, 229; Earache, Cure for, 224; Felon, Cure for a, 226; Frosted Fruit, 184; Fruit, to preserve by Drying, 184; Headache, 231; Hoarseness or Loaded Chest, 224; Hot Water, Medical Effects, 235; Humors, 230; Hydrophobia, 232; Itch, 229; Lumbago, 236; Measles, 230; Measles, Small-Pox, and Scarlet Fever, 237; Mortification, 229; Mumps, 231; Mustard Poultice, 228; Nails growing into the Toes, 233; Nauseous Taste of Medicine, 335; Neuralgia, 232; Opodeldoc, 224; Pimples, Sties, and Boils, 229; Polypus, 228; Proud Flesh, 231; Quinsy, 232; Rheumatism, 232, 233, 237; Ringworm, to cure, 226; Salt Rheum, 229; Scarlet Fever Remedy, 225; Senna, to take, 237; Sick-Room, to purify, 235; Sore Throat, 227; Spinal Difficulties, 231; Spitting Blood, 233; Stiff Joints, 232; Sties in the Eye, 236; Sting of a Bee, 224; Summer Complaint, 229; Thorns, to take out, 237; Toothache, 231; Vomiting, to stop, 228; Warts, 228; Weak Eyes, 234; Whitlow, 237; Worms in Children, 231
Apples, Baked, ...198
Apples and Rice, ...194
Apples for Dessert, ...194
Apples for Fritters, ...160
Apple Souffle, ...168
Artichokes, ... 90
Asparagus, ...84, 91, 239
Beans, ... 89
Beans, Lima, ... 90
Beans, String, ... 89

Beds, to clean, ...249
Beech, to stain the Color of Mahogany, ...252
BEEF, A LA MODE, ...23, 52
Beef à la Muskmelon, 53; Beef Balls, 53; Beef baked with Potatoes, 52; Broiling Beef, 21; Beef Cakes, 24, 25; Beef Cobbets, 43; Cooked in Onions, 23; Corned, to boil, 34, 52; Fricasseed Beef, 22; Fried Beef, 22; Beef, Frozen, 27; Frizzled, 26; Beef's Heart, 28; Hunter's Beef, 24; Beef, Jellied, à la Mode, 53; Liver, 26, 52; Olives, 25; Pickled, 16, 46; Pie, 28; Pressed, 52; Roast or Baked Beef, 22; Beef, Rolled, 23; Rump of, à la Bouillie, 41; or Veal, Stewed, 34; to stew, 26; Tongues or Dried Beef, a Pickle, for, 16
Beefsteak, Italian, ... 25
Beefsteak Pudding, ... 52
BERRIES:
Blackberries, 241; Gooseberries, 241; Raspberries, 241; Strawberries, 241.
Beeswax, to separate from the Comb, ...259
Beets, ... 85
Birds, to pot, ... 35
Birds, to stew, ... 34
Black Lace Vail, to wash, ...246
Blacking, Liquid, ...253
Blacking, to make, ...255
Bouilli, ... 23
BREAD, MAKING, ...147
Apple Bread, 152; Biscuit, 157; Hard Biscuit, 155; Biscuit, 153; Brentford Rolls, 154; Brown Bread, 152; Butter Crackers, 156; Corn Loaf, 153; Crackers from Bread Dough, 156; Cream of Tartar Bread, 151; Currant Bread, 153; English Rolls, 154; Excelsior Bread, 150; French Rolls, 155; Graham Bread, 150, 151; Indian, 151, 152; Milk Yeast, 149; Potato Bread, 151; Pumpkin Bread, 151; Rolls, 154; Rusk, 154; Rye Bread, 151; Salt Rising, 149; Soft Muffins, 136; Wheat Bread, 149; Yeast, Baker's, 149; Yeast Cakes, 147; Yeast, Potato, 148; Yeast, Soft, 148
Broccoli, ... 91
Brussels Spouts, ... 92

INDEX.

	PAGE
BUTTER AND CHEESE,	209

Brandy Cheese, 214; Butter, to make, 210; Cheese Cream, 215; Cheese, to make, 212, 214; Cheese, to preserve from the Fly, 214; Cottage or Dutch Cheese, 214; Cream, to raise, 215; Curd, to scald, 213; Rennet, to prepare, 212

Buttermilk, Flavored, ...209

Cabbage, ...84, 97
Cabbage Salad, ...88
Cabbages, to make grow, ...263
Cactus, the, ...242
CAKES:
Almond Cake, 105; Berwick Sponge, 119; Breakfast, 155; Champagne, 108; Cheap, 112; Cheese, 163; Cider, 121; Cocoa-Nut Cakes, 107, 113, 114; Coffee, 120; Coloring for Icing, 101; Composition Cake, 107, 114; Cookies, 105, 108, 119; Corn-Starch Cake, 121; Cream, 111; Cream Jelly, 120; Cream of Tartar Doughnuts, 108; Crullers, 105, 112; Cup Cake, 110, 111, 117; Cymbals, 109; Delicate Cake, 107; Directions for making, 102; Doughnuts, 106; Drop Cakes, 102; Elmsdale Cake, 121; English Seed Cake, 163; French Loaf, 103, 112; French Twist, 109; Frosting Cake, 101; Fruit, 103, 104, 107, 110, 111; Gingerbread, 105, 114, 115, 120; Gingerbread Nuts, 120; Ginger Crackers, 115; Ginger Snaps, 106; Gold Cake, 104, 117; Green Corn, 146; Hard Cookies, 118; Hickory-Nut Cake, 104; Honey, 112; Jam, 121; Jelly, 108, 113, 117; Jumbles, 109; Kisses, 105; Lady's Cake, 103; Lemon, 109; Lemon Cheese Cakes, 108; Lincoln, 118; Loaf without Eggs, 116; Luncheon, 115; Mock Sponge, 107; Mountain, 121; One-Two-Three-Four, 117; Pilgrim's Loaf, 121; Pork, 111; Pound, 103, 104, 116; Pound Cake Measured, 118; Plum Cake, 102; Queen's, 106, 110, 116; Railroad, 114; Rusk, 119; Rye Cake, 157, 158; Sally Lunn, 155; Savoy Cakes, 113; Scotch Cake, 104; Silver, 104, 110, 116; Snaps, 114; Soda Cake, 108, 110, 111, 115, 118, 120; Soda Crullers, 105; Soda Jumbles, 119; Soft, 112; Sponge, 110, 115, 116; Sponge Gingerbread, 106; Sugar-Drops, 109; Sugar Gingerbread, 118; Star Ginger Cakes, 108; Strawberry Cake, 111; Strawberry Short Cake, 157; Trifles, 155; Union Cake, 118; Vanities, 118; Wafers, 113; Wedding Cake, 106; West Point, 112; Whigs, 119; Whistles, 113; Wonders, 109

Calicoes that Fade, to wash, ...263
Calicoes, to wash, ...242
Callas, or Ethiopian Lily, ...242

	PAGE
Calves' Feet,	29
Calves' Head,	28
Camphor Spirits,	234
Carpet Rags, to dye all one Color,	271
Carpets,	249, 250
Carrots,	85
Carving,	17
Cauliflower,	84, 97, 239
Cecils,	25
Celeriac,	91
Celery,	239
Celery, to stew,	86, 92
CEMENT for Bottles,	251

Cement for Earthenware, 250; for Glass, etc., 250, 262; for Ironware, 251; for Knife-Handles, 250, 256; Invisible, 281; for Wood, 262, 263

CHICKENS,	30

Chickens and Oysters, 44; Boiled, 55; Broiled, 31; Fricassee, 30; Fried, 44, 55; Pie, 31; Pot-Pie, 31; Pudding, 31, 42; Salad, 32, 45

Chocolate and Cocoa,	203
Chowder,	39
Cider, to keep Sweet,	232
Cochineal, to color Woolen or Silk,	267
Coffee and Tea,	207

To COLOR:
Black, 269; Blue Cotton Goods, 268; Blue or Green per Pound, 270; Cinnamon, 271; Cotton, Lemon Color, 268; Green Cotton Goods, 268; Madder, 270; Nankeen, 270; Orange, 268; Royal Purple, 269; Scarlet, 271; Slate Color, 269; Tan, 271; Yellow on Cotton, 268

Collops, 28; Minced, 48

CONFECTIONERY,	215

Candy, Molasses, 184; Caramel, for Pastry, 216; Essence of Cinnamon, 217; Citron, to Candy, 216; Cream of Preserved Fruit, 217; Cream Snow, 216; Fruit, to Candy, 215, 216; Lemon Drops, 207; Lemons, to keep, 217; Sugar Candy, 217; Sugar Kisses, 216

Corn, Dry Green,	90
Corn, Sweet,	88
Cows, keeping of,	209

CREAMS, ETC.:
Blanched Cream, 171; Burnt, 171; Cake Trifle, 173; Cream, to whip, 172; Floating Island, 172; Ice Cream, 169, 170; Lemon, 170, 171; Orange, 171; Pompadour, 171; Rhenish, 170; Snow-Balls, 172; Snow Rice Cream, 171; Swiss, 170; Trifle, a, 172; Whip Cream, 169

Crumpets,	159
Cucumbers,	86
Curried Dishes,	35
DYEING,	267
Dahlias,	241
Dandelion Beer,	238
Duck or Rabbit, to boil,	33

INDEX.

Earthenware and Iron, to temper,..257
EGGS,............................. 69
  Eggs, Baked, 72; Cupped, 71; Boiling Eggs, 70; for Preserving, 69; done with Cheese, 71; Omelette, 71, 72; Omelette, Sweet, 71; Eggs, Poached, 71; to choose, 69; to poach in a Cup, 71
Egg Plant,........................87, 239
ESSENCES, EXTRACTS, ETC.:
  Blackberries, Pickled, 187; Compotes of Fruit, 193; Currants, Preserved, 187; Custard, Boiled, 195; Essence of Ginger, 188; Essence of Nutmeg, 188; Extract of Lemon and Orange, 188; Fruit Ice Cream, 195; Lemon Pickle, 190; Orange Custard, 195; Orange Jelly, 193; Orange Preserves, 193; Quinces, Baked, 194; Quinces preserved White, 190; Rice Jelly, 193; Rum Jelly, 194; Strawberries dried in Sugar, 187; Water-Melon Syrup, 196
Etceteras,..........................237

Feathers, to curl,..................257
Feathers, White, to clean,..........257
FISH,.............................. 72
  Black Fish, 75; Clams, 77; Clam Pancakes, 78; Codfish, 73, 74, 75; Eels, Baked, 82; Eels, Stewed, 75; Eels, to cook, 75; Fish, Broiled, 81; Fish Cakes, 77; Fish Force-Meat Balls, 76; Fish, Fresh, to cook, 76; Fish, Fresh, to crimp, 77; Fish, Potted, 81; Haddock, 81; Halibut, 73; Lobsters and Crabs, 77; Lobsters, Pickled, 80; Lobsters, to dress cold, 77; Mackerel, 75; Mackerel, Soused, 79; Oyster Pie, 78; Oyster Patties, 78; Oysters, Fried, 78; Oysters, Scolloped, 79; Oysters, Spiced, 80; Oysters, Stewed, 78, 79, 81; Oysters, to keep, 81; Oysters, to pickle, 79; Salmon, Pickled, 80; Salmon, Smoked, 75; Salmon, to boil, 74; Scollops, 77; Shad, Baked, 74; Shad, to Pickle, 80; Sounds and Tongues, 75; Sturgeons, 76; Sturgeon Steaks, 76; Trout, 76; Trout, Pickled, 80
Flowers, Different, from the same Stem, 240; Flowers, to hasten their Blowing, 241; Flowers, to restore, 240
Force-Meat Balls,................... 27
French Polish,.....................247
Fricandeau of Beef,................ 24
Fritters,....................159, 160, 161
Frogs,............................. 44
Furs and Flannels,.................252
GARDENING, HINTS ON,...............238
Geese or Ducks, Roast,............. 33
Geraniums,........................242
Gloves, to dye,...................253
Godfrey's Cordial.................236
Gold, to color,...................263
Goose, Mock,...................... 43

Goose, Pickled.................... 56
Grafting,.........................255
Grasses, to preserve,.............254
GRAVIES AND SAUCES,............... 57
  Apple Sauce, 58; Brown Gravies, 57; Brown Sauce, 58; Butter, Burnt, 57, 60; Butter, Clarified, 62; Butter, Drawn, 57, 60; Browning for Made Dishes, 59; Celery Sauce, 58; Celery Vinegar, 57; Cranberry Sauce, 58; Currant Sauce, 60; Curry Powder, 61; Dressing for Roast Pig, 62; Dressing for a Goose, 62; for Cold Meat, 60; for Goose, 61; for Roast Beef, 63; for Turtle, 59; for Venison, 63; French Sauce, 61; Herb Spirit, 59; Horse Radish, 62; Lemon Sauce, 62; Liver Sauce, 58; Lobster Sauce, 58; Mushroom Sauce, 62; Mustard to Mix, 61; Onion Sauce, 63
Grease, from Merinoes and Silks,...244
Green Corn Cake,..................156
Greens,........................... 89
GRIDDLE CAKES,....................161
  Bread Cakes, 162; Buckwheat, 161; Corn, 162; Cream, 163; Flannel, 161; Fruit, 163; Indian, 162; Potato, 162; Rice, 162; Rye, 162; Wheat, 161, 162, 163
Griddles, Fresh Meat,............. 28
Guinea and Pea Fowl,.............. 36

HAM, Boiled, 36, 37; Broiled, 36; Cold, Cooking, 36; Loaf, 43; Modes of Curing, 15, 16; Mutton Ham, Curing, 15; Roasted, 38; Southern Mode of Curing, 15; Toast, 56; to fry, 37; to keep, 37; with Madeira, 43
Hash Beef,........................ 25
Hash, Meat,....................... 40
Hash, Veal,....................... 40
Hash, Veal, with Toast,........... 41
Head-Cheese,...................... 37
Heat Marks, from Mahogany,........246
Hens, to make them lay in Winter,.248
Herbs, to dry,....................225
Hoarhound Candy,..................233
Hoe Cake,.........................156
Hog, Cutting up a,................ 17
Hominy,........................... 89
Horn, to stain,...................253
Hotch Potch,...................... 30
Husk Beds,........................238

Icing for Tarts,..................192
Ink, Black, Blue, Red,............254
Ink or Iron Rust,.................245
Ink, to mark Linen,...............253
Ink, with Type,...................253

Japan Varnish,....................257
JELLY, ETC.:
  Apple Jelly, 185, 195; Arrow-Root Blanc Mange, 167; Blackberry Syrup, 188, 189; Black Butter, 192; Blanc

INDEX.

Mange, 166; Calves' Feet Jelly, 185; Candied Plums, 192; Charlotte Russe, 167, 169; Coloring for Jellies or Creams, 186; Currant Jelly, 184; Elderberry Syrup, 189; Fruit for Children, 192; Fruit in Jelly, 186; Fruit, to candy, 191; Fruit, to prepare for Brandy, 192; Grapes in Brandy, 190; Isinglass Jelly, 189; Jacque Mange, Jaune Mange, 167; Lemon Jelly, 189; Lemon Juice, to preserve, 190; Orange Syrup, 188; Peach Jelly, 185; Plums in Brandy, 191; Puffs of Preserved Fruit, 190; Spiced Brandy, 188; Strawberry Jelly, 186; Strawberry Tart, 187; Strawberries for Cream, 187; Strawberries Souffle, 187; Wine Jelly, 189

Jersey Dish, a, ... 54
Johnny Cake, ...156, 158

Kale, Sea, ... 91
Kid Gloves, to clean, ...257
Knives and Forks, ...258

Lamb, Grilled, ... 30
Lamb, Roast, ... 51
Lamb, Shoulder of, ... 51
Lard, Frying, ... 17
Leather, to gild or silver, ...250
Lemon Sponge, ...168
Liver, Calf, ... 27

Macaroni, ...90, 208
Mad Dog, ...261
Mahogany, to polish, ...248
Malt Coffee, ...208
Maple Sugar, ...195
Marjoram, Sweet, to preserve, ...209
Martinoes, ...240
Matelote Meat, ... 45
Meat Turnovers, cold, ... 40
MEATS:
 Boiling, 19; Brolled, 21; Meat Cakes, 44; Fried, 20; Roast or Baked, 20
Mildew, from Linen, to remove, ...245
Mildew, to remove, ...257
Milk Punch, ...206
Milk Toast, ...164
Minute Dish, ... 45
Mirrors, etc., to clean, ...252
Mock Duck, ... 22
Muffins, ...158
Mushrooms, ... 86
MUTTON, ... 29
 Boiled, 51; Chops, 49; Cutlets, 48; Fillets, Stewed, 51; Ham, 49; Hung, 49; Leg, Stuffed, 48, 49, 50; Minced, 51; Roasted, 30; Sausages, 50; Shoulder, à la Turque, 50; Steaks, Broiled, 49; with Cream, 51

Nim's Puffs, ...146

Ochra, ... 90
Odor Delectabilis, ...279

Œufs Brouilles, ... 72
Oil of Flowers, ...255
Oil of Roses, ...275, 277
Onions, ... 83
Oranges for Dessert, ...194
Otto of Roses, British, ...278
Oyster Sausages, ... 42
Oysters, Vegetable, ... 86

PAINTS:
 Paint, a Cheap, 258; from Window Glass, 249; White, 258; from Clothing, 247; to clean, 249
Palma Christi Oil, ...279
Paregoric, to make, ...236
Parsnips, ... 85
PASTRY AND PIES, ...122
 Apple Custard Pie, 129; Apple, a Delicate, 125; Apple Puffs, 131; Apple Puffs, 125; Blackberry or Raspberry Pie, 127; Butternut, 128; Cherry, 130; Cocoa Nut, 123, 130; Cranberry Tarts, 131; Cream Pie, 131; Currant, 128; Custard, 126; Dried Apple, 129; Elderberry, 130; Gooseberry, 131; Grape, 125; Green Apple, 127, 128; Ground Cherry, 125; Lemon Cream, 131; Lemon, 123, 124, 129, 131; Maringoes or Cream Puffs, 125, 126; Marlborough Tarts, 123; Melon Pie, 124; Mince, 126, 129; Mince, without Meat, 124; Mock Apple, 127; Paste, Directions for making, 122; for Family Pies, 124; Peach Pie, 131; Pie Crust with very little butter, 123; Pumpkin Pie, 126, 128; Puff Paste, 122; Pyramid Paste, 124; Quince, 131; Quince Tarts, 128; Rhubarb Pie, 127; Rice, 129; Snow Balls, 126; Tarts, 129; Tart Pies, 129; Tomato, 130
Peas, ... 87
Peppers, ...240
Pheasants and Partridges, ... 85
PICKLING, ... 93
 Apples, Pickles, 98, 100; Beans, Green, 97; Blackberries and Currants, 99; Butternuts and Black Walnuts, 94, 96; Catsup, Mushroom, 99; Catsup, Tomato, 99; Cabbage, 97; Cauliflower, 97; Cucumbers, 96; Cucumbers, Pickling, 93; East-India Pickle, 98; Gherkins, to pickle, 99; Higdom, 98; Martinoes, 97; Melon Mangoes, 96; Mushrooms, 94; Nasturtions, 97; Onions, 97; Peaches, Pickled, 100; Peppers, 99; Pickle, a Delicate, 94; Plums, 97; Plums and Cherries, 101; Radish Pods, 96; Tomato Catsup, Green, 98; Tomato Catsup, Ripe, 98; Tomatoes, Green, 95; Tomato Pickalilly, 95; Tomatoes, Ripe, 95; Vinegar, Pepper, 100; Yellow Pickle, 95
Pig, Baked or Roasted, ... 86
Pigeons, ... 34

INDEX.

Pine-Apples, without preserving,...192
Pine-Apple Tarts,..................191
Pitch or Tar, to remove,..........245
Plaster-of-Plaster Figures, to enamel,254
Plum and Cherry Charlotte,........168
Poisons,......................260, 261
Polish for Silver and Brass,........251
PORK :
  Boiled, 41; Loin of, 41; Roast, 38; Rolled, 55; Salt, to fry, 28; Sausages, 29; Steaks, 38; Stew, 39; to pickle, 16
Potato Pie,........................ 40
Potatoes,.......................... 82
Potatoes, Fried,................... 92
Potatoes in Butter,................ 92
Potatoes, Sweet,................... 83
Pot Pourri,.......................275
PRESERVES AND SWEETMEATS,........173
  Apples, 174; Apple Butter, 183; Apricots, 176; Brandy Pears, 178; Canning Fruit, 183; Canning Maple Molasses, 196; Canning Peaches. 188; Canning Tomatoes, 183; Cherries or Small Plums, 180; Citron and Watermelon Rinds, 180; Crab-Apples, 175; Cranberries, 181; Cucumbers, 181; Currants, 177; Currant Marmalade, 177; Fruit, to bottle, 182; Gooseberries, 182; Grapes, 180; Green Gages, preserved, 179; Peaches, 176; Peaches in Brandy, 176, 191; Peach Jam, 177; Pears, 177; Plums, 179; Plums, to preserve, 179; Plum Jam, 180; Preserved Pumpkin, 183; Prunes, 182; Quinces, 178; Quince Marmalade, 179; Quinces with Molasses, 179; Raspberry Jam, 180; Rhubarb Jam, 182; Strawberries, 176; Sugar, to clarify, 174; Tomatoes, 180; Tomato Figs, 181; Tomato Jam, 181
PUDDINGS,........................132
  Almond Pudding, 132; Amber, 142; Apple Dumplings, 136, 144, 145; Apple Pudding with Rice, 142; Arrowroot, 132; Batter, 141; Bird's Nest, 146; Blueberry, 144; Boiled Bread, 141; Bread and Butter, 140; Bread, 138; Carrot, 135; Citron, 136; Cocoa-Nut, 135; Composition, 141; Corn Starch, 137; Cranberry, 147; Cream Almond, 143; Cream, 138; Crust for a Savoy Pie, 140; Directions for Puddings, 132; Egg Pudding, 138; English, 137; Eve's, 136; Family, 136; Flour, 139, 146; Fresh Fruit, 142; German, 144; Gooseberry, 141; Hasty, 145; Indian, 137, 146; Lemon Dumplings, 140; Lemons, for Puddings, 141; Lemon, 134, 135; Meringue, 140; Minute, 141; Nice, 144; Norfolk Dumplings, 133; Orange Pudding, 135, 145; Plum, 134, 136, 139, 143; Pound, 139; Pudding in Haste, 143; Puff Pudding, 139; Quaking, 141; Quince, 142; Ratafia, 134; Rice, 138,

140; Rich, 134; Rolly Pooly, 139; Sago, 137, 143; Salem, 143; Spring Fruit, 135; Squash, 133; Suet, 137, 143; Sweet Corn, 139; Sweet Potato, 144; Tapioca, 134, 146; Temperance Plum, 145; Transparent, 133; Vermicelli, 133; Wheat, 146; Wiltshire, 134

Rabbits, to fry,................... 56
Raspberry Charlotte,..............168
Raspberry Sponge,.................168
Rhubarb,..........................230
Rice Chicken Pie,.................. 41
Rice Paste,.......................247
Rice Puffs,.......................161
Rigolettes, etc., to wash,.........245
Rissoles,......................42, 46
Rose-Bushes,................262, 263
Roses, Monthly,...................242
Rose-Water, to make,..............275
Rules for Housekeepers,............ 7
Rust from Cutlery,................252
Ruta Baga,......................... 83

Sandwiches, Ham,.................. 40
Sangaree,.........................207
SAUCES :
  Oyster Dressing, 62; Oyster Sauce, 57; Pepper, 60; Pudding, 60; Rice, 58; Salad Dressing, 59; Scorched Flour, 62; Stock for Gravy, 63; Tomato Sauce, 59; Tomato Soy, 61; White Sauce, 63; Wine Sauce, 59
SAUSAGES, Bologna, 40; Sausages, Cases for, 17; Sausages in Summer, 40; Sausage Stew, 34
Scouring Boards,..................259
Scrapel,........................... 37
Shrubs,...........................240
SICK, PREPARATION OF FOOD FOR,....218
  Apple Marmalade, 175; Arrow-Root, 220; Barley Water, 218; Beef Tea, 220; Beef, Veal, or Chicken Broth, 221; Bread Jelly, 219; Calves' Feet Blanc-Mange, 219; Calves' Feet Broth, 219; Caudle, 219; Chicken Jelly, 219; Codfish Broth, 221; Crab-Apple Marmalade, 175; Cream of Tartar Whey, 221; Custard, Egg, 220; Egg for Invalids, 221; Flour Gruel, 221; Lemonade, Hot, 221; Milk Porridge, 218; Panada, 218; Pine-Apples, 175; Pine-Apple Marmalade, 175
SICK, SIMPLE DRINKS FOR,.........222
  Alum Whey, 222; Buttermilk Whey, 222; Cough Tea, 223; Egg Coffee, 223; Egg Tea, 223; Flax-Seed Jelly, 223; Flour Coffee, 222; Moss Jelly, 223; Thoroughwort Bitters, 223; Tomato Syrup, 222; Tonic for Indigestion, 224; Rice Gruel, 218; Sago, 220; Sassafras Jelly, 219; Tapioca Jelly, 219; Water Gruel, 218; Wine Whey, 220
Silks and Ribbons, to clean,....244, 266
Silk and Woolen Shawls, to clean,..244

Sirloin, Extra, ... 46
Skins, Dressing with the Fur on, ... 266
Slaw, ... 68
Snake Bites, ... 261
Snipes or Woodcocks, Roast, ... 33
SOAPS, HARD, SOFT, AND FANCY, to make, ... 263, 264, 265, 266, 267
Soufflé Français, ... 72
SOUPS, ... 63
  Bean Soup, 69; Beef, 64; Brown, 68; Chicken, 65; Clam, 66; Eel, 68; Force-Meat Balls, 65; Giblet Soup, 67; Gumbo, 68; Lobster, 67; Macaroni, 66, 67; Ochra, 68; Mock Turtle, 66; Oyster, 66, 82; Pea, 65; Pepper Pot, 67; Portable Soup, 64; Tomato, 65; Vegetable, 64; Vermicelli, 65; White 68
Sour Krout, ... 209
Souse, ... 37
Spare Rib, to roast, ... 87
Spinach, ... 87
Squash, ... 84
Squirrels, Stewed, ... 55
STAINS from Black Woolens, 246; from Broadcloth, 245; from Silks, 246; from the hands, 246
Starch, ... 247
Steaks, Cold, to warm, ... 53
Substitute for Court Plaster, ... 263
Substitute for Fresh Lemons, ... 190
Succotash, ... 88
Sweetbreads, ... 29
Sweet Potato Coffee, ... 208
Syrup for the Blood, ... 236

Tallow, Trying, ... 17
TOILET, ... 272
  Antidote for Acids, 260; Aromatic Vinegar, 277; Bandoline for the Hair, 279; Camphor Cerate, 278; Chapped Lips, 272; Cold Cream, 280, 281; Court Plaster, 255; Cream of Roses, 275; Eau de Cologne, to make, 279; Freckles, to remove, 272; Gowland's Lotion, 276; Hair Brushes, to clean, 280; Hair, Oil for the, 273; Hair, for the, 281; Hair, Superfluous, to remove, 277; Hair, to darken the, 273, 281; Hair, to prevent from falling off, 276; Hands and Arms, Skin of the, to improve, 273; Hands, to whiten, 279; Lavender Water, 277; Lip Salve, 272, 282; Macassar Oil, 273; Milk of Almonds, 276; Nails, the, 280; Pimples on the Face, 275, 281; Pomade Divine, 274; Pomatum for the Complexion, 281; Pomatum, Soft, to make, 274; Hard, to make, 274; Sunburn and Freckles, Lemon Cream for, 272; Sunburn, for, 275; Tooth Powder, 276, 278; Wash for Sunburn, 277; Wash for the Hair, 276, 278; Wrinkles, Lotion for, 272

TOMATOES, ... 91, 238
  Baked, 92; Dried, 196; Marmalade, 197; to dry for Pies, 196; to keep a Year, 196
Tongue, ... 46
Tongue, to Boil, ... 26
Transparent Crust, ... 191
Tripe, ... 26
Tripe, Fricassee, ... 46
Turkey, Boiled, ... 32
Turkey, Boned, ... 56
Turkey, Roast, ... 32
Turnips, ... 83

Union Dish, ... 44

Varnish, to make Wood look like Ivory, ... 262
VEAL, à la Mode, ... 47
  Veal, à la Française, 53; Balls, 85; Cold, 54; Cold Dressed, 47; Cones, 54; Cutlets, 27; Cutlets, French, 47; Fillet of, 27; Haricot, 34, 50; Leg in Surprise, 48; Marbled Pressed, 54; Patties, 54; Stew, 27; to Collar, 47; to Mince, 45; to Pot, 35
Velvet, to restore, ... 244
VENISON, ... 30
  Hash, 55; Haunch, to Roast, 55
Vermin, Household, ... 254
Vials and Bottles, to clean, ... 251
Vinegar, ... 199, 207
Vinegar, Berry, ... 205
Vinegar, Rhubarb, ... 204
Vinegar from Beets, ... 206

Waffles, ... 159
Walnuts for Medicine, ... 237
Wash-Balls, ... 266, 280
Washing Recipes, ... 256
Water-Proof Composition, ... 253, 281
Weights and Measures, ... 197
Welsh Rabbit, ... 215
White Clothes, to wash, ... 243
Whitewashes, ... 259
White Pot, ... 197
WINES, CORDIALS, ETC.:
Wine, Making, ... 197
  Apple Wine, 198; BEER, to make, 199, 200, 206; Blackberry Cordial, 203; Black Currant Wine, 201, 202; Blackberry or Raspberry Wine, 198; Cherry Bounce, 201; Cider Wine, 202; Currant Shrub, 205; Currant Wine, 198, 204; Elderberry Wine, 200, 202; Ginger Wine, 200; Grape Wine, 201, 202; Green Gooseberry Wine, 206; Harvest Drink, 200; Imperial, 202; Lemonade, 200; Lemon Cordial, 203; Lemon Water, 205; Mead, 202, 206; Peach Cordial, 203; Raisin Wine, 202; Raspberry Wine, 205; Ratafia, 204; Rhubarb Wine, 203, 204; Sherbet, 204; Tomato Wine, 198; Wine, a Rich, 201
Wool, Silk, and Straw, to bleach, ... 257
Woolens, to wash, ... 243

Yellow Dyes, ... 270

www.ingramcontent.com/pod-product-compliance
Lightning Source LLC
Chambersburg PA
CBHW031340230426
43670CB00006B/396